THE ANTI-MODERNIST READER

STUDIES ON THE NEW RELIGION OF VATICAN II

VOLUME TWO
THE MASS:
OLD, NEW, *MOTU, UNA CUM*

Edited by Rev. Anthony Cekada
Afterword by Rev. Tobias Bayer

Copyright © True Restoration Press 2025

ISBN: 979-8-9896052-7-9

All rights reserved. No part of this book may be reproduced or transmitted in any form or by any means, electronic, mechanical, or otherwise, without express written permission from the publisher, except that brief selections may be quoted or copied for non-profit use without permission.

TRUE RESTORATION PRESS

8399 Melrose Drive | Overland Park, KS 66214 | The United States of America
www.truerestorationpress.com

FOREWORD

This volume is the second in a pivotal series initiated by (the late) Father Anthony Cekada, to provide crucial information for the intellectual and spiritual fight against Modernism in the post-Vatican II era.

After covering the Papacy in Volume I, the progression is made herein to that of the Holy Sacrifice of the Mass.

Both the Catholic Roman Rite Mass ("known simply as, the "Old Mass"), and the various problems surrounding the Mass in modern times, such as the substitution with the *Novus Ordo Missae* (the "New Mass"), the *Motu Proprio* of Benedict XVI ("*Motu*") and the Mass offered in union with heretics/apostates/schismatics ("*Una Cum*") are all analysed in a thorough and theologically-sound manner.

Just as in Volume 1 of the Anti-Modernist Reader series, only the best articles on the subject are presented in this book. As a consequence of the authors being the most luminous anti-modernist clergy of the post-Vatican II period, including His Lordship Bishop Donald Sanborn, Reverend Anthony Cekada and the Most Reverend Daniel L. Dolan, the reader will certainly come away adequately enlightened with the correct Catholic attitude pertaining to these important topics!

Very many years of work have culminated in being able to bring this important collection to print. We offer the fruits of this labour to our patroness Mary Help of Christians, with gratitude for her ongoing help with our endeavours at True Restoration Press. May God be greatly glorified and Our Lady further honoured by these much-needed studies being made available in a much more lasting and convenient form.

Theresa Arthur
Director
True Restoration Press
The Feast of the Holy Name of Mary MMXXIV
Melbourne, Australia

Table of Contents

… TABLE OF CONTENTS …

THE MASS: OLD, NEW, *MOTU, UNA CUM*

CHAPTER 1 1

DID PAUL VI 'ILLEGALLY PROMULGATE' THE *NOVUS ORDO*?

by Rev. Anthony Cekada

1. Paul VI, who promulgated the New Mass, lost papal authority 2
2. Paul VI possessed papal authority but did not promulgate the New Mass lawfully. 2

SSPX and "Illegal Promulgation" 3
The Standard Arguments 3
What is "Promulgation"? 4
A Missing Decree? 5
Paul VI's Apostolic Constitution. 6
Same Terms as *Quo Primum* 7
"It is Our Will..." 7
Paul VI Revokes *Quo Primum* 8
The Obvious Conclusion 9
The October 1969 Instruction 10
The March 1970 Decree 11
The June 1971 Notification 11
The October 1974 Notification 12
No Immemorial Custom 13
Who Interprets a Pope's Laws? 14
Canon-Law Protestants? 14
Or the Pope and His Curia? 15
Not a Universal Law? 16
A Summary 17
The Unavoidable Consequences 18
Bibliography 19

CHAPTER 2 21

IS REJECTING THE PIUS XII LITURGICAL REFORMS "ILLEGAL"?

by Rev. Anthony Cekada
1. Lack of Stability (or Perpetuity) 22
2. Cessation 23

CHAPTER 3 25
LITURGICAL REVOLUTION [THE LITURGICAL REVOLUTION BEFORE VATICAN II]
by Rev. Francesco Ricossa

Illuminism 26
The Liturgical Movement 27
The Movement's Deviations 27
A Warning from Germany 28
Mediator Dei 28
Underestimating the Enemy 28
The Revolution Begins 29
The 1955 Holy Week: Anticipating the New Mass 31
The 1955 Holy Week: Other Innovations 33
Roncalli: Modernist Connections 34
The Revolution Advances 34
The "Anti-liturgical Heresy" in the John XXIII Reform 35

    1. Reduction of Matins to three lessons 35
    2. Replacing ecclesiastical formulae's style with Scripture 35
    3. Removal of saints' feasts from Sunday 35
    4. Preferring the ferial office over the saint's feast 36
    5. Excising miracles from the lives of the Saints 37
    6. Anti-Roman Spirit 37
    7. Suppression of the *Confiteor* before Communion 37
    8. Reform of Maundy Thursday, Good Friday and Holy Saturday 38
    9. Suppression of Octaves 38
    10. Make the Breviary as short as possible without any repetition 38
    11. Ecumenism in the Reform of John XXIII 38

12. The Office becomes "private devotional reading" 39
A Practical Conclusion... 39

CHAPTER 4 41
PRE-VATICAN II LITURGICAL CHANGES: ROAD TO THE NEW MASS

by Most Rev. Daniel L. Dolan

I. The "Experimental" Easter Vigil (1950) 43
II. The New Holy Week (1955) 44
    A. Key Features 44
    B. Palm Sunday 44
    C. The *Triduum* 44
III. **"Reform" of the Rubrics (1955)** 45
IV. **Consultation on Further Changes (1957)** 46
V. **Dialogue Masses and Commentators (1958)** 46
VI. The John XXIII Changes (1960–62) 47
VII. Liturgy in the Society of Saint Pius X 48
Say "No" to the Reformers.. 49

CHAPTER 5 51
PRIESTLY FRATERNITY OF SAINT PETER: SOME SALIENT PROBLEMS

by Rev. Anthony Cekada

CHAPTER 6 53
QUO PRIMUM: COULD A POPE CHANGE IT?

by Rev. Anthony Cekada

CHAPTER 7 55
RUSSIA AND THE LEONINE PRAYERS

by Rev. Anthony Cekada

I.		Origins of the Prayers	56
II.		A New Intention	58
III.		Two Dubious Stories	60
	A.	An Alleged Vision	60
	B.	Conspiracies and "Falsified" Texts	63
IV.		Law and the Leonine Prayers	67
	A.	Subsequent Legislation	67
	B.	Recent Developments in Russia	69
	C.	Cessation of the Law	72
V.		The Use of Other Prayers	75

Appendix: Prayer to Saint Michael from Exorcism against Satan and the Apostate Angels (Approved 18 May, 1890) 79

Bibliography 80

CHAPTER 8 83
THE *MOTU* MASS TRAP

by Rev. Anthony Cekada

I.		Positive Aspects	84
	1.	An Admission of Failure	84
	2.	Removing the Stigma	85
	3.	A Cause of Division in the Enemy Camp	86
	4.	Warning Flares for Committed Trads	86
	5.	Rubbing Priests' Noses in the New Mass	86
	6.	An Introduction to the Real Issues	87
II.		Negative Aspects	87
	1.	Co-opted by Modernist Subjectivism	87
	2.	A Side Chapel in an Ecumenical Church	88
	3.	Catholic Rituals, Modernist Doctrines	89
	4.	Non-Priests Offering Invalid Masses	90
III.		Say No to the *Motu*	91

CHAPTER 9 93

THE PIUS X AND JOHN XXIII MISSALS COMPARED
by Most Rev. Daniel L. Dolan

Missal of Saint Pius X vs. Missal of John XXIII 93
1. Promulgation 93
2. Basis 93
3. Accordance with Tradition 93
4. Prayers at the Foot of the Altar 94
5. The Collect 94
6. Commemorations 94
7. The Lessons on Ember Days 94
8. The Epistle 94
9. The Sequence 94
10. The Gospel 94
11. The Creed 94
12. The Canon of the Mass 94
13. The Communion of the People 95
14. The *Benedicamus Domino* 95
15. The Last Gospel 95
16. Changes in Feasts 95
17. Octaves of Feasts 96
18. Vigils of Feasts 96
Miscellaneous Rubrics 96
19. Tones of Voice 96
20. Bowing to the Cross 96
21. Holy Week Rites 96
Final Notes 97

CHAPTER 10 99
THE PIUS XII REFORMS: MORE ON THE "LEGAL" ISSUE
by Rev. Anthony Cekada

1. "Stability" and the Legislator's Intention 99
2. "Cessation" and Changed Circumstances? 101

3. Indefectibility of Church?..102
4. Are You "Pope-Sifting"?..103
5. Obedience to Lawful Authority?...103

CHAPTER 11 107
THE OTTAVIANI INTERVENTION: ITS ENDURING VALUE

by Rev. Anthony Cekada

Origins of the Intervention 108
Content of the Intervention... 109
Vatican Reaction 110
An Ottaviani Retraction?...112
"A Climate of Suspicion" 115
An Ephemeral Document..115
"The Cleverness of the Revisors"..117
A Theoretical Exercise..119
Conclusion... 120
Citations and Footnotes... 121

CHAPTER 12.. 123
UNA CUM: MASS IN UNION WITH OUR "POPE"

by Most Rev. Donald Sanborn

Naming the post-Vatican II "popes" in the Canon of the Mass............ 123
Introduction 123
Import of the *Una Cum* Phrase 124
A Declaration of Ecclesial Communion 125
Pope Benedict XIV.. 126
R. P. Pierre Le Brun... 127
Dom Ernest Graf, O.S.B. 127
Father William J. O'Shea, S.S., D.D. 128
F. Lucius Ferraris 128
An Ecclesiological Nightmare 128

Communion with Heretics.. 131
"But, John Paul II is a Heretic" 133
1. There is strong evidence that John Paul II is formal in his adherence to heresy. 134
2. The law of the Church presumes pertinacity unless the contrary be proven. 136
3. It is the practice of the Church to treat all those who publicly adhere to heresy as formal heretics in the external forum. 136
4. To recognize John Paul II as a member of the Catholic Church ruins the theological basis of resistance to the changes. 139
Conclusions of the Speculative Order... 144
Conclusions of the Moral Order... 146
A Neither-Nor Ecclesiological Twilight Zone 147
Answers to Objections 148
Conclusion... 150
Footnotes 151

CHAPTER 13.. 153

THE GRAIN OF INCENSE: SEDEVACANTISTS AND *UNA CUM* MASSES ~ Dedicated to Patrick Henry Omlor

by Rev. Anthony Cekada

Should we assist at Traditional Masses offered "together with Thy servant Benedict, our Pope"? 153

I. The Meaning of the Prayer... 156
    A. Linguistic Meaning 156
    B. Theological Meaning in the Liturgy 159
    C. Application to Ratzinger.. 162
II. Your Participation and Assent 163
    A. How You Actively Participate at Mass 164
    B. Active Participation = Your Approval... 166
    C. You Join with the Action of the Celebrant.. 167
    D. You Participate in and Ratify the Canon 168

III. Why You Should Not Participate 170
    A. A Pernicious Lie 171
    B. A Profession of Communion with Heretics 172
    C. Recognizing the One-World, Ecumenical Church 174
    D. Implicit Profession of a False Religion 174
    E. A Violation of Church Law 175
    F. Participation in a Sin 177
    G. Offering Mass with Ratzinger 177
    H. Recognition of a Usurper 178
    I. Sin of Scandal 179
    J. The "Resistance" Clergy 180
IV. Objections and Responses 186
    A. Pope Martin V and Cardinal de Lugo 186
    B. No Official Declaration 189
    C. Prayed for as Material Pope Only 190
    D. Can. 2261: Sacraments from Excommunicates 191
    E. The Sunday Obligation 191
    F. Toleration of Evil for a Greater Good 192
    G. The Priest Means Well 193
    H. Secret Sedevacantists in SSPX 193
    I. Conflicting Opinions among Priests 194
    J. No Place for Mass 195
V. Summary and Conclusion 196

CHAPTER 14 201
THE PROBLEM OF THE *UNA CUM* TRADITIONAL MASSES
by Most Rev. Donald Sanborn
A "valid" Mass does not equal a "Catholic Mass" 201

AFTERWORD 205

Chapter 1

Did Paul VI 'Illegally Promulgate' the *Novus Ordo*?

(2000)

by Rev. Anthony Cekada

The Society of Saint Pius X and a popular Traditionalist myth

Most Catholics who abandon the New Mass do so because they find it evil, irreverent or non-Catholic.

Instinctively, though, the Catholic knows that the Church of Christ *cannot* give us something evil, since the Church would then be leading us to hell, rather than heaven.

Catholic theologians, indeed, teach that the Church's universal disciplinary laws, including laws governing the sacred liturgy, are *infallible*. Here is a typical explanation from the theologian Herrmann:

> "The Church is infallible in her general discipline. By the term general discipline is understood the laws and practices which belong to the external ordering of the whole Church. Such things would be those which concern either external worship, such as *liturgy and rubrics*, or the *administration of the sacraments*...
>
> If she [the Church] were able to prescribe or command or tolerate in her discipline something against faith and morals, or something which tended to the detriment of the Church or to the *harm of the faithful*, she would turn away from her divine mission, which would be impossible."[1]

Sooner or later, then, the Catholic faces a dilemma: The New Mass is evil, but those who commanded us to use it (Paul VI, *et al.*) supposedly possessed the very authority of Christ. What should one do? Accept evil because of authority, or reject authority because of evil? Choose sacrilege, or choose schism?

---

[1] P. Herrmann, *Institutiones Theol. Dogm.*, Rome: 1904, 1:258. My emphasis. Other theologians such as Van Noort, Dorsch, Schultes, Zubizarreta, Irragui and Salaveri explain the teaching much the same way. For full quotes and citations, see my study *Traditionalists, Infallibility, and the Pope*.

How does a Catholic resolve this seeming dilemma: that Church authority commands evil?

Over the years, essentially only two explanations have been proposed:

1. Paul VI, who promulgated the New Mass, lost papal authority.

The argument is as follows: Once we recognize that the New Mass is evil, or harms souls, or destroys the Faith, we therefore also implicitly recognize something else: Paul VI, who promulgated (imposed) this evil rite in 1969, *could not have possessed true authority* in the Church when he did so. He somehow lost papal authority, if indeed he possessed it in the first place.

How could this have come about? Defection from the Faith, according to the teaching of at least two popes (Innocent III and Paul IV) and nearly all Catholic canonists and theologians, brings about automatic loss of papal office.

The evil of the New Mass, according to this argument, is like a giant neon arrow pointing back at the post-Vatican II popes and flashing the words: "No papal authority. Defectors from the Catholic faith."

2. Paul VI possessed papal authority but did not promulgate the New Mass lawfully.

This position argues that Paul VI did not follow the correct legal forms when he promulgated the New Mass. The New Mass, then, is not really a universal law, so we are not obliged to obey the legislation which supposedly imposed it; thus, the infallibility of the Church is "saved."

The theory has been extremely popular in the Traditionalist Movement since its beginnings in the 1960s.

This, it must be said, is the "have your cake and eat it too" argument. It allows you to "acknowledge" the Pope, but ignore his laws, denounce his New Mass, and keep the old Mass. It reassures simple souls fearful of schism that they are, despite appearances, still "loyal to the Holy Father."

I have treated the first position in my study *Traditionalists, Infallibility, and the Pope*.[2] Here I will discuss the second position, and

---

[2] For a free copy, contact: Saint Gertrude the Great Church, 11144 Reading Road, Cincinnati OH 45241, 513.769.5211, www.sgg.org

outline the considerable difficulties it presents as regards logic, Church authority, and Canon Law.

SSPX and "Illegal Promulgation"

While many Traditional Catholics adhere to the position that the New Mass was illegally promulgated, advocates are especially numerous among the members and supporters of Archbishop Marcel Lefebvre's Society of Saint Pius X (SSPX).

The theory fits neatly into what one can only term the Society's Jansenist/Gallican concept of the papacy: The pope is "recognized," but his laws and teachings must be "sifted." You get all the sentimental benefits of theoretically having a pope, but none of the practical inconveniences of actually obeying him.

(Over the years the position's emotional appeal for the laity has meant a fundraising bonanza for SSPX. This old Gallican goose really lays the golden egg.)

The Standard Arguments

For an explanation of the second position, therefore, we turn to two articles by SSPX's former U.S. District Superior, the Rev. François Laisney.

Father Laisney characterizes the New Mass as "evil in itself,"[3] and a danger to the Catholic faith.[4] He acknowledges in a general sense the principle upon which the first position is based — the Church cannot give a universal law that is evil or harmful to souls.

But, he argues, "the full strength of papal authority **was not engaged** in the promulgation of the New Mass,"[5] and that "Pope Paul VI did not oblige the use of his [New] Mass, but only permitted it... There is no clear order, command, or precept imposing it on any priest!"[6]

He makes the following arguments — they are typical of those who hold this position — against the legality of Paul VI's promulgation

---

[3] "Where Is the True Catholic Faith? Is the *Novus Ordo Missae* Evil?" Angelus 20 (March 1997) 38. Of course, it is hardly necessary to read the article in order to discover how SSPX answers the *first* question.

[4] "Was the Perpetual Indult Accorded by Saint Pius V Abrogated?" Angelus 22 (December 1999) 30-31.

[5] "Where is...?" 34. His emphasis.

[6] "Where is...?" 35.

of the New Mass:

- The *Novus Ordo Missae* was not promulgated according to the proper canonical form by the Sacred Congregation of Rites.
- A decree of the Sacred Congregation of Rites imposing the New Mass is not in the *Acta Apostolicae Sedis* (AAS — the official organ of the Catholic Church announcing new ordinances over the Church.).
- In later editions of the New Mass [this 1969 Decree] is replaced by a second decree (March 26, 1970) only *permitting* the use of the New Mass. This second decree which only permits — not orders — its use is in the *Acta Apostolicae Sedis*.
- In a 1971 Notification on the New Mass from the Congregation for Divine Worship, "one cannot find in this text any clear prohibition for any other priest to use the Traditional Mass nor an obligation to celebrate only the New Mass."
- Another Notification in 1974, says Father Laisney, *does* impose an obligation — but it does not appear in the *Acta*, and does not say Paul VI approved it, so it has no binding force.
- "Confused legislation" characterizes these reforms. "In this, one sees precisely the assistance of the Holy Ghost to the Church, because He did not allow the modernists to properly promulgate their reforms with perfect legal force."

Father Laisney then presents his conclusion: "The *Novus Ordo Missae* was promulgated by Pope Paul VI with so many deficiencies and especially **lacking even the proper juridical language to oblige** all priests and faithful, that it **cannot claim to be covered by the infallibility of the Pope in universal laws.**"[7]

To assess Father Laisney's claims, we will assume, as Father Laisney does, that Paul VI was indeed a true pope who, as such, possessed full legislative authority over the Church. This will allow us to hold Father to the objective criteria found in Canon Law which would flow from that assumption.

We will then demonstrate, by examining general principles of Canon Law and the specific legislative texts at issue, that Father Laisney's arguments and conclusions are false on every point.

What is "Promulgation"?

To "promulgate" a law means nothing more than to announce it

---

[7] Where is...?" 35-36. My emphasis.

publicly.

The essence of promulgation is the **public proposal** of a law to the community by the lawmaker himself, or on his authority, **so that the will of the lawmaker to impose an obligation can become known** to his subjects.[8]

The Code of Canon Law simply says: "Laws enacted by the Holy See are promulgated by their publication in the official commentary *Acta Apostolicae Sedis*, unless in particular cases another mode of promulgation is prescribed."[9]

This is all that the Code requires, and it suffices to make known the will of the legislator, the pope.

Unless another provision has been made in a particular law itself, a law becomes effective (binds) three months after its official publication date in the *Acta*.[10] The intervening period before the effective date is called the *vacatio legis*.

A Missing Decree?

The New Mass (*Novus Ordo Missae*) appeared in stages. The Vatican first published the new Ordinary in a small booklet in 1969, along with the General Instruction on the Roman Missal (a doctrinal and rubrical preface).[11]

In the front of this booklet appear Paul VI's lengthy Apostolic Constitution on the New Mass, *Missale Romanum*, and the 6 April, 1969 Decree *Ordine Missae* from the Congregation of Sacred Rites (*Consilium*).

The Decree, signed by Benno Cardinal Gut, states that Paul VI approved the accompanying Order of Mass, and that the Congregation was promulgating it by his special mandate. It set 30 November 1969 as the effective date for the legislation.

For reasons unknown, however, this Decree was never published in the *Acta*. And so, Father Laisney and countless others contend this omission means that the New Mass was, therefore, never "duly

---

[8] M. Lohmuller, *Promulgation of Law* (Washington: CUA Press 1947), 4.

[9] Canon 9. "*Leges ab Apostolica Sede latae promulgantur per editionem* in Actorum Apostolicae Sedis commentario officiali, *nisi in casibus particularibus alius promulgandi modus fuerit praescriptus.*"

[10] Canon 9. "*Et vim suam exserunt tantum expletis tribus mensibus a die qui* Actorum *numero appositus est, nisi ex natura rei illico ligent aut in ipsa lege brevior vel longior vacatio specialiter et expresse fuerit statuta.*"

[11] *Ordo Missae: Editio Typica* (*Typis Polyglottis Vaticanis:* 1969). The new order of Scripture readings appeared in May 1969.The full Missal, containing the new Orations for Sundays, seasons and feasts, would appear only in 1970.

promulgated, "and thus obliges no one."

But the argument over this bureaucratic slip is a red herring. The key question in Canon Law about the promulgation of any law is the *will of the legislator*. In this case, *did Paul VI manifest his will to impose on his subjects an obligation* (i.e., the New Mass)? And moreover, did he do so in the *Acta*?

Paul VI's Apostolic Constitution

The question is easily answered. In the 30 April, 1969 *Acta Apostolicae Sedis* we find the Apostolic Constitution *Missale Romanum*, bearing Paul VI's signature. Its heading: "Apostolic Constitution. By which the Roman Missal, restored by decree of Vatican Ecumenical Council II, is **promulgated**. Paul, Bishop, Servant of the Servants of God, for an Everlasting Memorial."[12]

The legislation, obviously, then meets the simple canonical norm for promulgation. The Supreme Legislator needs no Decree from a Cardinal for his law to "take." The New Mass is promulgated, and the law is binding.

In the text of the Constitution, moreover, Paul VI makes it abundantly clear that his will is to **impose the obligation of a law** on his subjects. Note in particular his language in the following passages:

- The General Instruction preceding the New Order of Mass "**imposes new rules** for celebrating the Eucharistic sacrifice."[13]
- "**We have decreed** that three new Canons be added to this Prayer [the Roman Canon]."[14]
- "**We have ordered** that the words of the Lord be one and the same formula in each Canon."[15]
- "And so, **it is Our will** that these words be thus said in every Eucharistic Prayer."[16]
- "All of which things **we have prescribed** by this, Our Constitution, shall begin to take effect from 30 November of this year."[17]
- "**It is Our will** that these laws and prescriptions be, and they shall

---

[12] AAS 61 (1969) 217-222.
[13] "...*novas normas...proponi.*" The verb employed ("*proponi*") has the post-classical sense of "to impose," as in "impose a law." See Lewis & Short, *A New Latin Dictionary* 2nd ed. (New York: 1907) 1471, col. 2.
[14] "*ut eidem Precationi tres novi Canones adderentur statuimus.*" "*Statuo*" with "ut" o[DA8] "*ne*" has the sense of "decree, order, prescribe." See Lewis & Short, 1753, col. 3.
[15] "*jussimus.*"
[16] "*volumus.*"
[17] "*Quae Constitutione hac Nostra praescripsimus vigere incipient.*"

be, firm and effective now and in the future."[18]

The standard Latin canonical terms a pope customarily employs to make a law are all present here: *normae, praescripta, statuta, proponimus, statuimus, jussimus, volumus, praescripsimus,* etc.

Same Terms as *Quo Primum*

This language is important for another reason: Some of it also appears in *Quo Primum,* the 1570 Bull by which Pope Saint Pius V promulgated the Tridentine Missal.

Father Laisney, like many others, claims that Paul VI's legislation did not impose an obligation. Rather, Paul VI merely "presented" or "permitted" the New Mass.[19]

This is false. Both *Quo Primum* and Paul VI use identical "lawmaking" terms in key passages: *norma, statuimus* and *volumus.* The Benedictine canonist Oppenheim says these are "preceptive" words that *"clearly indicate a strict obligation."*[20]

If such words made Pius V's *Quo Primum* obligatory, they did the same for Paul VI's *Missale Romanum.*

"It is Our Will..."

Earlier, we quoted the following passage as evidence that Paul VI intended to promulgate a law to bind his subjects:

"**It is Our will** [*volumus*] **that** these laws and prescriptions be, and they shall be, firm and effective now and in the future."[21]

The first English translations rendered the Latin verb *volumus* as "We wish that." Some priests and writers then argued that Paul VI was only wistfully "wishing" that Catholics would employ the New Mass — rather like wishing upon a star.

But in *Quo Primum,* Saint Pius V uses the *identical* verb to impose the Tridentine Missal:

"**It is Our will** [*volumus*], however — and We decree by **that** same authority — that, after the publication of the Missal and this,

---

[18] *"Nostra haec autem statuta et praescripta nunc et in posterum firma et efficacia esse et fore volumus."*
[19] "Perpetual Indult," 30.
[20] P. Oppenheim, *Tractatus de Iure Liturgico* (Turin: Marietti 1939) 2:56. *"verba autem... 'statuit,'... 'praecepit,' 'jussit,' et similia,* manifeste strictam obligationem denotat." His emphasis.
[21] Lest someone claim that it is unclear what this passage refers to, note that among the *"statuta et praescripta"* preceding it were the "new rules imposed" by the General Instruction (*"novas normas... proponi,"* see fn. above) for the celebration of Mass.

Our Constitution, priests present in the Roman Curia... be obliged to chant or read Mass according to this Missal."[22]

In both cases, the verb *volumus* expresses the essence of Church law-making: the legislator's will to impose an obligation on his subjects.[23]

Paul VI Revokes *Quo Primum*

Father Laisney trots out yet another old canard:[24] the tale that Paul VI did *not* abrogate (revoke) Saint Pius V's Bull *Quo Primum*.[25]

Advocates of this position sometimes cite a passage in the Code which states that "a more recent law given by competent authority, abrogates a former law, if it *expressly* orders abrogation."[26]

Paul VI, the argument goes, did not mention *Quo Primum* by name, so he did not expressly abrogate it. *Quo Primum*, then, never lost its force, and we are all still free to celebrate the old Mass.[27]

But proponents of this notion are engaging in wishful thinking.

Expressly, in the Canon quoted above, does not just mean "by name."[28] A legislator may "expressly" revoke a law in another way — and this is what occurred here, when Paul VI, after he gave his *volumus* to the New Mass, added the following clause:

"**Notwithstanding**, to the extent necessary, the **Apostolic Constitutions and Ordinances of Our Predecessors**, and other prescriptions, even those worthy of special mention and amendment."[29]

This clause *expressly* abrogates *Quo Primum*.

First, the Bull *Quo Primum* falls into the category of the most solemn

---

[22] "*Volumus autem et eadem auctoritate decernimus, ut post hujus Nostrae constitutionis, ac Missalis editionem, qui in Romana adsunt Curia Presbyteri, post mensem... juxta illud Missam decantare, vel legere teneantur.*"

[23] See Lewis & Short, *A New Latin Dictionary*, 2004, col. 1; 2006, col. 2. "of the wishes of those that have a right to command...it is my will."

[24] Canard = a hoax. It's also French for "duck" — highly appropriate here, because this particular duck (like the Gallican goose) never permanently "goes south."

[25] "Perpetual Indult," 28-29.

[26] Canon 22. "*Lex posterior, a competenti auctoritate lata, obrogat priori, si id expresse edicat, aut sit illi directe contraria, aut totam deintegro ordinet legis prioris materiam; sed firmo praescripto...*" The translation is Father O'Hara's in the Cicognani commentary.

[27] The discussion often centered around various technical canonical terms — abrogation, obrogation, derogation and subrogation. Participants usually didn't have a clue as to what they were talking about. But this was somewhat understandable: Even expert commentators on the Code are not always consistent with these terms.

[28] If the legislator's intent had been such, he could have used the Latin term for "by name" (*nominatim*) instead of the actual term "expressly" (*expresse*).

[29] "... *non obstantibus, quatenus opus sit, Constitutionibus et Ordinationibus Apostolicis a Decessoribus Nostris editis, ceterisquepraescriptionibus etiam peculiari mentione et derogatione dignis.*"

type of pontifical legal Act — a Papal or Apostolic Constitution.[30] And in the passage quoted from Paul VI's Apostolic Constitution, he specifically revokes the "**Apostolic Constitutions**" of his predecessors.

Second, in order to revoke a law *expressly*, a pope is not required to mention it by name. Express revocation also takes place, says the canonist Cicognani, if the legislator inserts "abrogatory or derogative clauses, as is common in decrees, rescripts, and other pontifical acts: *notwithstanding anything to the contrary, notwithstanding in any respect anything to the contrary, though worthy of special mention.*"[31]

Paul VI, in other words, used the exact type of language required to expressly revoke a prior law.

And in so doing, Paul VI again used some of the same phrases Saint Pius V employed in *Quo Primum* to revoke liturgical laws of *his* predecessors:

"**Notwithstanding preceding Apostolic constitutions** and ordinances... and whatever laws and customs there be to the contrary."[32]

Again, if this language worked in 1570, it also worked in 1969.[33]

In light of all the foregoing, one cannot continue to promote the myth that Paul VI's legislation did not expressly abrogate *Quo Primum*.

As for the other mistaken notions circulated about *Quo Primum*, these will be dealt with in a subsequent article.

The Obvious Conclusion

The technical law-making language, enumeration of specific laws, the setting of an effective date, language revoking his predecessors' Apostolic Constitutions, and the legislator's explicit expression of his will to impose these laws — nothing, it would seem, could be clearer. Paul VI is establishing a law here.

---

[30] See A. Cicognani, *Canon Law*, 2nd ed. (Westminster MD: Newman 1934) 81ff. "Papal Constitutions are Pontifical Acts which have the following characteristics: (1) they come immediately from the Supreme Pontiff, (2) they are presented *motu proprio*, (3) the solemn form of a Bull is attached to them, (4) they deal with matters of greater importance, namely, the welfare of the Church or the greater part thereof."

[31] *Canon Law*, 629. His emphasis.

[32] "*Non obstantibus praemissis, ac constitutionibus, et ordinationibus Apostolicis… statutis et consuetudinibus contrariis quibuscumque.*"

[33] In the 1980s, SSPX circulated a classic "Roman whispers" story: a group of canonists, convoked by the Vatican, had supposedly studied the legal status of the old Mass, and concluded that *Quo Primum* had never been abrogated. Even if true, the point is moot: 1) The legislator issued no authoritative and interpretive decree to that effect. 2) Abrogation is the only conclusion possible after examining the decrees the Vatican did promulgate. 3) The legislator (the modernist Vatican) allows the Traditional Mass only by an indult — a faculty or favor granted temporarily, either contrary to the law or outside the law. If the old law were not abrogated, an indult would be unnecessary.

All this is lost on Father Laisney. "There is no clear order, command, or precept imposing it on any priest," he says, adding that Paul VI "does not say" what a priest should do on the effective date.[34]

Ah, well — if the language of Paul VI's Constitution is not sufficiently "clear," we turn to subsequent legislation published in the *Acta Apostolicae Sedis*.

Once again, Paul VI clearly manifests his will — not only to impose his New Mass, but also quite specifically to **forbid** the old rite.

The October 1969 Instruction

The Instruction *Constitutione Apostolica* (20 October 1969) bears the title: "On gradually implementing the Apostolic Constitution *Missale Romanum*."[35]

The general purpose of the document was to resolve certain practical problems: the bishops' conferences were not able to complete vernacular translations of the new rite in time for the 30 November date Paul VI had prescribed as the effective date for the New Mass.

The Instruction begins by enumerating the three parts of the new Missal already approved by Paul VI: the *Ordo Missae*, the General Instruction and the new Lectionary, and then states:

"The foregoing documents **decreed** that, from 30 November of this year, the First Sunday of Advent, the **new rite and the new text be used**."[36]

To meet the practical problems this posed, the Congregation for Divine Worship, "**with the approval of the Supreme Pontiff, establishes the following rules.**"[37]

Among the various regulations are the following:

- "The individual conferences of bishops shall also **establish the day** from which (except for mentioned cases in paragraphs 19-20) it shall become **obligatory to employ** the [new] Order of Mass. This date, however, shall not be deferred beyond 28 November, 1971."[38]
- "The individual conferences of bishops shall **decree** the day from which use of the texts of the new Roman Missal (except for

---

[34] "Where is...?" 35, and fn.
[35] AAS 61 (1969) 749-753. *"gradatim ad effectum deducenda."*
[36] *"statuitur ut... adhibeantur."*
[37] *"approbante Summo Pontifice, eas quae sequuntur statuit normas."*
[38] *"diem...constituant." "necesse erit usurpare."*

mentioned cases in paragraphs 19-20) **shall be prescribed.**"³⁹

The exceptions were for older priests who offered private Mass and who experienced difficulties with the new texts or rites. With permission of the Ordinary they could continue to use the older rite.

The Instruction ends with the following statement.

"On 18 October, 1969 the Supreme Pontiff, Pope Paul VI, **approved** this Instruction, **ordered it to become public law**, so that it be faithfully observed by all those to whom it applies."⁴⁰

Here once again, we find the "preceptive" words of Church lawmaking which, as Oppenheim says, clearly indicate a strict obligation — in this case, to employ the New Order of Mass no later than 28 November 1971.

The March 1970 Decree

The Decree *Celebrationis Eucharistiae* (26 March 1970) is entitled: "The new edition of the Roman Missal is promulgated and declared the *editio typica*."⁴¹

This Decree accompanied the publication of the new Missal of Paul VI, which contained the previously-approved New Order of Mass, a revised General Instruction, and all the new Orations for the whole liturgical year.

It, too, contains the preceptive language of papal law-making:

"This Sacred Congregation for Divine Worship, **by the mandate of the same Supreme Pontiff, promulgates** this new edition of the Roman Missal, prepared according to the decrees of Vatican II, and declares it the typical edition."⁴²

Need one belabor the obvious? The New Missal is **the law**, by the command of Paul VI.

The June 1971 Notification

The Notification *Instructione de Constitutione* (14 June 1971) is entitled "On the use and the beginning of the obligation of the new

---

³⁹ "*decernant.*" "*adhiberi jubebuntur.*" Lest someone claim these paragraphs mean that bishops' conferences, not Paul VI, "promulgated" the New Mass, we point out that the provisions merely delegate the power to extend the *vacatio legis* — again, the period between which a law is promulgated and when it takes actual effect.
⁴⁰ "*Praesentem Instructionem Summus Pontifex Paulus Pp. VI die 18 mensis octobris 1969 approbavit, et publici juris fierijussit, ut ab omnibus ad quos spectat accurate servetur.*"
⁴¹ AAS 62 (1970), 554.
⁴² "*de mandato ejusdem Summi Pontificis... promulgat.*"

Roman Missal, [Breviary], and Calendar."[43]

This Notification, like the October 1969 Instruction, addresses some of the practical difficulties which delayed implementing the new liturgical legislation.

"Having attentively considered these things, the Sacred Congregation for Divine Worship, **with the approval of the Supreme Pontiff, lays down the following rules** on the use of the Roman Missal."[44]

It orders that in any given country, "from the day on which the translated texts **must be used** for celebrations in the vernacular, **only the revised form of the Mass** and [the breviary] **will be allowed, even for those who continue to use Latin.**"[45]

The plain sense of the text is that the new rite must be used, the Traditional rite is *forbidden*; the pope will sit, and all must obey.

The October 1974 Notification

Finally, there is the Notification *Conferentia Episcopalium* (28 October 1974).[46]

This specifies again that when a bishops' conference decrees that a translation of the new rite is obligatory, "Mass, whether in Latin or the vernacular, **may be celebrated lawfully only** according to the rite of the Roman Missal promulgated 3 April, 1969 by authority of Pope Paul VI."[47] The emphasis on the word "only" (*tantum modo*) is found in the original.

Ordinaries must ensure that all priests and people of the Roman Rite, "**notwithstanding the pretense of any custom, even immemorial custom,** duly accept the Order of Mass in the Roman Missal."[48]

Again, it is obvious that the New Mass has been duly promulgated and is obligatory: there are no exceptions.

Father Laisney admits that this Notification lays down an obligation to celebrate the New Mass. However, he dismisses its legal

---

[43] AAS 63 (1971) 712-715.
[44] "*approbante Summo Pontifice, quae sequuntur statuit normas.*" In English, "norm" has a weak sense of a mere idealized guideline. But in Latin, "*norma*" means a law, a rule, a precept. Thus, the first Book of the Code of Canon Law is denominated "*Normae generales.*"
[45] "*assumi debebunt, tum iis etiam qui lingua latina uti pergunt, instaurata tantum Missae et Liturgiae Horarum forma adhibenda erit.*"
[46] *Notitiae* 10 (1974), 353.
[47] "*tunc sive lingua latina sive lingua vernacula Missam celebrare licet* tantum modo *juxta ritum Missalis Romani auctoritate Pauli VI promulgati, die 3 mensis Aprilis 1969.*" Original emphasis.
[48] "*et nonobstante praetextu cujusvis consuetudinis etiam immemorabilis.*"

effect because it did not appear in *Acta Apostolicae Sedis* and because it does not state it was ratified by the Sovereign Pontiff.[49]

Father Laisney, alas, has misunderstood yet another principle of the Code regarding promulgation.

First, the Notification is not a *new law*. It is what canonists term an "authoritative and declarative interpretation" of a previous law. This, according to the Code, "merely declares the meaning of the words of the law that were certain in themselves." In such a case: "The interpretation need not be promulgated, and has retroactive effect."[50] It has force, in other words, *without* publication in the *Acta*.

And second, even though, strictly speaking, such a pronouncement would not need the express consent of the pope, Paul VI did nevertheless approve the final text of the Notification.[51]

No Immemorial Custom

The Notification addresses an interesting side issue: A number of Traditionalist writers who insisted that they recognized the authority of Paul VI, nevertheless claimed that "immemorial custom" allowed them to retain the old rite and reject Paul VI's New Mass.

On the face of it, this assertion makes no sense. Priests celebrated the Traditional Mass because a pope promulgated a written law prescribing it. Custom is a mere usage or unwritten law, which can be in accord with, contrary to, or beyond the written law.

The Notification, in any case, states that the New Mass is obligatory "**notwithstanding the pretense of any custom, even immemorial custom.**"

According to the Code, "a law does not revoke centenary or immemorial customs, unless it makes express mention of them."[52]

But canonists state that a "notwithstanding" (*non obstante*) clause like the foregoing does indeed expressly revoke an immemorial custom.[53] So, even if one *could* make a case that the old Mass constituted an immemorial custom, the Notification duly revoked it — dismissing

---

[49] "Where is...?" 36.
[50] Canon 17.2. "*et si verba legis in se certa declaret tantum, promulgatione non eget et valet retrorsum.*"
[51] A Bugnini, *La Riforma Liturgica* (1948-1975), (Rome: CLV-*Edizioni Liturgiche* 1983) 298: "*Il testo definitivo fu approvato dal Santo Padre,*" *il 28 ottobre 1974, con le parole "Sta bene. P."*
[52] Canon 30. "*...consuetudo contra legem vel praeter legem per contrariam consuetudinem aut legem revocatur; nisi expressamde iisdem mentionem fecerit, lex non revocat consuetudines centenarias aut immemorabiles.*"
[53] See Cicognani, 662-3.

the notion, moreover, as a "pretense."

But this merely brings us to what is in fact the *real* issue behind the dispute over whether Paul VI "illegally" promulgated the *Novus Ordo*:

Who Interprets a Pope's Laws?

For SSPX and many others, alas, the answer to this question is "anyone but the pope."

Father Laisney informs us, for instance, that Paul VI did not engage "the same plenitude of power" in his Apostolic Constitution as Pius V did in his. Paul VI did not mention the "nature of an obligation," its "subject," its "gravity."[54]

Father Laisney's argument is footnote-free. So, we are not able to identify the canonists who proposed these distinctions and criteria — to which each Catholic, lay or clerical, may evidently appeal in order to decide for himself whether he is bound by an Apostolic Constitution signed by the Supreme Pontiff of the Universal Church.

The swarms of expert Canon Lawyers in the Roman Curia who compose papal decrees could not (we are expected to believe) draft a legal text adequate to the simple juridical task of making a new rite of Mass obligatory. And this, mind you, not even after *five* attempts — an Apostolic Constitution and four (count'em!) Curial pronouncements implementing the Constitution.

Instead, lay controversialists and lower clergy throughout the world are free to judge the Supreme Legislator to be juridically inept in promulgating his own laws, and then to refuse him submission for decades on end.

Canon-Law Protestants?

Father Laisney's approach to a pope's laws, and that of this theory's other adherents is, in fact, "Canon-Law Protestantism" — interpret selected passages as you see fit, and no pope is ever going to tell you what they mean. And if you don't find the magic formula that you have decided is "required" to compel your obedience, well, too bad for the Vicar of Christ on earth.

This is the mentality of sects — Jansenists, Gallicans, Feeneyites. Profess recognition of Christ's Vicar in word *but* refuse him submission in deed — such is the precise and classic definition of schism.

---

[54] "Perpetual Indult," 30-31.

Or the Pope and His Curia?

The Catholic approach to interpretation of papal laws, on the other hand, is succinctly stated in the Code:

"Laws are authoritatively *interpreted by the lawmaker* and his successor, and by those to whom the lawmaker has committed the power to interpret the laws."[55]

Apart from the pope, who possesses this power to interpret his laws authoritatively? "The Sacred Congregations in matters proper to them," says the canonist Coronata. Their interpretations are issued "in the manner of a law."[56]

In the case of the New Mass, Paul VI committed the power to interpret his new liturgical legislation to the Congregation for Divine Worship.

The Congregation issued three documents — an Instruction, a Decree, and a Notification — which clearly state that the original legislation promulgating the New Mass is binding.

Such documents are classed among "authentic general interpretations" of the law,[57] and often generically referred to as "general decrees." The Congregation then promulgated these three documents, as required by the Code, in the *Acta Apostolicae Sedis*.

One of these documents, the October 1969 Instruction, is of particular interest here. It names Paul VI's Apostolic Constitution, the General Instruction on the Roman Missal, the New Order of Mass, the 6 April 1969 Decree, and the Order for the new Lectionary, and then states:

"The foregoing documents **decreed** that, from 30 November of this year, the First Sunday of Advent, **the new rite and the new text be used.**"[58]

Even if the initial legislation had been somehow defective or doubtful, this passage (and similar ones in the other documents) would cure the problem. It meets the Code's criteria for giving a previously doubtful law an *authoritative* interpretation. The lawgiver's representative (the Congregation for Divine Worship) states that the

---

[55] Canon 17.1. "*Leges authentice interpretatur legislator ejusve successor et is cui potestas interpretandi fuerit ab eisdem commissa.*"

[56] M. Coronata, *Institutiones Juris Canonici* 4th ed. (Turin: Marietti 1950) 1:24: *Quis interpretari possit… per modum legis ecclesiasticae leges interpretantur: Romanus Pontifex, Sacrae Congregationes pro sua quaequae provincia.*"

[57] See Abbo & Hannon, *The Sacred Canons* 2nd ed. (St. Louis: Herder 1960) 1:34.

[58] "*Praefatis autim documentis. Statuitur ut…adhibeantur.*"

earlier legislation did, in fact, "**decree**… that the new rite and the new text be used."

Any doubt you may have had, then, is resolved. This authoritative interpretation, says the Code, "**has the same force as the law itself.**"[59]

You therefore consider yourself bound by the law, because those responsible for interpreting it *told you* so. You then submit to the pope's law.

That, at least, is how a *real* Catholic — one for whom a pope is more than a cardboard wall-decoration, or an empty phrase in the *Te Igitur* — is supposed to act.

Not a Universal Law?

As we noted above, Father Laisney believed that the "legal deficiencies" he alleged existed with regard to the *Novus Ordo* prevented one from claiming it fell under the infallibility of universal laws.[60]

To this argument, the Rev. Peter Scott, Father Laisney's successor as SSPX U.S. District Superior, added another twist.

In a written debate with the English writer, Michael Davies, Father Scott stated: "It would be a preposterous and intolerable insult to Eastern rite Catholics (many of whom are Traditional) to claim [as Mr. Davies does] that 'the Roman rite…is… equivalent to the universal Church,' simply on account of numerical preponderance. A decree for the Roman Rite, even rightly promulgated, is not for the universal Church."[61]

Others have made essentially the same argument: Paul VI's legislation on the New Mass is not truly "universal," because it does not apply to Eastern rite Catholics.

Father Scott, alas, has confused some common technical terms in Canon Law.

Church law is indeed divided by *rite* into Western and Eastern, but this has nothing to do with the matter at hand.

When a canonist calls a law "universal," he is not referring to it applying in the Latin and Eastern rites simultaneously. Rather, he is referring to a law's *extension*, i.e., the *territory* where it has force.

Thus, a *particular* law binds only within a certain determined territory. A universal law, on the other hand, "*binds throughout the whole Christian world.*"[62]

---

[59] Canon 17.2. "*Interpretatio authentica, per modum legis exhibita, eandem vim habet ac lex ipsa.*"
[60] "Where is…?" 36.
[61] "Debate over New Order Mass Status Continues," *Remnant*, 31 May 1997, 1.
[62] See D. Prümmer, *Manuale Juris Canonici* (Freiburg: Herder 1927) 4. "b) *Ratione exten-*

The legislation promulgating the New Mass, obviously, was intended to be obligatory throughout the world.

The principle also applies to various Declarations, Directories, Instructions, Notifications, Replies, etc. of the Congregation of Sacred Rites (Divine Worship).

No one, says the canonist Oppenheim, doubts that all such decrees for the Universal Church (sometimes known collectively as "general decrees") have the character of true law.[63] Indeed, "general decrees which are addressed to the universal Church (of the Roman Rite) *have the force of universal law."*[64] According to a Decree of the Congregation of Sacred Rites, moreover, they possess the same authority as if they emanated directly from the Roman Pontiff, himself.[65]

It is therefore impossible to deny that the liturgical legislation of Paul VI would qualify as universal disciplinary law.

A Summary

After what we have presented concerning Paul VI's legislation on the New Mass, we wish in conclusion to sum up what has been said, and then insist on one point in particular:[66]

We have examined the claim, put forth by Father Laisney and countless other Traditionalist writers, that Paul VI imposed the *Novus Ordo* "illegally," and we have demonstrated the following:

1. The purpose of promulgating a law is to manifest the lawmaker's will to impose an obligation on his subjects.
2. In his Apostolic Constitution *Missale Romanum* Paul VI manifested his will to impose the New Mass as an obligation. This is evident in the document from:
   a. At least six particular passages.
   b. Standard lawmaking vocabulary of Canon Law.
   c. Parallels to *Quo Primum*.

---

sionis jus ecclesiasticum dividitur: a. *injus universale*, quod obligat in toto orbe christiano, et *jus particulare*, quod viget tantum in aliquo territorio determinate... e)*Ratione ritus* jus distinguitur in *jus Ecclesiae occidentalis* et *jus Ecclesiase orientalis*." His emphasis. See also G. Michiels *Normae Generales Juris Canonici* 2nd ed. (Paris: Desclée 1949) 1:14.

[63] Oppenheim 2:54. "*Quae decreta pro universa Ecclesia ... rationem* verae legis *habere, nemo est qui dubitet*." His emphasis.

[64] Oppenheim 2:63. "*Decreta generalia* quae ad universam Ecclesiam (ritus romani) diriguntur, *vim legis habent universalis*." His emphasis.

[65] SRC Decr. 2916, 23 May 1846. "*An Decreta a Sacra Rituum Congregatione emanata et responsiones quaecumque ab ipsapropositis dubiis scripto formiter editae, eamdem habeant auctoritatem ac si immediate ab ipso Summo Pontifice promanarent, quamvis nulla facta fuerit de iisdem relatio Sanctitati Suae?... Affirmative.*"

[66] "*...quiddam nunc cogere et efficere placet.*"

    d. Promulgation in *Acta Apostolicae Sedis*.
3. Paul VI's Apostolic Constitution expressly abrogated (revoked) *Quo Primum* by using a standard clause customarily employed for that purpose.
4. The Congregation for Divine Worship (CDW) subsequently promulgated three documents (which are, in fact, "general decrees") that implement Paul VI's Constitution. These documents:
    a. Impose the New Mass as obligatory.
    b. Forbid (save in certain cases) the old Mass.
    c. Employ standard lawmaking vocabulary.
    d. Expressly state they had Paul VI's approval.
    e. Were duly promulgated in the *Acta*.
5. The CDW also issued a 1974 Notification, which reiterated that *only* the New Mass may be celebrated and that the old Mass was forbidden. It dismissed the claim of "immemorial custom" as "a pretense." This document was a declarative interpretation of a law, and as such, did not have to be promulgated in the *Acta* to have effect.
6. The documents issued by the CDW were "authoritative interpretations of law" which, according to the Code, would have "the same force as the law itself," because they were issued by a Roman congregation "to whom the lawmaker has committed the power to interpret the laws."
7. The objection against classifying Paul VI's legislation as universal disciplinary law because it does not bind the Eastern rites is based on a misunderstanding of the term "universal." The term refers not to rite but to a law's *territorial extension*.

The Unavoidable Consequences

For all the foregoing reasons, therefore, if you insist that Paul VI was indeed a true pope possessing plenary legislative powers as the Vicar of Christ, you must also accept the following as the unavoidable consequences of his exercise of papal authority:

1. The New Mass was legally promulgated.
2. The New Mass is obligatory.
3. The Traditional Mass was forbidden.

If you then still insist that the New Mass is **evil**, logic compels you to conclude what the Faith and Christ's promises preclude: **the Church of Christ has defected**.

For the Successor of Peter, who possesses the *authority* of Christ, has used that same authority to destroy the *Faith* of Christ by imposing a Mass that is evil. For you, then, Christ's promise to Peter and his successors is a lie and a deception — the gates of hell have prevailed.

*   *   *   *   *

This in turn, brings us back to the starting point for our study: the evil of the New Mass and the principle that the Church cannot give evil.

Paul VI followed all the correct legal forms which those invested with true papal authority customarily employed to impose universal disciplinary laws. Canonically, he dotted the i's and crossed the t's.

But what Paul VI imposed was evil, sacrilegious, and faith-destroying. This is why as Catholics we reject it.

Because we know that the authority of the Church is incapable of imposing evil universal laws, we must therefore conclude that Paul VI, the giver of evil law, did not in reality possess papal authority.

For while it is impossible for the Church herself to defect, it is possible — as popes, canonists and theologians teach — for a pope as an individual to defect from the Faith, and automatically lose papal office and authority.

Once we recognize, in a word, that the New Mass is not Catholic, we also recognize that its promulgator, Paul VI, was neither a true Catholic nor a true pope.

(*St. Gertrude the Great Newsletter 49*, February 2000).

Bibliography

ABBO, J. & HANNON, J. *The Sacred Canons*, 2nd ed. Saint Louis: Herder 1960. 2 volumes.
BUGNINI, A. *La Riforma Liturgica* (1948-1975). Rome: CLV-*Edizioni Liturgiche* 1983.
CEKADA, A. *Traditionalists, Infallibility, and the Pope*. Cincinnati: Saint Gertrude the Great Church 1995
CICOGNANI, A. *Canon Law*, 2nd. ed. Westminster MD: Newman 1934.
DIVINE WORSHIP, CONGREGATION FOR. Decree *Celebrationis Eucharistiae* (26 March 1970). AAS 62 (1970) 554.
— Notification *Conferentia Episcopalium* (28 October 1974). Notitiae 10 (1974) 353.
— Instruction *Constitutione Apostolica* (20 October 1969). AAS 61 (1969) 749-753.
— Notification *Instructione de Constitutione* (14 June 1971). AAS 712-715.

CODEX JURIS CANONICI. 1917.

CORONATA, M. *Institutiones Juris Canonici* 4th ed. Turin: Mariettti 1950. 3 volumes.

HERRMANN, P. *Institutiones Theologiae Dogmaticae.* Rome: Della Pace 1904. 2 volumes.

LAISNEY, F. "Was the Perpetual Indult Accorded by Saint Pius V Abrogated?" *Angelus* 22 (December 1999).

— "Where is the True Catholic Faith? Is the *Novus Ordo Missae* Evil?" *Angelus* 20 (March 1997).

LEWIS & SHORT. *A New Latin Dictionary,* 2nd ed. New York: 1907.

LOHMULLER, M. *Promulgation of Law.* Washington: CUA Press 1947.

MICHIELS, G. *Normae Generales Juris Canonici,* 2nd ed. Paris: Desclée 1949. 2 volumes. OPPENHEIM, P. *Tractatus de Jure Liturgico.* Turin: Marietti 1939. 2 vol.

ORDO MISSAE. Ed. *Typica. Typis Polyglottis Vaticanis*: 1969.

PAUL VI. Apostolic Constitution *Missale Romanum* (3 April 1969). AAS 61 (1969) 217-222.

PIUS V, (SAINT). Bull *Quo Primum Tempore* (19 July 1570).

PRÜMMER, D. *Manuale Juris Canonici.* Freiburg: Herder 1927.

RITES, CONGREGATION OF SACRED. Decree *Ordinis Praedicatorum* (23 May 1846) 2916.

SCOTT, P. "Debate over New Order Mass Status Continues," *Remnant,* 31 May 1997, 1ff.

Chapter 2

Is Rejecting the Pius XII Liturgical Reforms "Illegal"?

(2006)

by Rev. Anthony Cekada

Q. I was just wondering how you justify rejection of the Holy Week "reforms" under Pius XII. If the principle of "epikeia" is invoked, it would seem this does not apply given the validity of the reigning Pontiff, and his rightful authority to make such "changes." I was under the impression that epikeia only applied when a law began to work against the common good and needed to be ignored. I would appreciate your insight. Thank you for your fantastic work and time.

Q. Thank you for sending me these links to your wonderful website and for the beautiful ceremonies presented in the pictures. Regarding the 1955 Holy Week Changes: in reading the arguments from 1955 for the reasons in the changes, the "innovators" talked of "returning to earlier traditions" and of "simplification of the ceremonies," etc.: the same arguments made later for the entire *Novus Ordo*. Admittedly, the whole thing stinks of Bugnini. Annibale admitted in his memoirs that this was an important step towards the liturgical anarchy he later created with Paul VI and all their Protestant friends and bishops. I have no doubt in my mind that the 1955 changes should have been thrown out (like the rest of Bugnini's "innovations").

However, I have two main questions: what does this say to us of Pope Pius XII in those latter years for permitting and utilizing this new ceremony, and also, since we have been Interregnum since 1958, what justifications do we utilize to individually celebrate the older ceremonies which were replaced before 1958 without making it appear that we are "picking and choosing" which ceremonies we want to utilize? Is it because of the belief that Pope Pius XII would never have agreed with the changes if he knew what occurred afterwards like we do know? Is it because he never really promulgated the changes (as some believe)? Or is it simply because Bugnini was behind it all? I would greatly appreciate your thoughts on this as this topic has puzzled me for quite some time.

A. Over the years we have been repeatedly asked these questions. The answer is quite simple, and is based on the common-sense principles that underlie all the Church's legislation.

The laws promulgating the Pius XII liturgical reforms were human ecclesiastical laws, subject to the general principles of interpretation for all Church laws. As such, they no longer bind on two grounds:

I. LACK OF STABILITY (OR PERPETUITY). Stability is an essential quality of a true law. The 1955 reforms were merely transitional norms; this is self-evident from subsequent legislation and contemporaneous comments by those responsible for creating them.

In his 1955 book on the changes, *The Simplification of the Rubrics*, Bugnini, himself, makes this abundantly clear in the following passages:

- "The present decree has a contingent character. It is essentially **a bridge between the old and the new**, and if you will, **an arrow indicating the direction** taken by the current restoration..."
- "The simplification does not embrace all areas which would deserve a reform, but *for the moment only the* things that are easiest and most obvious and with an immediate and tangible effect... In the simplification, being **a 'bridge' between the present state and the general reform,** compromise was inevitable..."
- "This reform is **only the first step toward measures of a wider scope,** and it is not possible to judge accurately of a part except when it is placed in its whole."

In a 1956 commentary on the new Holy Week rite (*Bibliotheca Ephemerides Lit.* 25, p.1.), Bugnini says:

- "The decree '*Maxima redemptionis nostrae mysteria*,' promulgated by the Sacred Congregation of Rites on 16 November, 1955 [and introducing the new Holy Week] is **the third step towards a general liturgical reform.**"

Such norms (as we now realize), thus lacked one of the essential qualities of a law — stability or perpetuity — and are therefore no longer binding.

2. CESSATION. A human ecclesiastical law that was obligatory when promulgated can become harmful (*nociva*) through a change of circumstances after the passage of time. When this happens, such a law ceases to bind. (I have written several articles that touch upon this topic.)

Traditionalists apply this principle (at least implicitly) to a great number of ecclesiastical laws, and it applies equally to the 1955 reforms.

The many parallels in principles and practices between the Missal of Paul VI and the 1955 reforms now render continued use of the latter harmful, because such a use promotes (at least implicitly) the dangerous error that Paul VI's "reform" was merely one more step in the organic development of the Catholic liturgy.

Indeed, this is the very lie that Paul VI proclaimed in the first two paragraphs of *Missale Romanum*, his 1969 Apostolic Constitution promulgating the *Novus Ordo*.

It makes no sense to support this deception by insisting that the 1955 legislation still binds — especially when we now know that it was all part of a long-range plot by Annibale Bugnini's modernist cabal to destroy the Mass.

Here, from his 1955 book, *The Simplification of the Rubrics*, is Bugnini announcing the long-term goal of these changes:

- "We are concerned with 'restoring' [the liturgy]… [making it] **a new city in which the man of our age can live and feel at ease…**"
- "No doubt it is still too early to assess the full portent of this document, which marks an **important turning point** in the history of the rites of the Roman liturgy…"
- "Those who are eager for a more wholesome, realistic liturgical renewal are once more — I should say — almost invited, tacitly, to **keep their eyes open** and make an accurate investigation of the principles here put forward, to see their possible applications…"
- "More than in any other field, a reform in the liturgy must be the fruit of an intelligent, **enlightened collaboration of all the active forces.**"

And here is Bugnini describing how his "reform" commission got the liturgical changes approved by Pius XII:

> "The commission enjoyed the full confidence of the Pope, who was kept abreast of its work by Monsignor Montini [Paul VI, the modernist who would promulgate the *Novus Ordo Missae*] and even more, on a weekly basis, by Father Bea [half-Jew, modernist, and premier ecumenist at Vatican II], confessor of Pius XII. **Thanks to them, the commission was able to achieve important results even during periods when the Pope's illness kept everyone else from approaching him.**" (*The Liturgical Reform*, p.9).

Thus, the Mason's liturgical creations were presented to the sick pope for his approval by the two scheming modernists who will be major players in destroying the Church at Vatican II.

Bugnini in his memoirs, indeed, entitles the chapter on his involvement with the pre-Vatican II changes as "The Key to the Liturgical Reform." It prepared the ground for what would follow.

I devote two weeks of my seminary liturgy course on the "Modern Era" to an examination of the pre-Vatican II antecedents to the later "reforms." The problems outlined in the articles by Bp. Dolan and Fr. Ricossa on our website thus far are only the tip of the iceberg.

Traditionalists rightly set aside as inapplicable many other ecclesiastical laws. *A fortiori*, they should ignore liturgical laws that were the dirty work of the man who destroyed the Mass.

(Internet, 27 April 2006).

Chapter 3
The Liturgical Revolution Before Vatican II
(1987)

by Rev. Francesco Ricossa

The New Mass just was the final stage of a long process.

"The Liturgy, considered as a whole, is the collection of symbols, chants and acts by means of which the Church expresses and manifests its religion towards God."

In the Old Testament, God Himself, so to speak, is the liturgist. He specifies the most minute details of the worship which the faithful had to render to Him: the importance attached to a form of worship which was but the shadow of that sublime worship in the New Testament which Christ the High Priest wanted His Church to continue until the end of the world. In the Liturgy of the Catholic Church, everything is important, everything is sublime, down to the tiniest details, a truth which moved Saint Teresa of Avila to say: "I would give my life for the smallest ceremony of Holy Church."

The reader, therefore, should not be surprised at the importance we will attach to the rubrics of the Liturgy, and the close attention we will pay to the "reforms" which preceded the Second Vatican Council.

In any case, the Church's enemies were all too well aware of the importance of the Liturgy—heretics corrupted the Liturgy in order to attack the Faith itself. Such was the case with the ancient Christological heresies, then with Lutheranism and Anglicanism in the 16th century, then with the Illuminist and Jansenist reforms in the 18th century, and finally with Vatican II, beginning with its Constitution on the Liturgy and culminating in the *Novus Ordo Missae*.

The liturgical "reform" desired by Vatican II and realized in the post-Conciliar period is nothing short of a revolution. No revolution has ever come about spontaneously. It always results from prolonged attacks, slow concessions, and a gradual giving way. The purpose of this article is to show the reader how the liturgical revolution came about, with special reference to the pre-Conciliar changes in 1955 and 1960.

Monsignor. Klaus Gamber, a German liturgist, pointed out that the liturgical debacle pre-dates Vatican II. "If," he said, "a radical break with Tradition has been completed in our days with the introduction of the *Novus Ordo* the new liturgical books, it is our duty to ask ourselves where its roots are. It should be obvious to anyone with common sense that these roots are not to be looked for exclusively in the Second Vatican Council. The Constitution on the Liturgy of December 4, 1963 represents the temporal conclusion of an evolution whose multiple and not all homogenous causes go back into the distant past."

Illuminism

According to Monsignor Gamber: "The flowering of church life in the Baroque era (the Counter-Reformation and the Council of Trent) was stricken towards the end of the 18th century, with the blight of Illuminism. People were dissatisfied with the Traditional liturgy, because they felt it did not correspond with the concrete problems of the times." Rationalist Illuminism found the ground already prepared by the Jansenist heresy, which, like Protestantism, opposed the traditional Roman Liturgy.

Emperor Joseph II, the Gallican bishops of France, and of Tuscany in Italy, meeting together for the Synod of Pistoia, carried out reforms and liturgical experiments "which resemble to an amazing extent the present reforms; they are just as strongly orientated towards Man and social problems."..."We can say, therefore, that the deepest roots of the present liturgical desolation are grounded in Illuminism."

The aversion for Tradition, the frenzy for novelty and reforms, the gradual replacement of Latin by the vernacular, and of ecclesiastical and patristic texts by Scripture alone, the diminution of the cult of the Blessed Virgin and the saints, the suppression of liturgical symbolism and mystery, and finally the shortening of the Liturgy, it judged to be excessively and uselessly long and repetitive — we find all these elements of the Jansenist liturgical reforms in the present reforms, and see them reflected especially in the reforms of John XXIII. In the most serious cases the Church condemned the innovators: thus, Clement IX condemned the Ritual of the Diocese of Alet in 1668, Clement XI condemned the *Oratorian Pasquier Quesnel* (1634-1719) in 1713, Pius VI condemned the Synod of Pistoia and Bishop Scipio de' Ricci in his bull *Auctorem Fidei* in 1794.

The Liturgical Movement

"A reaction to the Illuminist plague," says Monsignor Gamber, "is represented by the restoration of the 19th century. There arose at this time the great French Benedictine abbey of Solesmes, and the German Congregation of Beuron." Dom Prosper Guéranger (1805-1875), Abbot of Solesmes, restored the old Latin liturgy in France.

His work led to a movement, later called the "Liturgical Movement," which sought to defend the Traditional liturgy of the Church, and to make it loved. This movement greatly benefited the Church up to and throughout the reign of Saint Pius X, who restored Gregorian Chant to its position of honor and created an admirable balance between the Temporal Cycle (feasts of Our Lord, Sundays, and ferias) and the Sanctoral Cycle (feasts of the saints).

The Movement's Deviations

After Saint Pius X, little by little, the so-called "Liturgical Movement" strayed from its original path, and came full circle to embrace the theories which it had been founded to combat. All the ideas of the anti-liturgical heresy — as Dom Guéranger called the liturgical theories of the 18th century — were now taken up again in the 1920s and 30s by liturgists like Dom Lambert Beauduin (1873-1960) in Belgium and France, and by Dom Pius Parsch and Romano Guardini in Austria and Germany.

The "reformers" of the 1930s and 1940s introduced the "Dialogue Mass," because of their "excessive emphasis on the active participation of the faithful in the liturgical functions." In some cases — in scout camps, and other youth and student organizations — the innovators succeeded in introducing Mass in the vernacular, the celebration of Mass on a table facing the people, and even concelebration. Among the young priests who took a delight in liturgical experiments in Rome in 1933 was the chaplain of the Catholic youth movement, a certain Father Giovanni Battista Montini.

In Belgium, Dom Beauduin gave the Liturgical Movement an ecumenical purpose, theorizing that the Anglican Church could be "united [to the Catholic Church] but not absorbed." He also founded a "Monastery for Union" with the Eastern Orthodox Churches, which resulted in many of his monks "converting" to the eastern schism. Rome intervened: the encyclical against the Ecumenical Movement, *Mortalium Animos* (1928) resulted in Dom Beauduin being discreetly recalled, a temporary diversion. The great protector of Beauduin was Cardinal Mercier, founder of "Catholic" ecumenism, and described by the anti-modernists of the time as the "friend of all the betrayers of the Church."

In the 1940s, liturgical saboteurs had already obtained the support of a large part of the hierarchy, especially in France (through the CPL — Center for Pastoral Liturgy) and in Germany.

A Warning from Germany

On January 18, 1943, the most serious attack against the Liturgical Movement was launched by an eloquent and outspoken member of the German hierarchy, the Archbishop of Freiburg, Conrad Grober. In a long letter addressed to his fellow bishops, Grober gathered together seventeen points expressing his criticisms of the Liturgical Movement. He criticized the theology of the charismatics, the Schoenstatt Movement, but above all the Liturgical Movement, involving implicitly also Theodor Cardinal Innitzer of Vienna.

Few people know that Father Karl Rahner, S.J., who then lived in Vienna, wrote a response to Grober. We shall meet Karl Rahner again as the German hierarchy's conciliar "expert" at the Second Vatican Council, together with Hans Küng and Schillebeeckx.

Mediator Dei

The dispute ended up in Rome. In 1947, Pius XII's encyclical on the liturgy, *Mediator Dei*, ratified the condemnation of the deviating Liturgical Movement.

Pius XII "strongly espoused Catholic doctrine, but the sense of this encyclical was distorted in the commentaries made on it by the innovators — and Pius XII, even though he remembered the principles, did not have the courage to take effective measures against those responsible; he should have suppressed the French CPL and prohibited a good number of publications. But these measures would have resulted in an open conflict with the French hierarchy."

Having seen the weakness of Rome, the reformers saw that they could move forward: from experiments they now passed to official Roman reforms.

Underestimating the Enemy

Pius XII underestimated the seriousness of the liturgical problem: "It produces in us a strange impression," he wrote to Bishop Grober, "if, almost from outside the world and time, the liturgical question has been presented as the problem of the moment."

The reformers thus hoped to bring their Trojan Horse into the Church, through the almost unguarded gate of the Liturgy, profiting from the scant attention that Pope Pius XII paid to the matter, and helped by persons very close to the Pontiff, such as his own confessor Agostino Bea, future cardinal and "super-ecumenist."

The following testimony of Annibale Bugnini is enlightening:

> "The Commission (for the reform of the Liturgy instituted in 1948) enjoyed the full confidence of the Pope, who was kept informed by Mgr. Montini, and even more so, weekly, by Fr. Bea, the confessor of Pius Xll. Thanks to this intermediary, we could arrive at remarkable results, even during the periods when the Pope's illness prevented anyone else getting near him."

The Revolution Begins

Father Bea was involved with Pius XII's first liturgical reform, the new liturgical translation of the Psalms, which replaced that of Saint Jerome's Vulgate, so disliked by the Protestants, since it was the official translation of the Holy Scripture in the Church, and declared to be authentic by the Council of Trent. (*Motu proprio, In cotidianis precibus,* of March 24, 1945.) The use of the New Psalter was optional, and enjoyed little success.

After this reform, came others which would last longer and be more serious:

- May 18, 1948: establishment of a Pontifical Commission for the Reform of the Liturgy, with Annibale Bugnini as its secretary January 6, 1953: the Apostolic Constitution *Christus Dominus* on the reform of the Eucharistic fast.
- March 23, 1955: the decree *Cum hac nostra aetate*, not published in the *Acta Apostolicae Sedis* and not printed in the liturgical books, on the reform of the rubrics of the Missal and Breviary.
- November 19, 1955: the decree *Maxima Redemptionis*, new rite of Holy Week, already introduced experimentally for Holy Saturday in 1951.

The following section will discuss the reform of Holy Week.

Meanwhile, what of the rubrical reforms made in 1956 by Pius XII? They were an important stage in the liturgical reforms, as we will see when we examine the reforms of John XXIII. For now it is enough to say that the reforms tended to shorten the Divine Office and diminish the cult of the saints. All the feasts of semi-double and simple ranks became simple commemorations; in Lent and Passiontide one could choose between the Office of a saint and that of the feria; the number of Vigils was diminished and Octaves were reduced to three. The *Pater, Ave* and *Credo* recited at the beginning of each liturgical hour were suppressed; even the final antiphon to Our Lady was taken away, except at Compline. The Creed of Saint Athanasius was suppressed except for once a year.

In his book, Father Bonneterre admits that the reforms at the end of the pontificate of Pius XII are "the first stages of the self-destruction of the Roman Liturgy." Nevertheless, he defends them because of the "holiness" of the pope who promulgated them.

"Pius XII," he writes, "undertook these reforms with complete purity of intention, reforms which were rendered necessary by the need of souls. He did not realize — he could not realize — that he was shaking discipline and the liturgy in one of the most crucial periods of the Church's history; above all, he did not realize that he was putting into practice the program of the straying Liturgical Movement."

Jean Crete comments on this:

> "Fr. Bonneterre recognizes that this decree signaled the beginning of the subversion of the liturgy, and yet seeks to excuse Pius XII on the grounds that at the time no one, except those who were party to the subversion, was able to realize what was going on. I can, on the contrary, give a categorical testimony on this point. I realized very well that this decree was just the beginning of a total subversion of the liturgy, and I was not the only one. All the true liturgists, all the priests who were attached to tradition, were dismayed.
>
> The Sacred Congregation of Rites was not favorable toward this decree, the work of a special commission. When, five weeks later, Pius XII announced the feast of Saint Joseph the Worker (which caused the ancient feast of Ss. Philip and James to be transferred, and which replaced the Solemnity of St Joseph, Patron of the Church), there was open opposition to it.

For more than a year the Sacred Congregation of Rites refused to compose the Office and Mass for the new feast. Many interventions of the pope were necessary before the Congregation of Rites agreed, against their will, to publish the Office in 1956 — an Office so badly composed that one might suspect it had been deliberately sabotaged. And it was only in 1960 that the melodies of the Mass and Office were composed — melodies based on models of the worst taste.

We relate this little-known episode to give an idea of the violence of the reaction to the first liturgical reforms of Pius XII."

The 1955 Holy Week: Anticipating the New Mass

"The liturgical renewal has clearly demonstrated that the formulae of the Roman Missal have to be revised and enriched. The renewal was begun by the same Pius XII with the restoration of the Easter Vigil and the Order of Holy Week, which constituted the first stage of the adaptation of the Roman Missal to the needs of our times."

These are the very words of Paul VI when he promulgated the New Mass on April 3, 1969. This clearly demonstrates how the pre-Conciliar and post-Conciliar changes are related. Likewise, Monsignor Gamber wrote that:

"The first Pontiff to bring a real and proper change to the traditional missal was Pius XII, with the introduction of the new liturgy of Holy Week. To move the ceremony of Holy Saturday to the night before Easter would have been possible without any great modification. But then along came John XXIII with the new ordering of the rubrics. Even on these occasions, however, the Canon of the Mass remained intact. [Also John XXIII introduced the name of Saint Joseph into the Canon during the council, violating the tradition that only the names of martyrs be mentioned in the Canon.] It was not even slightly altered. But after these precedents, it is true, the doors were opened to a radically new ordering of the Roman Liturgy."

The decree, *Maxima Redemptionis*, which introduced the new rite in 1955, speaks exclusively of changing the times of the ceremonies of Maundy Thursday, Good Friday, and Holy Saturday, to make it easier for the faithful to assist at the sacred rites, now transferred after centuries to the evenings of those days.

But no passage in the decree makes the slightest mention of the drastic changes in the texts and ceremonies themselves. In fact, the new rite of Holy Week was nothing but a trial balloon for post-Conciliar reform which would follow. The modernist Dominican Father Chenu testifies to this:

> "Fr. Duployé followed all this with passionate lucidity. I remember that he said to me one day, much later on. 'If we succeed in restoring the Easter Vigil to its original value, the liturgical movement will have won; I give myself ten years to achieve this.' Ten years later it was a *fait accompli*."

In fact, the new rite of Holy Week, is an alien body introduced into the heart of the Traditional Missal. It is based on principles which occur in Paul VI's 1965 reforms.

Here are some examples:

- Paul VI suppressed the Last Gospel in 1965; in 1955 it was suppressed for the Masses of Holy Week.
- Paul VI suppressed the psalm *Judica me* for the Prayers at the Foot of the Altar; the same had been anticipated by the 1955 Holy Week.
- Paul VI (following the example of Luther) wanted Mass celebrated facing the people; the 1955 Holy Week initiated this practice by introducing it wherever possible (especially on Palm Sunday).
- Paul VI wanted the role of the priest to be diminished, replaced at every turn by ministers; in 1955 already, the celebrant no longer read the Lessons, Epistles, or Gospels (Passion) which were sung by the ministers — even though they form part of the Mass. The priest sat down, forgotten, in a corner.

In his New Mass, Paul VI suppresses from the Mass all the elements of the Gallican liturgy (dating from before Charlemagne), following the wicked doctrine of "archaeologism" condemned by Pius XII. Thus, the Offertory disappeared (to the great joy of Protestants), to be replaced by a Jewish grace before meals. Following the same principle, the New Rite of Holy Week had suppressed all the prayers in the ceremony of blessing the palms (except one), the Epistle, Offertory and Preface which came first, and the Mass of the Presanctified on Good Friday.

- Paul VI, challenging the anathemas of the Council of Trent, suppressed the sacred order of the subdiaconate; the new rite of Holy Week suppressed many of the subdeacon's functions. The deacon replaced the subdeacon for some of the prayers (the *Levate* on Good Friday) the choir and celebrant replaced him for others (at the Adoration of the Cross).

CHAPTER 3

The 1955 Holy Week: Other Innovations

Here is a partial list of other innovations introduced by the new Holy Week:

- The Prayer for the Conversion of Heretics became the "Prayer for Church Unity."
- The genuflection at the Prayer for the Jews, a practice the Church spurned for centuries in horror at the crime they committed on the first Good Friday.
- The new rite suppressed much medieval symbolism (the opening of the door of the church at the *Gloria Laus* for example).
- The new rite introduced the vernacular in some places (renewal of baptismal promises).
- The *Pater Noster* was recited by all present (Good Friday).
- The prayers for the emperor were replaced by a prayer for those governing the republic, all with a very modern flavor.
- In the Breviary, the very moving psalm *Miserere*, repeated at all of the Offices, was suppressed.
- For Holy Saturday the *Exultet* was changed and much of the symbolism of its words suppressed.
- Also on Holy Saturday, eight of the twelve prophecies were suppressed.
- Sections of the Passion were suppressed, even the Last Supper disappeared, in which Our Lord, already betrayed, celebrated for the first time in history the Sacrifice of the Mass.
- On Good Friday, communion was now distributed, contrary to the tradition of the Church, and condemned by Saint Pius X when people had wanted to initiate this practice.
- All the rubrics of the 1955 Holy Week rite, then, insisted continually on the "participation" of the faithful, and they scorned as abuses many of the popular devotions (so dear to the faithful) connected with Holy Week.

This brief examination of the reform of Holy Week should allow the reader to realize how the "experts" who would come up with the New Mass fourteen years later had used and taken advantage of the 1955 Holy Week rites to test their revolutionary experiments before applying them to the whole liturgy.

Roncalli: Modernist Connections

Pius XII was succeeded by John XXIII, Angelo Roncalli. Throughout his ecclesiastical career, Roncalli was involved in affairs that place his orthodoxy under a cloud. Here are a few facts:

As professor at the seminary of Bergamo, Roncalli was investigated for following the theories of Monsignor Duchesne, which were forbidden under Saint Pius X in all Italian seminaries. Monsignor Duchesne's work, *Histoire Ancienne de l'Eglise*, ended up on the Index.

While papal nuncio to Paris, Roncalli revealed his adhesion to the teachings of *Sillon*, a movement condemned by Saint Pius X. In a letter to the widow of Marc Sagnier, the founder of the condemned movement, he wrote: "The powerful fascination of his [Sagnier's] words, his spirit, had enchanted me; and from my early years as a priest, I maintained a vivid memory of his personality, his political and social activity."

Named as Patriarch of Venice, Monsignor Roncalli gave a public blessing to the socialists meeting there for their party convention. As John XXIII, he made Monsignor Montini a cardinal and called the Second Vatican Council. He also wrote the encyclical *Pacem in Terris*. The encyclical uses a deliberately ambiguous phrase, which foreshadows the same false religious liberty the Council would later proclaim.

The Revolution Advances

John XXIII's attitude in matters liturgical, then, comes as no surprise.

Dom Lambert Beauduin, quasi-founder of the modernist Liturgical Movement, was a friend of Roncalli from 1924 onwards. At the death of Pius XII, Beauduin remarked: "If they elect Roncalli, everything will be saved; he would be capable of calling a council and consecrating ecumenism..."'

On July 25, 1960, John XXIII published the *Motu Proprio Rubricarum Instructum*. He had already decided to call Vatican II and to proceed with changing Canon Law. John XXIII incorporates the rubrical innovations of 1955–1956 into this *Motu Proprio* and makes them still worse. "We have reached the decision," he writes, "that the fundamental principles concerning the liturgical reform must be presented to the Fathers of the future Council, but that the reform of the rubrics of the Breviary and Roman Missal must not be delayed any longer."

In this framework, so far from being orthodox, with such dubious authors, in a climate which was already "Conciliar," the Breviary and Missal of John XXIII were born. They formed a "Liturgy of transition" destined to last — as it in fact did last — for three or four years. It is a transition between the Catholic liturgy consecrated at the Council of Trent and that heterodox liturgy begun at Vatican II.

The "Anti-liturgical Heresy" in the John XXIII Reform

We have already seen how the great Dom Guéranger defined as "liturgical heresy" the collection of false liturgical principles of the 18th century inspired by Illuminism and Jansenism. I would like to demonstrate in this section the resemblance between these innovations and those of John XXIII.

Since John XXIII's innovations touched the Breviary as well as the Missal, I will provide some information on his changes in the Breviary also. Lay readers may be unfamiliar with some of the terms concerning the Breviary, but I have included as much as possible to provide the "flavor" and scope of the innovations.

1. Reduction of Matins to three lessons

Archbishop Vintimille of Paris, a Jansenist sympathizer, in his reform of the Breviary in 1736, "reduced the Office for most days to three lessons, to make it shorter." In 1960, John XXIII also reduced the Office of Matins to only three lessons on most days. This meant the suppression of a third of Holy Scripture, two-thirds of the lives of the saints, and the whole of the commentaries of the Church Fathers on Holy Scripture. Matins, of course, forms a considerable part of the Breviary.

2. Replacing ecclesiastical formulae's style with Scripture

"The second principle of the anti-liturgical sect," said Dom Guéranger, "is to replace the formulae in ecclesiastical style with readings from Holy Scripture." While the Breviary of Saint Pius X had the commentaries on Holy Scripture by the Fathers of the Church, John XXIII's Breviary suppressed most commentaries written by the Fathers of the Church. On Sundays, only five or six lines from the Fathers remains.

3. Removal of saints' feasts from Sunday

Dom Guéranger gives the Jansenists' position: "It is their [the Jansenists'] great principle of the sanctity of Sunday which will not permit this day to be 'degraded' by consecrating it to the veneration of a saint, not even the Blessed Virgin Mary. A fortiori, the feasts with a rank of double or double major which make such an agreeable change for the faithful from the monotony of the Sundays, reminding them of the friends of God, their virtues and their protection —shouldn't they be deferred always to weekdays, when their feasts would pass by silently and unnoticed?"

John XXIII, going well beyond the well-balanced reform of Saint Pius X, fulfills almost to the letter the ideal of the Jansenist heretics: only nine feasts of the saints can take precedence over the Sunday (two feasts of Saint Joseph three feasts of Our Lady, Saint John the Baptist, Saints Peter and Paul, Saint Michael, and All Saints). By contrast, the calendar of Saint Pius X included 32 feasts which took precedence, many of which were former holydays of obligation. What is worse, John XXIII abolished even the commemoration of the saints on Sunday.

4. Preferring the ferial office over the saint's feast

Dom Guéranger goes on to describe the moves of the Jansenists as follows: "The calendar would then be purged, and the aim, acknowledged by Grancolas (1727) and his accomplices, would be to make the clergy prefer the ferial office to that of the saints. What a pitiful spectacle! To see the putrid principles of Calvinism, so vulgarly opposed to those of the Holy See, which for two centuries has not ceased fortifying the Church's calendar with the inclusion of new protectors, penetrate into our churches!"

John XXIII totally suppressed ten feasts from the calendar (eleven in Italy with the feast of Our Lady of Loreto), reduced 29 feasts of simple rank and nine of more elevated rank to mere commemorations, thus causing the ferial office to take precedence. He suppressed almost all the Octaves and Vigils, and replaced another 24 saints' days with the ferial office. Finally, with the new rules for Lent, the feasts of another nine saints, officially in the calendar, are never celebrated. In sum, the reform of John XXIII purged about 81 or 82 feasts of saints, sacrificing them to "Calvinist principles."

Dom Guéranger also notes that the Jansenists suppressed the feasts of the saints in Lent. John XXIII did the same, keeping only the feasts of first and second class. Since they always fall during Lent, the feasts of Saint Thomas Aquinas, Saint Gregory the Great, Saint Benedict, Saint Patrick, and Saint Gabriel the Archangel would never be celebrated.

5. Excising miracles from the lives of the Saints

Speaking of the principle of the Illuminist liturgists, Dom Guéranger notes: "the lives of the saints were stripped of their miracles on the one hand, and of their pious stories on the other."

We have seen that the reform of 1960 suppresses two out of three lessons of the Second Nocturn of Matins, in which the lives of the saints are read. But this was not enough. As we mentioned, eleven feasts were totally suppressed by the pre-Conciliar rationalists. For example, Saint Vitus, the Invention of the Holy Cross, Saint John before the Latin Gate, the Apparition of Saint Michael on Mount Gargano, Saint Anacletus, Saint Peter in Chains, the Finding of Saint Stephen, Our Lady of Loreto ("A flying house! How can we believe that in the twentieth century!"); among the votive feasts, Saint Philomena (the Curé of Ars was so "stupid" to have believed in her).

Other saints were eliminated more discreetly: Our Lady of Mount Carmel, Our Lady of Ransom, Saint George, Saint Alexis, Saint Eustace, the Stigmata of Saint Francis—these all remain, but only as a commemoration on a ferial day.

Two popes are also removed, seemingly without reason: Saint Sylvester (was he too triumphalistic?) and Saint Leo II (the latter, perhaps, because he condemned Pope Honorius).

We note finally a "masterwork" which touches us closely. From the prayer to Our Lady of Good Counsel, the 1960 reform removed the words which speak of the miraculous apparition of her image, if the House of Nazareth cannot fly to Loreto, how can we imagine that a picture which was in Albania can fly to Genzzano?

6. Anti-Roman Spirit

The Jansenists suppressed one of the two feasts of the Chair of Saint Peter (January 18), and also the Octave of Saint Peter. Identical measures were taken by John XXIII.

7. Suppression of the *Confiteor* before Communion

The suspect Missal of Trojes suppressed the *Confiteor*. John XXIII did the same thing in 1960.

8. Reform of Maundy Thursday, Good Friday and Holy Saturday

This happened in 1736, with the suspect Breviary of Vintimille ("a very grave action, and what is more, most grievous for the piety of the faithful," said Dom Guéranger.) John XXIII had his precedent here, as we have seen!

9. Suppression of Octaves

The same thing goes for the suppression of nearly all the Octaves (a usage we find already in the Old Testament, to solemnize the great feasts over eight days), anticipated by the Jansenists in 1736 and repeated in 1955-1960.

10. Make the Breviary as short as possible and without any repetition

This was the dream of the Renaissance liturgists (the Breviary of the Holy Cross, for example, abolished by Saint Pius V), and then of the Illuminists. Dom Guéranger said that the innovators wanted a Breviary "without those complicated rubrics which oblige the priest to make a serious study of the Divine Office; moreover, the rubrics themselves are traditions, and it is only right they should disappear. Without repetitions...and as short as possible... They want a short Breviary. They will have it; and it will be up to the Jansenists to write it."

These three principles will be the public boast of the reform of 1955 and 1960: the long petitions in the Office called *Preces* disappear; so too, the commemorations, the suffrages, the *Pater, Ave,* and *Credo,* the antiphons to Our Lady, the Athanasian Creed, two-thirds of Matins, and so on.

11. Ecumenism in the Reform of John XXIII

The Jansenists hadn't thought of this one. The reform of 1960 suppresses from the prayers of Good Friday the Latin adjective *perfidis* (faithless) with reference to the Jews, and the noun *perfidiam* (impiety) with reference to Judaism. It left the door open for John Paul II's visit to the synagogue.

Number 181 of the 1960 Rubrics states: "The Mass against the

Pagans shall be called the Mass for the Defense of the Church. The Mass to Take Away Schism shall be called the Mass for the Unity of the Church."

These changes reveal the liberalism, pacifism, and false ecumenism of those who conceived and promulgated them.

12. The Office becomes "private devotional reading"

One last point, but one of the most serious: *The Ottaviani Intervention* rightly declared that "when the priest celebrates without a server the suppression of all the salutations (i.e., *Dominus Vobiscum,* etc.) and of the final blessing is a clear attack on the dogma of the communion of the saints." The priest, even if he is alone, when celebrating Mass or saying his Breviary, is praying in the name of the whole Church, and with the whole Church. This truth was denied by Luther.

Now this attack on dogma was already included in the Breviary of John XXIII, it obliged the priest when reciting it alone to say *Domine exaudi orationem meam* (O Lord, hear my prayer) instead of *Dominus vobiscum* (The Lord be with you). The idea, "a profession of purely rational faith," was that the Breviary was not the public prayer of the Church anymore, but merely private devotional reading.

A Practical Conclusion

Theory is of no use to anyone, unless it is applied in practice. This article cannot conclude without a warm invitation, above all to priests to return to the liturgy "canonized" by the Council of Trent, and to the rubrics promulgated by Saint Pius X.

Monsignor Gamber writes: "Many of the innovations promulgated in the last twenty-five years — beginning with the decree on the renewal of the liturgy of Holy Week of February 9, 1951 [still under Pius XII] and with the new Code of rubrics of July 25, 1960, by continuous small modifications, right up to the reform of the *Ordo Missae* of April 3, 1969 — have been shown to be useless and dangerous to their spiritual life."

Unfortunately, in the "Traditionalist" camp, confusion reigns: one stops at 1955; another at 1965 or 1967. Archbishop Lefebvre's followers, having first adopted the reform of 1965, returned to the 1960 rubrics of John XXIII even while permitting the introduction of earlier or later uses! There, in Germany, England, and the United States, where the Breviary of Saint Pius X had been recited, the Archbishop attempted to impose the changes of John XXIII. This was not only for legal motives, but as a matter of principle; meanwhile, the Archbishop's followers barely tolerated the private recitation of the Breviary of Saint Pius X.

We hope that this and other studies will help people understand that these changes are part of the same reform and that all of it must be rejected if all is not accepted. Only with the help of God — and clear thinking — will a true restoration of Catholic worship be possible.

(*The Roman Catholic*, February–April 1987).

Chapter 4
Pre-Vatican II Liturgical Changes: Road to the New Mass
(1983)

by Most Rev. Daniel L. Dolan

Was it Pius XII and John XXIII? Or was it really Bugnini?

The recent attempt by Archbishop Lefebvre to impose the reformed liturgy of John XXIII upon Catholic clergy and laity faithful to Tradition is nothing short of a tragedy, as recent events have demonstrated. But for all this, it contains the certain ironies — but ironies which sting rather than amuse.

The Society dedicated to Saint Pius X, the great foe of Modernism, has attempted to compel its members to abandon the liturgical books bearing its holy Patron's name, a guarantee of orthodoxy, in favor of the provisional reforms of John XXIII, a man long suspected of Modernism, as he himself personally told Archbishop Lefebvre. The reforms of John XXIII were intended merely to "tide the Church over" until Vatican II could revise everything, and now they are being used to divide those who have been attempting to salvage what souls remained after the mass destruction of that Council.

The Society has rightly resisted the abuses of authority by the Conciliar Church. But it now attempts to legislate in matters liturgical — a right which it does not have, for such power belongs to the Holy See alone (Canon 1257). Instead of following its own prudent practice of keeping the custom of each country (sanctioned by the General Chapter of 1976 and never revoked), it now demands an unquestioning obedience in the name of "liturgical unity." Priests who are unwilling to give an unquestioning obedience to the demands that they "reform" the way they say Mass are first subjected to threats and finally, if that fails, they are made the objects of bitter denunciations. It is as though history is repeating itself before our eyes.

Another irony is that the Liturgy of John XXIII is not really his at all, any more than the new Holy Week can be attributed to Pope

Pius XII. These interim changes which prepared the way for the *Novus Ordo Missae* were prepared under the direction of two men: Rev. (later Cardinal) Ferdinando Antonelli, O.F.M., and Rev. (later Archbishop) Annibale Bugnini, C.M.

In 1969 Antonelli would sign the decree promulgating the *Novus Ordo*. And Bugnini, who supervised the liturgical reform from its inception in 1948 to its culmination in 1969 with the New Order of Mass, is the one Vatican prelate against whom the oft-raised charges of complicity with Masonry seem to stick. In fact, Archbishop Lefebvre himself, based on his personal experience, thinks it highly probable that Father Bugnini was a Mason.

But now we are asked to accept all the liturgical mischief done during the fifties and sixties by Father Bugnini, all the while rejecting what he produced a mere eight years later! Perhaps Catholics are right to feel they are being "set-up" for a compromise! Not irony, but tragedy!

How many times have you heard someone ask, "How could it have happened?" The answer is that it did not happen overnight. Those responsible for replacing our Holy Mass with a Community Celebration were content for years to work slowly — very slowly. A detective who examines what seems to be the corpse of Catholicism (as the world judges: truly She lives yet!) would find irrefutable evidence of the murderers' *modus operandi*: their method is one of gradualism, the very same one employed by Satan in slaying souls. This was as much as admitted by Cardinal Heenan of Westminster who said the changes had to be made gradually, or the people would never have accepted them.

Let us look at the history of "the first stages in the destruction of the Roman Liturgy" — the phrase is taken from a book on the pre-Conciliar reforms to which Archbishop Lefebvre himself wrote the preface. We shall see how by design the liturgical changes — the ones we are now asked to accept — followed each other every few years until the clergy were accustomed to living in an atmosphere of constant change, so that most of them inevitably gave in to the confusion. They no longer considered themselves bound to know and apply properly the body of rubrics, or even felt "at home" anymore in the sanctuary. In the name of "simplification," the rules and principles which governed the liturgy for centuries were slowly exchanged for the constant state of flux which presently obtains in the Conciliar Church.

After studying this cleverly conceived chronology of change you will find it no wonder that most priests were left bewildered and confused, with no more sure or unchanging principle to cling to than blind obedience, expressed by a ready acceptance of whatever new rubrics were to be found in the morning mail.

I. The "Experimental" Easter Vigil (1950)

This work of gradual change began on May 28, 1948, by the appointment of a **Commission for Liturgical Reform** with Father **Antonelli as General Director,** and Father **Bugnini as Secretary,** the men who respectively imposed and composed the *Novus Ordo Missae*.

Two years later on November 22, 1950, Cardinal Liénart, in his capacity as head of the French assembly of bishops, formally petitioned the Holy See for permission to celebrate the Easter Vigil at night rather than in the morning for "pastoral reasons." He got more than he bargained for. Under the guise of a simple change of times, a substantially rewritten rite was slipped in, even as later the "English Mass" was imposed in the name of the vernacular, with little reference to the fact that only 30% of the text of the Traditional Mass remains.

The first jarring, discordant strains of the "New Order Symphony" were already heard in this new Easter Vigil:

1. The principle of **optional rites** used experimentally was introduced.
2. For the first time, the **vernacular was introduced into the liturgy proper.** (This was Cranmer's first step as well in 1548)
3. The rubric directing the **celebrant to "sit and listen"** (*sedentes auscultant*) to the lessons rather than reading them at the altar is introduced for the first time and is immediately interpreted as justifying the exclusive use of the vernacular in this part of the liturgy.

In 1953 the immemorial midnight Eucharistic fast was mitigated to three hours under certain conditions as a concession to modern weakness. The modernist liturgists, however, saw in this the beginning of the gradual destruction of the Church's sacramental discipline, which would end with Paul VI's "fifteen minutes."

Already in 1954, the first rumblings of liturgical anarchy were heard, and Pope Pius XII warned priests in an allocution not to change anything in the liturgy on their own authority. But still changes continued.

II. The New Holy Week (1955)

The whole of the Church's venerable Holy Week got the axe in 1955 with the publication of *Maxima Redemptionis*. The lie is repeated and extended: this is merely a change of times. The drastic overhauling of most of the ceremonies of the Church's most sacred week receives no justification. How could it?

A. **KEY FEATURES:** The new Holy Week was a kind of trial balloon for the *Novus Ordo*. What were some of the key features?
   1. Everything must be **short and simple**.
   2. Key rites are to be performed by the priest with his back to the altar, **facing the people**: the Blessing of Palms, the final prayer of the Palm Sunday Procession, the Holy Saturday Blessing of the Baptismal Water, etc.
   3. The **Prayers at the Foot of the Altar** and the **Last Gospel** are suppressed for the first time.
   4. Everyone, priest and laity, must **recite together the Our Father** on Good Friday.
B. **PALM SUNDAY:** In particular, the Palm Sunday service lost its ancient rite of blessing which incorporates many prayers of the Mass, thus associating the sacramental palm with the Blessed Sacrament. The seven Collects were reduced to one, the Fore-Mass of the Blessing entirely disappeared, as did the ceremony of the *Gloria Laus* at the door of the Church. The Passion account was shortened, omitting the Anointing at Bethany and the Last Supper.
C. **THE *TRIDUUM*:** The whole of the balance of the *Triduum Sacrum*, the last three days of Holy Week, was upset. The beautiful Office of *Tenebrae* practically disappeared, as did the popular devotion of the *Tre Ore*.

The ancient **Mass of the Presanctified** on Good Friday was **abolished** and replaced with a simple Communion Service for the people. Contrary to immemorial custom, a genuflection was prescribed at the prayer for the Jews.

1. The **Holy Saturday Vigil** was **entirely changed**, with its lessons reduced from twelve to four, and there was a drastic modification of the traditional rite of the Blessing of the New Fire and Paschal Candle. (In 1955 as well, the equally ancient Vigil Service for Pentecost Eve was entirely suppressed.)

Even this necessarily superficial overview of the new Holy Week rite will enable us to understand how it was that a noted liturgical modernist, Father Duployé, could say, "If we succeed in restoring the Paschal Vigil in its original value, the Liturgical Movement will have triumphed; I give myself ten years to do that." The modernist theologian Father Chenu comments: "Ten years later it was done."

III. "Reform" of the Rubrics (1955)

The year 1955 was a bad one for the Roman Liturgy; it saw as well a modernist-oriented reform of the rubrics of the Missal and Breviary, with the decree *Cum Nostra Hac Aetate*.

So called "undesirable accretions" were removed from the Sacred Liturgy "in the light of modern scholarship," to wit:

1. The **ancient ranks** of semi-double and simple feasts were abolished.
2. Most **vigils of feast days were suppressed**, leaving the celebration of vigils "a shadow of its former self." (Vigils such as All Saints, the Apostles, Our Lady, etc.)
3. The number of **octaves** was reduced from fifteen to three. Some of the suppressed octaves went back to the 7th century!
4. For the first time a **distinction between "public" and "private" recitation of the Divine Office** was introduced, even though tradition teaches us that the Office is by its very nature a public prayer. This foreshadows the *Novus Ordo* distinction between Masses with and without people.
5. The **Our Fathers** recited in the Office were reduced from sixteen to five, and the ten **Hail Marys** and three **Creeds** were entirely omitted, as were certain other prayers before and after the Office.
6. The penitential **ferial prayers** were abolished with two minor exceptions.
7. The **Suffrage of the Saints** and the **Commemoration of the Cross** were abolished, and the beautiful Athanasian Creed (dating from the 8th century) was said but once a year.
8. The **additional Collects** said at Mass during the different seasons of the year (such as those of Our Lady and Against the Persecutors of the Church) were abolished.
9. The **Proper Last Gospel** was abolished. Here again we have been obliged to content ourselves with a brief overview of these changes which were described as "provisional" — but which so altered the sacred liturgy as to discourage all but the most dedicated priest

from learning them. Why should he bother, anyway? In five years the rubrics would change again.

Finally, in 1955 the **Solemnity of Saint Joseph**, Patron of the Universal Church, was suppressed. It was replaced with a kind of Feast Day of Labor, Saint Joseph the Worker, on the international socialist holiday of May Day.

In 1957, further changes in the Holy Week were introduced, including provision for a **Solemn High Mass** without a subdeacon.

IV. Consultation on Further Changes (1957)

In 1957 as well, the bishops of the world were consulted about further liturgical changes. The majority asked that the traditional structure of the Divine Office be preserved. Father Thomas Richstatter, in his book *Liturgical Law. New Style, New Spirit*, gives the following account:

> "One bishop quotes Saint Thomas (*Summa*, I-II, q. 97, art. 2) where he states that the modification of any positive law will naturally bring with it a certain lessening of discipline. Consequently, if there is to be a change, it must be not just for something 'a little better' but for something 'much better' in order to compensate for this falling off of discipline which necessarily accompanies any change in legislation. Therefore, the bishop states, we must be very cautious in this matter. It is not easy to say 'no' to requests for change, but that is the proper action here. The bishop concludes by stating that he is among that large number who are not only satisfied with the liturgy as it is, but who consider any change not only undesirable but dangerous to the Church."

V. Dialogue Masses and Commentators (1958)

On September 3, 1958, one month before the death of the beleaguered Pius XII, the *Instruction on Sacred Music* was issued. The use of the "Dialogue Mass," first conceded in 1922, was extended and encouraged, so that the congregation would recite much of the Mass along with the priest: the *Introit, Kyrie, Gloria,* etc., as well as all the responses. It should be noted here that the traditional form of congregational participation is Gregorian Chant. Popular recitation of Mass prayers was never done until the "Dialogue Mass" was introduced.

Under the cover of participation, lay commentators made their appearance for the first time. Their role was to read in the vernacular while the priest read in Latin.

On October 28 of that same year John XXIII was elected. He wasted no time in calling a general Council which would "consecrate Ecumenism." The following year, in June of 1960, **John XXIII appointed Father Bugnini** to serve as secretary of the Preparatory Liturgical Commission for the Council.

In the meantime, Father Bugnini continued his work with the commission for the reform of the liturgy, producing yet another series of provisional changes, to last until the conciliar reforms. The Missal and Breviary were again changed, as was the Calendar, and for the first time, the Pontifical and the Ritual.

VI. The John XXIII Changes (1960–62)

At last we come to "the liturgy of John XXIII," more properly called that of "middle Bugnini." The following changes were instituted in the Mass, the Divine Office and the Calendar:

1. The **lives of the saints** at Matins were reduced to brief summaries.
2. The **lessons from the Fathers of the Church** were reduced to the briefest possible passages, with the somewhat naive wish that the clergy would continue to nourish their souls with patristic writings on their own.
3. The **solitary recitation** of the Divine Office was no longer held to be public prayer, and thus the sacred greeting *Dominus vobiscum* was suppressed.
4. The **Last Gospel** was suppressed on more occasions.
5. The **proper conclusion** of the Office Hymns was suppressed.
6. Many **feast days were abolished**, as being redundant or not "historical, for example: (a) The Finding of the Holy Cross. (b) Saint John Before the Latin Gate. (c) The Apparition of Saint Michael. (d) Saint Peter's Chair at Antioch. (e) Saint Peter's Chains, etc.
7. During the Council, the principle of the unchanging Canon of the Mass was destroyed with the addition **of the name of Saint Joseph**.
8. The *Confiteor* **before Communion** was suppressed.

It is to be noted that the "Liturgy of John XXIII" was in vigor for all of three years, until it came to its logical conclusion with the promulgation of the Conciliar Decree on the Liturgy — also the work of Bugnini.

VII. Liturgy in the Society of Saint Pius X

A question: "Isn't this Liturgy of John XXIII the one in which you priests were trained and ordained at Ecône?"

The answer is no. We received no appreciable liturgical training whatever at Ecône, and until September of 1976 the Mass was that of the early years of Paul VI. (Indeed, concelebration was permitted in our first statutes.) The celebrant sat on the side and listened to readings, or himself performed them at lecterns facing the people. The only reason the readings were done in Latin and not French, we were told, is that the seminary is an international one! (Interestingly enough, the *Ordinances* of the Society, signed by Archbishop Lefebvre and currently in force, allow for the reading of the Epistle and the Gospel *in the vernacular* — without reading them first in Latin.)

It would be difficult to say what liturgy was followed at Ecône, because the rubrics were a mishmash of different elements, one priest saying Mass somewhat differently from the next. No one set of rubrics was systematically observed or taught. As a matter of fact, no rubrics were taught at all.

The best I can say is that over the years a certain eclectic blend of rubrics developed based on the double principle of (a) what the Archbishop liked, and (b) what one did in France. These rubrics range rather freely from the Liturgy of Saint Pius X to that of Paul VI in 1968. It is simply the "Rite of Ecône," a law unto itself.

To this day it would be impossible to study a rubrical textbook and then function, say, in a Pontifical Mass at Ecône. There is no uniformity, because there is no principle of uniformity — certainly not the "Liturgy of John XXIII." Perhaps one day someone will codify this Rite of Ecône for posterity.

As for our seminary training, we were never taught how to celebrate Mass. Preparation for this rather important part of the priestly life was to be seen to in our spare time and on our own. The majority of the seminarians there seem never to have applied themselves to a rigid or systematic study of the rubrics, as may be seen from the way in which they celebrate Mass today.

The Traditional Mass is a work of discipline and of art — every little gesture is carefully prescribed and provided for. It is a pity that today so many priests trained at Ecône are content with saying Mass "more or less" properly. But with no training and the bad example of older priests who had been subjected to 20 years of constant confusing changes, could anything else be expected?

Another happier result emerged from the liturgical chaos at Ecône. Some seminarians simply went back to the unreformed rubrics of the Church. After all, had they not been told by Archbishop Lefebvre himself that this Bugnini was a Freemason? And didn't he have his finger in the liturgical pie since 1948?

Say "No" to the Reformers

At one time we were taught to reject the Vatican Council II entirely, since, again according to the Archbishop, so many of its actions "began in heresy and ended in heresy." Why then follow the provisional liturgy which paved its way? Why, indeed? Archbishop Lefebvre saw no need in 1976 to attempt to force a liturgical "reform" on England, Germany and America which were following the unreformed liturgy.

I do not claim that the "Liturgy of John XXIII" is heretical or offensive to God in any way like the *Novus Ordo* is. I do know it to be a step towards the *Novus Ordo*, authored by the same men who produced the *Novus Ordo*. I do believe, finally, that to accept these "reforms" today with the benefit of 20 years' hindsight would be wrong. I know as well — I have seen with my own eyes — that the cumulative effect of these gradual changes on priests is disastrous.

The Church today must be rebuilt practically from the ground up. Will we look to the man glowing with health or the one slowly dying as our model? Will we take as our principle the same adage of Saint Vincent of Lerins: "*Quod semper, quod ubique, quod ab omnibus*" (What always, what everywhere, what by everyone was done) or the "laws" (if indeed they could be considered such) which in the proven intent of their creators served only to pave the way for the destruction of the "most beautiful thing this side of Heaven," the Holy Sacrifice of the Mass?

(*The Roman Catholic*, June 1983).

Chapter 5
Priestly Fraternity of Saint Peter: Some Salient Problems
(1995)

by Rev. Anthony Cekada

QUESTION: Recently, the Fraternity of Saint Peter has started operating near to where I offer the traditional Latin Mass every week. Fraternity priests tell people not to receive the sacraments at my Mass center because I do not have faculties from the local bishop, who is of course a complete modernist.

The Fraternity's criticisms of me aside, their operation leaves me very uneasy. I suspect I should tell my people to steer clear, but I can't figure out how exactly to explain the reasons.

I am not a sedevacantist. Do you have any reflections on the problems with the Fraternity of Saint Peter apart from the pope question?

REPLY: Apart from the question of John Paul II's legitimacy, working with or supporting the Priestly Fraternity of Saint Peter (FSSP) poses a whole slew of ecclesiological, doctrinal and moral problems. Whether an FSSP supporter is willing to admit it or not, he implicitly accepts the orthodoxy, legitimacy and/or intrinsic goodness of the *Novus Ordo*, ecumenism, religious liberty, communion in the hand, liturgical dance, server-ettes, patently phony annulments, the new catechism, subjection to heretical bishops, legally-sanctioned intercommunion with eastern schismatics, etc.

FSSP priests cannot condemn any of these things; Fraternity members purchase "official approval" with the coin of their silence. Nor, logically speaking, *could* FSSP condemn such things — for while their organization is enjoying official approval in its side chapel of the Conciliar Church, John Paul II is at the main altar with the dancers for the African Synod Mass, an officially-approved female in another chapel is popping hosts in the officially-approved way into people's hands, and someone else in still another chapel is running kiddy Masses according to the officially-approved Children's Directory.

The Traditional Mass and the Traditional Faith are thus reduced to nothing more than one dish among the many officially approved for the post-Vatican II smorgasbord. Worship and belief become nothing more than a matter of "preference" — I like the old way, you like the new way, and we're all one big happy post-Vatican II family.

Lay people sometimes are oblivious to this broader picture. They see a Traditional Mass, and presume all is well. It's not. In reality, the Fraternity of Saint Peter is leading its lay adherents bit by bit into the high-church, nostalgia wing of the ecumenical, post-Vatican II religion.

Such an aim, to be sure, may be far from the minds of priests and seminarians in the FSSP. But it is difficult to discern what reason they could give for adhering to the old Mass, other than pure, sentimental "preference." All FSSP members must accept the legitimacy and "doctrinal rectitude" of the *Novus Ordo*. Why refrain from celebrating a valid, licit and doctrinally-sound rite of Mass if the pope himself celebrates it? It would be interesting to hear FSSP explain the theory behind its practice.

(*Sacerdotium* 14, Spring 1995).

Chapter 6

Quo Primum: Could a Pope Change It?

(2007)

by Rev. Anthony Cekada

QUESTION: *During a recent argument with a* Novus Ordo *friend, she told me that (according to her priest) popes can change whatever they want, as long as it is not dogmatic. We were discussing* "Quo Primum." *I told her that it was forever, but she said that even if the pope said "forever" another pope can change it. What would you say to that?*

REPLY: On this point, she's right.

A (true) pope is the supreme legislator for ecclesiastical law and has the power to change ecclesiastical laws enacted by his predecessors. *Quo Primum* was an ecclesiastical law, and a true pope did indeed have the power to abrogate it or modify any of its provisions.

The "forever" clause was merely a type of legal boilerplate common in all sorts of papal legislation.

In the 1960s faithful Catholics seized upon this language as a justification for disobeying the new liturgical legislation while simultaneously "recognizing" Paul VI as a true pope. This was unfortunate, because anyone who knows a bit about Canon Law can refute the argument very easily.

The argument also obscures the *real* reason for adhering to the Traditional Mass and rejecting the New Mass: The old rite is Catholic. The new rite is evil, inimical to Catholic doctrine (on the Real Presence, the priesthood, the nature of the Mass, etc.) and a sacrilege.

If you send me your postal address, though, I'll send you a consolation prize: some copies of a booklet I wrote, *Welcome to the Traditional Latin Mass*, that compares the old Mass and the New Mass. Give a copy to your friend and tell her to give it to her priest. That should keep him busy for quite a while!

QUESTION: *So you are saying that a real pope can change a Papal Bull decree that another pope has made in perpetuity? Why would a pope decree something for all time, if another pope could change it?*

REPLY: If it was a *disciplinary* Bull (establishing a Church law), yes, another pope could change it. The language was simply a standard formula in church legislation that referred to one of the qualities a law is supposed to have: stability.

Frequent changes in laws harm the common good because people do not know how to act — hence, laws are supposed to be relatively stable. But a human legislator (unlike God) cannot foresee all future circumstances, so his successor has the power to change existing laws if he decides the circumstances warrant it.

This reflects a general principle in law: An equal does not have power over another equal. No pope who used "perpetuity" in his disciplinary decrees understood the term to mean that no future pope could ever amend or replace his legislation.

And popes did in fact change some of the provisions of *Quo Primum*, even before Vatican II. In 1604, for instance, Pope Clement VIII issued new regulations for the Blessing at Mass, and in 1634 Pope Urban VIII changed the wording of the Missal's rubrics and hymn texts.

Traditionalists should stop using the *Quo Primum* argument. It's a Canon Law urban-legend — as in "alligators in the sewers," rather than Urban VIII!

This was written by Rev. Anthony Cekada. Posted on Thursday, May 17, 2007, at 12:33 pm.

Chapter 7
Russia and the Leonine Prayers
(1992)

by Rev. Anthony Cekada

The Prayers after Low Mass and recent events in Russia

After my ordination to the priesthood in 1977, I followed the lead of other Traditional priests in the U.S., and began announcing that the Leonine Prayers — the three Hail Marys, the *Salve Regina* and the Saint Michael prayer recited after Low Mass — were recited "for the conversion of Russia."

Having heard this intention announced for the umpteenth time, a faithful traditional Catholic in a church I serve recently inquired: "Why do we always have to pray for the conversion of *Russia*? Why can't we pray for *America* instead?"

It seemed like a fair question. I therefore set out to document what was surely the correct answer: that the Church, responding to Our Lady's 13 July, 1917, request at Fatima, had decreed that the object of these prayers was to obtain Russia's conversion to the Catholic faith. End of story — or so I thought.

I consulted about 20 standard commentaries on the Mass and encountered something surprising: not *one* of them stated that the Leonine Prayers were connected with the Fatima Message. And not one of them said that the object of the prayers was to bring about Russia's conversion to Catholicism.

Having drawn a blank, I turned to a multi-volume work containing the texts of all the laws the Holy See has promulgated since 1917.[1] The work contained a number of official decrees on the Leonine Prayers — but none of the decrees tied the prayers to the Fatima Message. And again, none of them stated that the object of the prayers was to obtain Russia's conversion to the Catholic faith.

Traditional Catholic priests, it thus appears, have unwittingly promoted a notion about these prayers which is false. Obviously this should be corrected, since we do, after all, profess adherence to the

---
[1] Xaverius Ochoa ed., *Leges Ecclesiae post Codicem Juris Canonici*, (Rome: Polyglot 1969).

Church's traditions and laws.

The history of the Leonine Prayers is also more than a little intriguing, tied as it is to various crises the Church has faced over the past century and a half. Recent developments in Russia, moreover, raise certain legal and practical questions regarding the use of the prayers.

Here we will consider the following issues:

1. The origins of the Leonine Prayers.
2. The object (or intention) Pope Pius XI decreed for them.
3. Two dubious stories which have been circulated about the prayer to Saint Michael the Archangel.
4. Past legislation on the Leonine Prayers, and whether, in light of recent events in Russia, the law prescribing their recitation has accordingly ceased.
5. Whether it would thus now be permissible to recite in place of the Leonine Prayers other prayers for other intentions.

I. ORIGINS OF THE PRAYERS

From the onset of the Napoleonic wars in the late 18th century, the position of the popes as temporal rulers of the Papal States (the civil territories they governed in central Italy) became increasingly more precarious.

Though the Congress of Vienna (1815) had restored the pope's sovereignty over his temporal domains, Masonry and other secret societies, such as the Carbonari, conspired to stir up revolts against him. In 1830 and 1832 rebellions broke out in the Papal States, and in 1848 the revolutionaries succeeded in driving Pope Pius IX from Rome.

In 1850 Napoleon III sent his army into Italy, restored Pius to his temporal throne and garrisoned Rome with imperial troops — an act prompted not so much by the French Emperor's devotion to the Holy See as by his desire to undermine Austrian influence in Italy. Meanwhile, the adepts of the secret societies, supported by aid from abroad, took over the governments of the city-states which bordered the papal domains.[2]

---

[2] For a concise and excellent account of the history of the Papal States, see E. Jarry, "Les États Pontificaux," *Tu es Petrus: Encyclopédie Populaire sur la Papauté*, ed. by G. Jacquemet, (Paris: Bloud 1934), 551–617. See also Gustav Schnürer, "States of the Church," *The Catholic Encyclopedia*, ed. by Charles G. Habermann et al., (New York: Encyclopedia Press 1912), 14:257–268.

CHAPTER 7

Surrounded by hostile states, undermined by secret societies, and supported by a half-hearted ally, Pius IX feared that the triumph of the revolutionaries was imminent.

Early in 1859, the Pontiff ordered that special public prayers — three Hail Marys, the *Salve Regina*, a versicle and a Collect — be recited after Mass in all churches within the Papal States. The prayers were not obligatory in other countries. But Pius urged Catholics everywhere to pray for the defeat of the enemies of his temporal sovereignty,[3] and granted indulgences to all who would recite the prayers for his intentions.[4]

In 1870 Rome fell to the revolutionaries and the army of the royal House of Savoy. Pius IX shut himself up in the Vatican, excommunicated those who had seized the papal territories and refused to recognize the legitimacy of the government the usurpers had set up. Thus began the "Roman Question" — the issue of what accommodation, if any, could be reached between the legitimate temporal claims of the Supreme Pontiff and the government of the new Italian state which exercised *de facto* control over the pope's states. The question would weigh heavily on the hearts of popes for nearly 60 years.

In the 1880s, anti-clerical mobs, egged on by the Masonic lodges, repeatedly demonstrated against Pope Leo XIII, and even attempted to throw the remains of Pius IX into the Tiber. The government enacted a series of laws against the Catholic clergy, and by the end of the decade would confiscate the goods of Catholic charitable associations.

On 6 January, 1884, therefore, Leo XIII decreed that the prayers Pius IX had prescribed for churches in the Papal States be recited after Low Mass in churches throughout the world, "so that the Christian people would implore God with common prayer for that very thing which benefits the whole Christian commonwealth."[5]

The Collect which Pope Leo first prescribed is different from the version we are accustomed to. Here is the 1884 version, with the variants noted in *italics*:

> O God, our refuge and our strength, *hearken to the devout prayers of Thy Church, and* through the intercession of the glorious and immac-

---

[3] Encyclical *Qui Nuper*, 18 June 1859.
[4] Encyclical *Cum Sancta Mater Ecclesia*, 27 April 1859.
[5] S.R.C. Decree *Iam Inde ab Anno*, 6 January 1884, in *Acta Sanctae Sedis* 16 (1884), 249–250. "*Iamvero gravibus adhuc insidientibus malis nec satis remota suspicione graviorum, cum Ecclesia catholica singulari Dei praesideo tantopere indigeat, Sanctissimus Dominus Noster Leo Papa XIII opportunum iudicavit, eas ipsas preces nonnullis partibus immutatas toto orbe persolvi, ut quod christianae reipublicae in commune expedit, id communi prece populus christianus a Deo condendat, auctoque supplicantium numero divinae beneficia misericordiae facilius assequatur.*"

ulate Virgin Mary, Mother of God, of blessed Joseph, of Thy blessed apostles Peter and Paul, and of all the saints, *grant that what we humbly seek in our present needs, we may readily obtain.*[6]

Parts of the prayer will sound familiar. The text is an expanded version of the oration for the 22nd Sunday after Pentecost.

In 1886 the text of the Collect was changed to the following:

> O God, our refuge and our strength, look down with mercy on Thy people who cry to Thee, and through the intercession of the glorious and immaculate Virgin Mary, Mother of God, of blessed Joseph, of Thy blessed apostles Peter and Paul, and of all the saints, in mercy and goodness hear the prayers we pour forth to Thee for the conversion of sinners and for the freedom and exaltation of Holy Mother Church.

While two other small changes were later made in the Latin text, this version of the Collect is the one we all know so well.

At the same time, the Prayer to Saint Michael the Archangel was added. The opening words of the invocation are similar to the *Alleluia* verse for Saint Michael's feasts on May 8 and September 29.

The 1886 changes, by the way, present a curious legal anomaly. Before a liturgical practice can be made legally binding for the whole Church, the decree prescribing it must be promulgated in an official publication. There is no decree, however, in either the 1886 acts of the Holy See,[7] or in the six-volume collection of the authentic decrees of the Sacred Congregation of Rites[8] which authorizes the 1886 changes. (Indeed, I can find no decree for these changes anywhere.) The explanation, I suspect, is simply that a curial official forgot to have it registered.

In 1904, in any case, Saint Pius X allowed priests to add the threefold invocation "Most Sacred Heart of Jesus, have mercy on us" after the prayer to Saint Michael. He did not make the practice obligatory, but it was generally adopted by priests throughout the world.

II. A NEW INTENTION

During the pontificates of Leo XIII, Saint Pius X and Benedict XV, little progress was made toward resolving the Roman Question, due to the complex and volatile political situation in Italy. The negotiating

---

[6] Ibid., 250. "...*adesto piis Ecclesiae tuae precibus, et praesta; ut ... quod in praesentibus necessitatibus humiliter petimus, efficaciter consequamur.*"
[7] *Acta Sanctae Sedis* 18 (1886).
[8] *Decreta Authentica Congregationis Sacrorum Rituum*, (Rome: Polyglot Press 1898).

process finally began to gain momentum after the election of Pius XI in 1922.

On 12 February, 1929, the Vatican announced that the Holy See and Italy had signed a treaty which settled the Roman Question, regulated relations between the Church and the Italian state, and stipulated how the Holy See would be remunerated for the territory it had lost. The accord was ratified at the Lateran Palace on 9 June, 1929,[9] and was followed by a cordial exchange of telegrams between the Pope and the King of Italy.

In Article 26 of the Lateran Treaty, the Holy See declared "the Roman question definitely and irrevocably settled and therefore eliminated."[10] The purpose for which the Leonine Prayers had been instituted was therefore achieved.

The Supreme Pontiff, however, had another important intention that he wished to recommend to the prayers of the faithful. The Communist government in Russia had begun a systematic persecution of Catholics. Pius XI asked Catholics in Russia and throughout the world to observe a day of prayer to implore Saint Joseph for his aid. On the day appointed, even the eastern schismatics honored the Pope's request.

In a 1930 address to the College of Cardinals, Pius XI discussed both the Lateran Treaty and Russia. He spoke of the day of prayer for the Church in Russia, expressing his hope that the prayers which had been offered for those suffering would be more fruitful in the future.

The Pontiff then noted sadly that "not so long ago the enemies of God and religion throughout the aforementioned regions kindled a very fierce persecution of the Church." He immediately added:

> "Christ, the Redeemer of the human race, is therefore to be implored to permit tranquility and freedom to profess the faith to be restored to the afflicted people of Russia. And, that all may be able to make this prayer with very little trouble and difficulty, We desire that those same prayers which Our Predecessor of happy memory, Leo XIII, ordered priests to recite with the people after Mass, shall be said for this intention, that is, for Russia. Bishops and the clergy, both secular and religious, should be most zealous in giving notice of this to their people or to all who assist at Mass, and should frequently remind them of it."[11]

---

[9] For the text of the treaty, see Appendix A to Wilfred Parsons SJ, *The Pope and Italy*, (New York: America Press 1929).

[10] In Parsons, 93.

[11] Pius XI, Allocution *Indictam ante*, 30 June 1930, *Acta Apostolicae Sedis* 22 (1930), 301. "... *fecundiorem eam posthac evasuram sperare licet, etsi, non ita pridem, divini nominis cultusque, per eas quas diximus regiones, inimici ad Ecclesiae insectationem exarsere acrius. Christo igitur*

The new intention which the Pontiff decreed for the Prayers after Low Mass, therefore, was that Christ "permit tranquility and freedom to profess the faith to be restored to the afflicted people of Russia."

An action taken by the Pontifical Commission for Russia reconfirms that this is indeed the actual intention the Pontiff laid down. While the Pope's decree applied only to priests of the Latin Rite, the Commission promptly prepared another decree for Catholic Uniates who employed the Byzantine Rite. The Commission ordered the insertion into the Byzantine Rite Mass of prayers for peace for the clergy, "the brethren," and "all our people."[12]

The "freedom of the Church in Russia" (as the liturgist Wuest succinctly put it),[13] therefore — and not the conversion of Russia to the Catholic faith in fulfillment of the Fatima promises — was the intention for which these prayers continued to be prescribed.

III. TWO DUBIOUS STORIES

The two foregoing sections outlined the origins of the Leonine Prayers as a unit. One of these prayers, the Invocation to Saint Michael the Archangel, merits special attention, since some intriguing but rather dubious stories have come to be associated with it.

A. An Alleged Vision

A pamphlet dealing with a diabolical possession, written in the

---

humani generis Redemptori instandum, ut afflicitis Russiae filiis tranquillitatem fideique profitendae libertatem restitui sinat; atque ut instare omnes, modico sane negotio atque incommodo, queant volumus, quas fel. rec. decessor Noster Leo XIII sacerdotes cum populo post sacrum expletum preces recitare iussit, eaedem ad hanc ipsam mentem, scilicet pro Russia, dicantur; id ipsum Episcopi atque uterque clerus populares suos, vel sacro adstantes quoslibet, studiosissime moneant, in eorundemque memoriam saepenumero revocent."

[12] *Pontificia Commissio pro Russia*, Decree *Cum Summus*, 11 July 1930, *Acta Apostolicae Sedis* 22 (1930), 366. "*Cum Summus Pontifex Pius div. Prov. Papa XI in Consistorio secreto diei 30 Junii c. a. praeceperit ut latini sacerdotes toto orbe terrarum preces, post sacrum expletum iussu Leonis Papae XIII recitandas, nunc pro Russia applicent, haec Pontificia Commissio sacerdotes non latinos sibi subditos hortatur, ut dum Sacram Liturgiam celebrant, eandem intentionem Deo commendent. Ideo: (1) in sic dicta Ectenia Magna, inter preces seu invocationes (…) post verba* [in Cyrillic: For this city and every city] *haec addantur:* [in Cyrillic: and for all our brethren, let us pray to the Lord]. (2) *In fine Liturgiae, in oratione sic dicta post ambonem (…), post verba* [in Cyrillic: Give peace to all Thy people and Thy Church], *haec addantur:* [in Cyrillic: and to His Holiness, the first among bishops, Pius XI, Pope of Rome, and to all priests and to all of our brethren and to all of our people]."

[13] Joseph Wuest CSsR, *Matters Liturgical: The Collectio Rerum Liturgicarum*, trans. by Thomas W. Mullaney CSsR and rearranged and enlarged by William T. Barry CSsR, (New York: Pustet 1956), 440.

early 1930s and still popular in Traditional Catholic circles, relates the following about the Saint Michael prayer:

> "A rather peculiar circumstance induced Pope Leo XIII to compose this powerful prayer. After celebrating Mass one day he was in conference with the Cardinals. Suddenly he sank to the floor. A doctor was summoned and several came at once. There was no sign of any pulse-beating[;] the very life seemed to have ebbed away from the already weakened and aged body. Suddenly he recovered and said: "What a horrible picture I was permitted to see!" He saw what was going to happen in the future, the misleading powers and the ravings of the devils against the Church in all countries. But Saint Michael had appeared in the nick of time and cast Satan and his cohorts back into the abyss of hell. Such was the occasion that caused Pope Leo XIII to have this prayer recited over the entire world at the end of Mass."[14]

The foregoing passage appears as a digression in an account of an exorcism. The author gives no date for the alleged vision.

An article written in 1933 repeats the same account, virtually word for word, adding: "And so, shortly after 1880, Leo decreed the general prayer to Saint Michael."[15] Note the date given for the supposed vision: 1880 — four years before Leo XIII prescribed the Prayers after Low Mass *without* the Saint Michael prayer, and six years before the prayer itself was actually prescribed.

A more recent variant of the story adds another detail: It quotes a dialogue between Our Lord and Satan that Pope Leo supposedly heard during the vision. One writer says the dialogue occurred at the foot of the altar, where Leo stopped after Mass. He gives no date.[16] Another writer tells the same story, but he gives a date: 13 October, 1884.[17]

Still another writer tells essentially the same variant of the story

---

[14] Carl Vogl, *Begone Satan: A Soul-Stirring Account of Diabolical Possession in Iowa*, trans. by Celestine Kapsner OSB, (St. Cloud MN: 1935), reprinted Rockford IL: TAN Books 1973, 24. The exorcism took place in Earling, Iowa in 1928, and was the basis for William Peter Blatty's novel The Exorcist, which was itself later made into a film.

[15] Hg. Schnell, *Konnersreuther Sonntagsblattes* (1933), no. 39, "*Nachdem Leo XIII. eines Morgens die heilege Messe zelebriert hatte, begab er sich zu einer Besprechung mit den Kardinälen. Aber plötzlich sank er in Ohnmacht zusammen. Die herbeigeeilten Arzte fanden keinen Grund zu dieser Ohnmacht, obwohl der Pulsschlag fast aufhörte. Plötzlich erwachte er wieder und war frisch wie zuvor. Er erzählte dann, er hätte ein furchtbares Bild gesehen. Er durfte die Verführungskünste und das Wüten der Teufel der kommenden Zeiten in allen Ländern sehen. In dieser Not erschien Saint Michael, der Erzengel, und warf den Satan mit allen seinen Teufeln in den höllischen Abgrund zurück. Daraufhin ordnete Leo XIII. kurz nach 1880 das allgemeine Gebet zum heiligen Michael an.*" Quoted in Bers "*Die Gebete nach der hl. Messe,*" *Theol-Prakt. Quartalschrift* 87 (1934), 161.

[16] See "An Interesting Story," The *Maryfaithful* (Sept–Oct 1978), 19.

[17] Arthur H. Durand, "Satan's Hundred Year War," *The Remnant* (15 January 1984), 9–10.

as these two writers, but he has the event taking place when "the aged Pontiff was in a conference with the Cardinals."[18]

And the most recently circulated version of the story gives yet another date for the supposed vision: 25 September, 1888.[19] Here again, remember that the Saint Michael prayer in fact appeared two years *earlier* (in 1886) than this account would have it.[20]

Now while all six accounts cited connect the Saint Michael prayer with a supposed vision, they differ as to when, where, and how the alleged vision took place. None of them, moreover, gives a source, even the two accounts from the 1930s. All six authors merely assert that the incident took place.

Taken together, these factors should be a cause for suspicion.

In 1934 a German writer, Father Bers, investigated the origins of the story of Leo's vision. "Wherever one looks," he observed, "one may find this claim — but nowhere a trace of proof."

Sources contemporaneous with the institution of the prayer were silent on the matter. Father Bers quoted a priest who visited with Leo XIII when the prayer was instituted in 1886:

> "When the prayers which the priest says after Mass were being instituted, I happened to have a short audience with the Holy Father. During the conversation Leo XIII mentioned what he was going to prescribe and recited all the prayers from memory. This he did with such deep-seated conviction of the power of the cosmic rulers of this darkness and of the beguilement which they cause, that I was quite struck by it."[21]

Commenting on this passage, Father Bers concluded:

> "Therefore it can be safely assumed that the Holy Father would have spoken of the vision if he had had it — or that at least the reporter would have mentioned it — since it would have been most relevant to the general purport of the statement. Consequently, the argument 'from silence' seems to indicate clearly that the 'vision' had been invented in later times for some reason, and was now feeding upon itself 'like a perpetual sickness.'"[22]

The problems with the story connecting the institution of the Saint

---

[18] *Saint Michael and the Angels*, compiled from Approved Sources, (Rockford IL: TAN 1988), 84–85.
[19] Gary Giuffré, "Exile of the Pope-Elect, Part VII: Warnings from Heaven Suppressed," *Sangre de Cristo Newsnotes* 69–70 (1991), 4.
[20] See *Irish Ecclesiastical Review* 7 (1886), 1050.
[21] *Kölner Pastoralblatt* (1891) 179, cited in Bers 162–163.
[22] Bers, 162–163.

Michael prayer and a supposed vision of Leo XIII may be summarized as follows:

- Writings which promote the story give no references to sources.
- The various accounts contradict each other as to where the vision supposedly took place — after Mass at the foot of the altar, or in a conference with cardinals.
- The various accounts are inconsistent about the date of the vision.
- The dates the accounts give for the alleged vision (1880, 1884 and 1888) do not correspond with the date when the Saint Michael prayer was actually instituted (1886).
- There appears to be no corroboration for the story in a contemporary account which one would expect to have mentioned the event, had it indeed taken place.

These considerations all tend to support the conclusion Father Bers arrived at in the 1930s: "that the 'vision' had been invented in later times for some reason," and that the story was simply feeding upon itself.

B. Conspiracies and "Falsified" Texts

Another story which has recently gained currency in Traditionalist circles alleges that the Saint Michael prayer is a "falsified" version of a longer prayer Leo XIII wrote. The longer prayer, we are told, warned that Judaeo-Masonic infiltrators would achieve their long-time goal of usurping the papal chair, so conspirators "censored" it twice after Leo's death.[23]

This is the sort of juicy tale that certain types on the Traditional Catholic scene really love to promote. It incorporates some familiar elements: private revelations, infiltrators, altered documents, a deceived Pontiff, and prophecies of an evil intruder sitting on the Chair of Peter. For those who understand how the enemies of the Church operate, parts of the account may sound plausible at first. It also (as contemporary book reviewers like to say) makes for "a rollicking good read."

Unfortunately, it's the type of conspiracy story which exposes Traditional Catholics to ridicule — because when you look closely at the facts adduced as "proof" for a conspiracy, you discover that the story's originators managed to get just about everything wrong.

---

[23] Thus Giuffré, 4–7.

To understand how, we turn first to the background of the prayer which — the story goes — is the "original" version of the prayer to Saint Michael recited after Low Mass.

On 25 September, 1888, Pope Leo XIII approved a prayer to Saint Michael the Archangel and granted an indulgence of 300 days for its recitation.[24] By this time, of course, the text of the prayer to Saint Michael we know from the Prayers after Low Mass had already been in use for two years.[25] The text Leo approved in 1888 was, in fact, a completely *new* prayer.

Like the 1886 text, the 1888 prayer also invokes Saint Michael's aid for us in our warfare against the devil. But it is a very lengthy text, filled with line after line of vivid and striking imagery about the devil and his minions.

The prayer describes the devil as one who pours out on "men of depraved mind and corrupt heart, the spirit of lying, of impiety, of blasphemy, and the pestilent breath of impurity, and of every vice and iniquity." Of these servants of Satan, the prayer adds:

> These most crafty enemies have filled and inebriated with gall and bitterness the Church, the spouse of the Immaculate Lamb, and have laid impious hands on her most sacred possessions.

The prayer then expands upon this description with the following:

> In the Holy Place itself, where has been set up the See of the most holy Peter and the Chair of Truth for the light of the world, they have raised the throne of the abominable impiety, with the iniquitous design that when the Pastor has been struck, the sheep may be scattered.[26]

These two passages, needless to say, are the ones which the censored-text theorists claim "predict" the effects of Vatican II.

---

[24] For the Italian text, see *Enchiridion Indulgentiarum: Preces et Pia Opera Omnium Christifidelium*, (Vatican: Polyglot Press 1950), 446. A search of the *Acta Sanctae Sedis* for 1888 failed to turn up the text of the *Motu proprio* mentioned in the *Enchiridion*. The 300 Days indulgence, therefore, was most likely granted *viva voce* by Pope Leo during the course of an audience and simply noted in a curial diary. The indulgence was increased to 500 days in 1934. It may be that Leo XIII had some sort of vision or locution in connection with the institution of *this* prayer to Saint Michael, rather than the prayer to Saint Michael recited after Low Mass.

[25] For the Latin version, see *Irish Ecclesiastical Review* 7 (1886), 1050. "*Sancte Michael Archangele, defende nos in praelio; contra nequitiam et insidias diaboli esto praesidium. — Imperet illi Deus, supplices deprecamur; tuque, Princeps militiae coelestis, Satanam aliosque spiritus malignos, qui ad perditionem animarum pervagantur in mundo, divina virtute in infernum detrude. Amen.*"

[26] These two texts are from a translation in Ambrose Saint John, *The Raccolta or Collection of Indulgenced Prayers and Good Works*, 11th ed., (London: Burns Oates 1930), 407.

After its approval, the 1888 text was at some point included in *The Raccolta* (the Church's official collection of indulgenced prayers). In an audience two years later, moreover, Leo XIII approved a new and lengthy "Exorcism against Satan and Apostate Angels," intended to be used by bishops and by priests who received special permission from their ordinaries.[27] This rite employed the 1888 prayer to Saint Michael, including the two passages quoted above, as sort of a preface to a series of prayers of exorcism.[28] The rite was then incorporated into the Appendix of *The Roman Ritual* (the book containing the official texts for sacramental rites and various blessings) among the more recent blessings (*Benedictiones Novissimae*).[29]

Later editions of *The Raccolta* omitted the conclusion of the 1888 prayer, beginning with the passage which spoke of the "throne of abominable impiety" raised where the See of Peter stood. Later editions of *The Roman Ritual* went even further: they omitted not only that passage, but also the one referring those who have laid impious hands on the Church's most sacred possessions. Other passages were deleted as well, leaving only about one-third of the 1888 text. (See the Appendix below.)

Now, having misidentified an 1888 prayer as the antecedent to an 1886 prayer, the proponents of the censored-text theory contend that unnamed infiltrators in the Vatican, fearing exposure of their plot to seize control of the See of Peter, stealthily deleted these passages from the *Raccolta* and the *Ritual* after Leo's death.

All of it is nonsense.

First, the passages were not removed after Leo XIII's death. They were already suppressed in 1902 — a year and a half *before* the Pontiff died.

Second, this suppression was not, as we are told, an "ambiguous forgery" perpetrated "mysteriously" by some "unnamed Vatican official." The Sacred Congregation of Rites, in consultation with the Congregation for Indulgences, revised the 1888 prayer and issued a new edition. This was printed in 1902, bearing the seal of the Congrega-

---

[27] S.C. de Propaganda Fide, *ex audientia Sanctissimi* 18 May 1890, *Acta Sanctae Sedis* 23 (1890–91), 747. "...omnibus Reverendissimis Episcopis, nec non Sacerdotibus ab Ordinariis suis legitime ad id auctoritatem habentibus..."

[28] S.C. de Propaganda Fide. "Exorcismus in satanam et angelos apostaticos iussu Leonis XIII P.M. editus," *Acta Sanctae Sedis* 23 (1890–91), 743–4. "*Ecclesiam, Agni immaculati sponsam, vaferrimi hostes repleverunt amaritudinibus, inebriarunt absinthio; ad omnia desiderabilia ejus impias miserunt manus. Ubi sedes beatissimi Petri et Cathedra veritatis ad lucem gentium constituta est, ibi thronum posuerunt abominationis impietatis suae; ut percusso Pastore, et gregem disperdere valeant.*"

[29] See *Rituale Romanum*, 6th ed. *post typicam*, (Ratisbon: Pustet 1898), 163*ff.

tion's Prefect, Cardinal Ferrata, and the signature of the Congregation's Secretary, Archbishop D. Panici.[30]

Third, the passages in question, please note, were not written in the *future* tense, as one would expect for a prophecy. They were written in the past tense, and thus referred to events which had already *taken place* in 1888.

To whom, then, do the passages refer? One has but to look to the situation the Pope faced in Italy in the late 1880s.

The "crafty enemies" of the Church who "laid impious hands on her most sacred possessions" were none other than the revolutionaries who (as we have seen above) invaded the Papal States and despoiled the Church's properties.

And the "throne of abominable impiety" raised up in "the Holy Place itself, where there has been set up the See of the most holy Peter and the Chair of truth for the light of the world"? This was the throne of the King of Italy, set up in the Quirinale Palace.

Prior to its seizure in 1870 by the excommunicated King of Italy, Victor Emmanuel, the Quirinale was the principal papal palace in Rome. It was the customary location for papal conclaves. It was also one of the places where the pope had held court, sitting, of course, on a throne — the "Chair of truth for the light of the world." When the 1888 prayer was composed, the throne of a usurping and excommunicated monarch then stood in this palace which had been stolen from the pope.

Why, finally, were the texts altered toward the end of the Leo's reign? Again, we look to historical situation.

By 1902 Leo XIII had been carrying on secret negotiations for years with the new King, Umberto. The King at one point appeared willing to return a substantial part of the city of Rome to the Pope's control — a proposal that could have infuriated Parliament enough to call for the King's deposition.[31] Had Umberto made such a risky concession, he would have expected (and received) official recognition of his status from the Pope. Further references to the King in the Church's *Ritual* as occupying "a throne of abominable impiety," needless to say, would have been at odds with papal acknowledgement of the King's

---

[30] See supplementary material bound into back of Pustet *Rituale Romanum*, 6th ed., (1898). "*Concordat cum suo Originali, asservato penes Secretariam S. Congregationis Indulgentiis sacrisque Reliquiis praepositae. In fidem etc. Ex Secretaria Sacror. Rituum Congregationis, die 7. Januarii 1902. [l.s.] + D. Panici Archiep. Laodicen. S.R.C. Secretarius.*"
[31] See Jarry, 610.

legitimacy.[32] The prayer also linked the establishment of the King's throne with the devil, who pours out on "men of depraved mind and corrupt heart, the spirit of lying, of impiety, of blasphemy, and the pestilent breath of impurity, and of every vice and iniquity." Since the King gave signs of wanting to make amends, it probably seemed appropriate to alter the prayer.

To sum up, then: The lengthy 1888 prayer to Saint Michael was composed after the Saint Michael prayer in the Leonine Prayers appeared. The passages in the 1888 text which are supposedly "prophetic" refer in fact to the Italian government's seizure of Church property. Once the King of Italy appeared willing to arrive at a settlement of the Roman Question, the Vatican dropped from the prayer, passages which he, and the Italian government, would have found offensive.

IV. LAW AND THE LEONINE PRAYERS

Apologists for the New Mass sometimes make the false claim that various popes introduced substantial "changes" into the Mass of Saint Pius V.

When Leo XIII ordered the recitation of the Leonine Prayers, however, he did not legislate a "change" in the Mass. The prayers, unlike, say, the *Ite Missa Est* or the Last Gospel, are not part of the Ordinary of the Mass. They are always referred to as prayers recited *after* Mass. The rubrics in the front of the priest's altar Missal remained unchanged, and do not mention the Leonine Prayers at all.

In this section we will consider subsequent legislation on the Leonine Prayers, and, in light of the recent achievement of the object for these prayers, discuss the consequent cessation of the law regarding them.

A. Subsequent Legislation

The original legislation prescribing the Leonine Prayers says they are to be recited after every *Low* Mass (i.e., Mass without singing),[33] while subsequent decrees speak rather of reciting the prayers after

---

[32] This issue was finally settled with the Lateran Treaty. In Article 26 the Holy See recognized the Kingdom of Italy and its royal dynasty, the House of Savoy. Article 12 of the accompanying Concordat prescribed that on Sundays and Church holidays, the celebrant of High Mass in major churches would sing a prayer "for the prosperity of the King of Italy and the Italian State." For texts, see Parsons, 93, 99.
[33] See S.R.C. Decree, 6 January 1884, in *Acta Sanctae Sedis* 16 (1884), 250. "...*in fine cuiusque Missae sine cantu celebratae.*"

Private Mass. Over the years, a number of questions arose over the issue of when it would be lawful to omit the prayers. The Sacred Congregation of Rites issued a number of decrees on the subject. The meaning of some of the decrees is not absolutely clear, and rubricists (experts in liturgical law) were not able to reach complete agreement in interpreting them.[34]

The Leonine Prayers may be omitted after a Low Mass which:

- Takes the place of a Solemn Mass (e.g., an ordination or a funeral Mass).
- Has the privileges of a Solemn Votive Mass *pro re gravi* (e.g., the Sacred Heart Votive Mass on First Friday).
- Is celebrated with a certain solemnity (e.g., a Nuptial Mass, the Mass following the Blessing of Ashes on Ash Wednesday).
- Takes the place of the main ("parochial") Mass on Sunday and is "celebrated with a certain solemnity" (e.g., *Asperges* beforehand, prayer for the government afterwards, etc.).
- Is followed by a sacred function or pious exercise, without the celebrant departing from the sanctuary (e.g., Benediction, Novena, etc. after Mass).

The foregoing list is not exhaustive, and is taken from a classic work written in 1941 by the great English rubricist O'Connell.[35] Subsequently, the Congregation of Rites granted an Indult to the clergy of the Archdiocese of Bologna, allowing them to omit the prayers at Masses where a homily was given.[36] A 1960 decree clarified some previous decisions on the matter, and gave permission to priests everywhere to omit the Leonine Prayers at a "Dialogue" Mass, or at a Mass where a homily was given.[37]

Vatican II (1962–1965), of course, had refused to condemn Communism, while Paul VI after his election in 1963 began to take the first tentative steps toward building what would come to be known as the "Vatican-Moscow Axis." Since the Leonine Prayers were a reminder that Moscow was conducting a persecution, they were among the first

---

[34] Richard E. Brennan, "The Leonine Prayers," *American Ecclesiastical Review* 125 (1951), 92.
[35] See J. O'Connell, *The Celebration of Mass: A Study of the Rubrics of the Roman Missal*, (Milwaukee: Bruce 1941) 1:210–11. This three-volume work is the clearest and most systematic treatment of the rubrics of the Mass available. Every priest who celebrates the Traditional Mass should have a copy of it.
[36] S.C. *Rituum*, Indult *Excellentissimus*, 22 July 1955, Ochoa 2513.
[37] S.C. *Rituum*, Decree *A Nonnullis Locorum*, 9 March 1960, Ochoa 2895. "*Preces sic dictas Leoninas omitti posse: … 3. cum infra Missae celebrationem habeatur homilia. 4. cum fit Missa dialogata, diebus Dominicis et Festis tantum.*"

things to go.

In 1964, even before the Council closed, the Vatican issued a liturgical instruction which contained the memorably brutal phrase: "The Last Gospel is omitted; the Leonine Prayers are suppressed."[38] Under the circumstances, a more appropriate verb would have been "liquidated" or "purged."[39]

Only a handful of priests resisted the post-Vatican II liturgical changes at first, but not everyone retained the Leonine Prayers. I suspect this was the case in France, since at the Saint Pius X Seminary in Ecône in the 1970s we never said the prayers publicly.[40] (I recited them publicly after my first Mass in 1977, an act considered rather daring at the time.)

Most priests in America who first resisted the changes were well-known as dedicated patriots and vocal anti-Communists. These few stalwart men kept the Leonine Prayers alive when no one else in America did. It is to their eternal credit that they handed down the practice to a future generation which would see the prayers at long last bear fruit.

B. Recent Developments in Russia

The intention Pope Pius XI decreed in 1930 for the Leonine Prayers, as we noted above, was the freedom of the Church in Russia — that "tranquility and freedom to profess the faith," as he said, "be restored to the afflicted people of Russia."

The people of Russia are indeed afflicted by many things these days — corrupt politicians, scarce goods, Western immorality, socialism, international bankers, and the "New World Order." But it seems certain that they do enjoy at least one thing: "the tranquility and freedom to profess the faith."

On 1 October, 1990, the Soviet Union enacted a law on freedom of conscience and religious organizations. It was a lengthy and detailed statute, running in translation to nearly 500 lines of miniscule print.

---

[38] S.C. *Rituum (Consilium)*, Instruction *Inter Oecumenici* on the orderly carrying out of the Constitution on the Liturgy, 26 September 1964, ¶48, in *Documents on the Liturgy, 1963-1979: Conciliar, Papal, and Curial Texts*, trans., compiled and arr. by International Committee on English in the Liturgy, (Collegeville: Liturgical Press 1982), 340.

[39] I have a vague childhood memory of the priest telling us as the changes began that we would henceforth pray for Russia in the Prayer of the Faithful. *That* didn't last long. A few years later in the diocesan seminary, we were praying not for persecuted Catholics but for leftist guerrillas in South America.

[40] At Ecône during the 1975–1976 academic year, we followed many of the initial changes Paul VI introduced into the Order of the Mass in 1964.

The law's stated purpose was to guarantee the rights of citizens "to determine and express their attitude toward religion, to hold corresponding convictions and to profess a religion and perform religious rites without hindrance."[41]

Article 3 of the law is of particular interest to us here:

> "In accordance with the right to freedom of conscience, every citizen independently determines his attitude toward religion and has the right, individually or in conjunction with others, to profess any religion or not to profess any, and to express and disseminate convictions associated with his attitude toward religion."

We note, for the sake of emphasis, the phrase "the right… to profess any religion."

In Article 4, the law creates legal liability for restricting this right:

> Any direct or indirect restriction of rights or the establishment of any advantages for citizens depending on their attitude toward religion, as well as the incitement of hostility and hatred in this connection or any insulting of citizens' feelings, entails liability as established by law.

This would forbid persecuting someone for his religious beliefs.

The statute deals exhaustively with the manner in which these rights are exercised in practice. It guarantees the right to form religious organizations (Art. 7), religious congregations (Art. 8), religious associations (Art. 9), religious orders (Art. 10), and religious educational institutions (Art. 11). It allows a religious group to formulate its own statutes (Art. 12), to acquire civil/legal existence (Arts. 13, 14), to terminate voluntarily its own existence (Art. 16), to use state properties (Art. 17),[42] to own property (Art. 18), to dispose of property (Art. 20), to establish and maintain places of worship (Art. 21), to conduct worship services without hindrance (Art. 21), to acquire and produce religious literature and objects (Art. 22), to create charitable organizations (Art. 23) and to maintain ties with international religious organizations (Art. 24).

---

[41] Law of the Union of Soviet Socialist Republics: *On Freedom of Conscience and Religious Organizations*, 1 October 1990, Pravda, 9 October 1990, 4, trans. in *The Current Digest of the Soviet Press* 42.40 (1990), 6–8, 31. "The Aims of the Law. This law guarantees the rights of citizens to determine and express their attitude toward religion, to hold corresponding convictions and to profess a religion and perform religious rites without hindrance, as well as social justice, equality and the protection of citizens' rights and interests regardless of their attitude toward religion, and it regulates relations connected with the activity of religious organizations." (Art. 1)

[42] Any governmental body in the U.S. which allowed this would be hauled into court by the A.C.L.U.

Given the Communists' track record, we looked at all this from afar and took it with a grain (if not a pillar) of salt.

Others more familiar with current affairs in Russia, however, say that the status of believers underwent a real change. In an exhaustive commentary on the new law, one Western legal scholar noted that a comparison of past Soviet legislation with the 1990 law reveals that "there is no doubt about the intent of the legislator to endow freedom of conscience with a content quite different from that of the past."[43] Professor Jerry G. Pankhurst, a Russian-speaking American who actually spent some time in the Soviet Union after the law was passed, assured me that Catholics were indeed then quite free to profess their religion and that they suffered no persecution.

In 1991 events took an even more dramatic turn. Gorbachev fell, the Communist Party was dissolved and the Soviet Union broke up. The new Russian Republic adopted a law on religious freedom similar to the 1990 Soviet law. Professor Parkhurst believes that the new law "while totally compatible, is even more tolerant in the freedoms it grants."

But is it put into practice? For well over a year now, the conservative Catholic press has been carrying extensive reports on the changed situation for Catholics in Russia. A seminary has been founded. Members of the intelligentsia have converted. Archbishop Tadeusz Kondrusiewicz, appointed Apostolic Administrator of the European part of the Russian Republic by John Paul II, now resides in Moscow and ministers to a growing flock. Bishop Joseph Werth, a Jesuit, now travels around Siberia seeking out scattered groups of Catholics. Some church properties have been returned, and new religious publications have sprung up.

Nor are the adepts of the *Novus Ordo* the only ones to benefit from the new climate: Two Russians are now studying for the priesthood at the Society of Saint Pius X's seminary in Ecône, Switzerland. And one of the Ecône seminary professors, Father Rulleau, now travels to Moscow several times a year to offer the Traditional Mass for a group of Catholics.

Another Russian-speaking academic — a graduate student in Russian history — told me how she had recently spent time with Catholics in Moscow and Saint Petersburg. Their numbers, she noted, are small. But like everyone else, she said, Catholics are entirely free to profess their religion and now suffer no persecution.

All this leads one to conclude that Catholics in Russia are now

---

[43] Giovanni Codevilla, "Commentary on the New Soviet Law on Freedom of Conscience and Religious Organizations," *Religion in Communist Lands* 19 (Summer 1991), 131.

free to profess the Faith. The object for which the Leonine Prayers were prescribed for all these years, therefore, has been obtained.

C. Cessation of the Law

Immediately, however, we are confronted by a practical question: What then of the Leonine Prayers? If their object has been obtained, should they continue to be recited after Low Mass?

Strictly speaking — according to the principles of Church law — no.

First, we should recall the classic definition theologians and canonists give for the word "law": An ordinance of reason for the common good promulgated by the person who has care of the community.[44]

The canonist (and later cardinal) Giovanni Cicognani points out that, while laws are normally stable, the *reasons* or *purposes* for which a law was promulgated can later change. A law then becomes useless, harmful or — the very antithesis of what a law is supposed to be — *unreasonable*.

Obviously, the superior should revoke a law that has become unreasonable. But what if a superior has not done so? Cicognani adds:

> [I]f [such a law] has not actually been revoked, it is to be reasonably presumed to be revoked. For its purpose is the soul of law, and a law without a soul lapses, ceases to exist, dies.[45]

The technical term for the "death" of a law which loses its purpose is *intrinsic cessation of the law (cessatio legis ab intrinseco)*.[46] Intrinsic here simply means, as Cicognani put it, that "the law ceases of itself."[47]

The Bouscaren-Ellis commentary on the Code of Canon Law notes

---

[44] Dominic M. Prümmer OP, *Manuale Theologiae Moralis*, 10th ed., (Barcelona: Herder 1946), 1:142. "*Quaedam rationis ordinatio ad bonum commune ab eo, qui communitatis curam habet, promulgata.*"

[45] Amleto Giovanni Cicognani, *Canon Law*, 2nd rev. ed., trans. by Joseph M. O'Hara (Westminster MD: Newman 1934), 625. "In treating the elements of law we saw that it is proper and fitting that a law should be stable and firm. However, every law has its element of uncertainty, for the reasons and the purpose for which the law was made can change, and consequently, since law is an ordinance in accordance with reason, it ought to be revoked if it becomes useless, harmful or unreasonable; and if it has not actually been revoked, it is to be reasonably presumed to be revoked. For its purpose is the soul of law, and a law without a soul lapses, ceases to exist, dies."

[46] This is distinguished from *extrinsic cessation of the law,* i.e., when it is revoked by the superior. A lay woman once told me that, whenever a priest used the words *intrinsic* or *extrinsic* in an article directed to Traditional Catholics, she immediately judged the article "too deep," and promptly chucked it into the garbage. If she reads this article, I hope she makes it past the sentence above.

[47] Cicognani, 627

that this is common doctrine.[48] Indeed, Prümmer,[49] Beste,[50] Coronata,[51] Cappello,[52] Lanza,[53] McHugh-Callan,[54] Regatillo,[55] and Wernz-Vidal[56] speak of a law whose "purpose," "end," or "total cause" ceases, "loses its force" or "falls." By that very fact, it is then no longer a "rational norm," having lost the purpose for which it was promulgated. Such a law, as the Wernz-Vidal commentary on the Code of Canon Law says, then "has fallen without a special act of a legislator." Or as Regatillo put it, the law "ceases *ipso facto* without a legislator's declaration."

McHugh-Callan[57] and Cicognani[58] give as examples, laws which

---

[48] T. Lincoln Bouscaren SJ & Adam C. Ellis SJ, *Canon Law: A Text and Commentary*, (Milwaukee: Bruce 1946), 35. "A law may cease to bind in two ways: either by repeal, which is called extrinsic cessation, or by becoming inoperative without repeal, which is called intrinsic cessation. It is common doctrine that a law ceases to bind without repeal in two cases: first, if the circumstances are such that the law has become positively harmful or unreasonable; second, if the purpose of the law has entirely ceased for the entire community."

[49] *Man. Theol. Moralis*, 1:269–71. "*Lex ipsa tripliciter cessare potest: ... 2. per cessationem finis totalis. ... Cessatio finis totalis, seu causae motivae* adaequate, *ob quam lex lata est, producit cessationem ipsius legis. Ratio est, quia cessante causa totali, etiam effectus cesset oportet.*" His emphasis.

[50] Udalricus Beste OSB, *Introductio in Codicem*, (Collegeville: Saint John's 1946), 89. "...ab intrinseco per cessationem finis seu causae motivae, quae legislatorem induxit ad legem ferendam."

[51] Matthaeus Conte a Coronata OFMCap, *Institutiones Juris Canonici*, (Rome: Marietti: 1950), 1:28. "*Ipsa lex non sola eius obligatio dupliciter cessare potest:* ab intrinseco *et* ab extrinsico." His emphasis.

[52] Felix M. Cappello SJ, *Summa Juris Canonici*, 4th ed., (Rome: Gregorian 1945), 1:101. "*Lex cessare potest* ab intrinseco *et* ab extrinseco, *prout corruit ex se ipsa, vel tollitur per actum positivum externum competentis Superioris.* ... *1. Cessatio ab intrinseco. — 1. Si lex non est amplius* norma rationabilis *ammittit eo ipso vim suam. Id autem pendet ex* fine, *qui habet rationem boni, cuius intuitu praecise lex fertur.*" His emphasis.

[53] Antonius Lanza, *Theologia Moralis*, (Rome: Marietti 1949), 1:252. "Lex ab intrinseco cessat, aut transacto tempore ad quod lata est, aut cessante eius fine."

[54] John A. McHugh OP and Charles J. Callan OP, *Moral Theology: A Complete Course*, (New York: Wagner 1929), 1:500. "A law ceases *from within* (i.e., of itself), when through a change of conditions the purpose for which it was made no longer exists, or is no longer served by the law.... A law no longer serves its purpose, if, from having been useful, it *has become useless*, inasmuch as it is no longer necessary for the end intended by the lawgiver. In this case the law ceases, for regulations should not be imposed needlessly." His emphasis.

[55] Eduardus F. Regatillo SJ, *Institutiones Juris Canonici*, 5th ed., (Santander: Sal Terrae 1956), 1:98. "*Cessatio ab intrinseco. — A. Cessante fine pro communitate:... in casis praecedentibus lex* ipso facto *cessat absque legislatoris declaratione.*"

[56] F.X. Wernz SJ and P. Vidal SJ, *Jus Canonicum*, (Rome: Gregorian 1938), 1:187. "...*cessatio* ab intrinseco *cum lex corruit sine* speciali *actu legislatoris.*" His emphasis.

[57] *Moral Theology*, 1:501. "Example: The Council of Jerusalem made a law that the faithful should abstain from using as food animals that had been strangled (Acts, XV.20). The purpose of the law was to avoid offense to the Jewish converts, who at that time formed a large part of the Christian community and who had a religious abhorrence for such food. But shortly afterwards, the Gentile element having become stronger in the Church, no attention was paid to ceremonial rules of Judaism."

[58] *Canon Law,* 627. "The end (either its purpose or cause) of the law ceases adequately when all its purposes cease; *inadequately*, when only some particular purpose of the law ceases (e.g., fasting is enjoined in order to end an epidemic and to obtain rain; and the rain comes but the epidemic continues its ravages)." His emphasis. If both rain were to come and the

prescribe abstinence from certain foods, or decree a fast to obtain relief from various dangers.

Of particular interest to us here are laws which prescribe that certain prayers be recited to obtain some specific end. Once the end either *can no longer* be obtained or *has been* obtained, the law prescribing the prayer goes out of existence.

Moralists and canonists give the following examples:

- "If a bishop has prescribed a prayer for the recovery of the king's health, once the king is dead, by that very fact the prayer must be omitted."[59]
- "... when the health of the Pontiff is to be obtained, for example, if his health would be obtained, or if the Pontiff would die."[60]
- "If a bishop should prescribe prayers to obtain peace and good weather, the obligation would cease once both purposes together are obtained."[61]

A historical commentary on the Mass, written in 1949, speaks even more directly to our case. The author, Father Bede Lebbe, observed that Leo XIII prescribed the October Rosary Devotions[62] for the resolution of the Roman Question, and that the Devotions ceased to be obligatory once the Lateran Treaty was signed in 1929.[63]

The Leonine Prayers, Father Lebbe said, were offered for the same intention, and likewise became optional when the Lateran Treaty was signed — until, of course, Pius XI decreed that they be applied to the intentions of the persecuted Church in Russia. Father Lebbe then added:

> As the situation in that country continues to be far from favourable, it is clear that the obligation still exists of reciting after Mass the three Aves, the *Salve Regina* and the two prayers.[64]

According to his line of reasoning, obviously, a change in the sit-

---

epidemic were to cease, obviously, both purposes of the law would cease, and the law along with it.

[59] Prümmer, 1:271. "*Sic e.gr. si episcopus praescripsit orationem pro recuperanda regis sanitate, mortuo rege, eo ipso haec oratio omittenda est.*"

[60] Benedictus H. Merkelbach OP, *Summa Theologiae Moralis*, (Paris: Desclée 1946), 1:398. "*Cessat quando iam est obtentus vel amplius obtineri nequit, v.g. sanitas pontificis obtinenda si obtenta fuerit vel si pontifex moriatur.*"

[61] Beste, 89. "*Quare si episcopus preces praescripserit ad obtinendam pacem et aeris serenitatem, obligatio desinit obtento utroque fine simul, non autem alterutro dumtaxat.*"

[62] These consisted of the recitation of the Rosary, Litany of Loreto and Prayer to Saint Joseph, either during Mass or before the Blessed Sacrament exposed, each day from October 1 through November 2.

[63] Bede Lebbe OSB, *The Mass: A Historical Commentary*, (Westminster MD: Newman 1949), 167.

[64] Lebbe, 167–68.

uation would mean that the obligation to recite the Leonine Prayers would no longer exist.

It remains, then, to apply the principles to the case of the Leonine Prayers:

1. Catholic moralists and canonists teach that a law ceases (or dies) when the end for which it was instituted is obtained.
2. The end Pope Pius XI prescribed for the Leonine Prayers was that "tranquility and freedom to profess the faith be restored to the afflicted people of Russia."
3. This end has recently been obtained.
4. The law prescribing the recitation of the Leonine Prayers has therefore ceased.

Finally, what if Russia would again begin persecuting Catholics? Would one again be obliged to recite the Leonine Prayers?

No. For once a law ceases this way, Regatillo[65] and Cardinal Palazzini[66] explain, a new act from the legislator would be required to reintroduce it.

V. THE USE OF OTHER PRAYERS

If the law on the Leonine Prayers has ceased, could the priest then publicly "pray for America" (as our friend suggested), or for some other intention?

The mind of the Church, it appears, is that *some* types of prayers, at least, may indeed be recited after Low Mass on certain occasions.

Some countries had their own special customs in this regard. In England, for instance, the Prayer for the King was said, in Latin or English, depending on diocesan law.[67] In Ireland, Psalm 129 (the *De Profundis*) and a Collect for the Faithful Departed were recited before the Leonine Prayers.[68]

---

[65] *Institutiones*, 1:98. "... nec reviviscit redeunte causa finali, materia aut subjecto, sed debet denuo promulgari."
[66] Petrus Palazzini, *Dictionarium Morale et Canonicum*, (Rome: Catholic Book Agency 1962), 1:657. "... non reviviscit redeunte causa finali, ut iterum obliget, requiritur novus actus legislatoris ecclesiastici, eam iterum introduceret."
[67] E.J. Mahoney, *Priests' Problems*, ed. by L.L. McReavy, (New York: Benziger 1958), 118.
[68] Of the origin of this practice, Lebbe, 168, says: "Some liturgists see in it a compensation for the numerous endowments and foundation Masses for the Dead, all records of which were wantonly destroyed by Protestantism; or else a prayer of the Church for all those who were killed during the years and the persecutions of the 17th century, and in the Penal Times and buried without the comforting presence of a priest, or the blessing and prayers of the Liturgy." The Irish clergy apparently introduced this practice in Australia — to avoid, some said, having to recite the Prayer for the King of England.

General legislation made allowances for adding other prayers. In response to an inquiry, the Sacred Congregation of Rites decided that the priest could recite some prayers at the altar after Mass, as long as they were said with the permission of the Ordinary (diocesan bishop).[69] In his book of replies on various liturgical questions, Father Mahoney says that the Ordinary's permission may sometimes be presumed "when there exists some good reason for adding prayers."[70] One sacristy manual notes that the Divine Praises or indulgenced prayers for the dead may be added.[71]

While it is not advisable to add extra prayers after Low Mass each time it is celebrated,[72] the addition from time to time of some prayer or short devotion after Low Mass — the opportunity to venerate a relic, for example — is certainly in keeping with the legislation and the commentaries cited above. With a little thought and foresight, moreover, one can harmonize the prayer with the feastday or particular liturgical season (always the ideal, of course).

Not just any prayer will do. The priest should not use the invariable, devotional, novena-type prayers because of their essentially private character. For the same reason, the priest should not recite aloud with the people prayers intended for thanksgiving after Holy Communion. Nor should this be an occasion to recite prayers for what are purely private intentions — for some individual's health, prosperity, etc.

The texts of the prayers, rather, should have a "public" or "universal" character. (They should also, if possible, be indulgenced.)

---

[69] S.R.C. Decree Mechlin., 31 August 1867, 3157. "VII. Quaeritur: An possint praecipi, aut saltem permitti aliquae preces recitandae ad Altare post Missam, non depositis sacris vestibus. Obstare videtur Decretum in Conversanen. die 31 Augusti 1669. Ad VII. Affirmative; dummodo preces dicantur assentiente Ordinario."

[70] Priests' Problems, 119–20. "If he desires to add to those ordered, the above reply leaves it with the local Ordinary to determine its legality, and the writers concede a certain latitude on the supposition that the Ordinary's permission may sometimes be presumed; in fact, the replies of the Sacred Congregation of Rites in nn. 3537, 1, and 3805, can be harmonised with the n. 3157 above only by supposing that a presumed permission suffices. It may be presumed when there exists some good reason for adding prayers."

[71] Joseph Wuest CSsR, *Matters Liturgical: The Collectio Rerum Liturgicarum*, trans. and rev. by Thomas W. Mullaney CSsR, (New York: Pustet 1925), 188.

[72] A priest who regularly tacks onto the end of the Mass lengthy vernacular prayers of his own choosing imparts a false idea to his people: That while liturgical functions (the Mass, etc.) are good as far as they go, to have "real prayer," you must add something afterwards in the vernacular. Some priests in the Traditional Movement, unfortunately, already add not only a lengthy series of vernacular prayers *after* Mass, but also an equally-lengthy series *before* as well. Repeatedly sandwiching the Mass between elements that are not part of the Church's official worship diminishes its importance as the prayer *par excellence*. Their attitude reflects the sort of wrong-headed view of the Sacred Liturgy illustrated by a well-known story: A group of Canons were chanting Vespers in a great cathedral when a terrifying thunderstorm erupted. The Dean signalled the clergy to cease their chanting, and announced: "Because of the danger from the storm, Fathers, we will stop the Office so we can say some prayers together."

This is implicit in Rome's requirement that one have the permission of the Ordinary, who possesses the authority locally to regulate public worship.

If a priest "presumes" this permission (as Father Mahoney would allow), he should turn to the prayers the hierarchy of the Church has *already* approved for public recitation at the altar. These he will find collected in altar manuals approved before Vatican II.[73] Among the prayers authorized were the approved Litanies, Psalm 129 for the Dead, a prayer for the civil government[74] or sovereign, the Act of Consecration to the Sacred Heart, the Pentecost Novena, the Prayer for Peace, the Devotion for Church Unity, and a handful of other prayers. All of them are profound, well-phrased, traditional, dignified, universal in character, and easily harmonized with the Sacred Liturgy.

None of the approved altar manuals I have come across break up the texts with asterisks or otherwise indicate that the priest and the congregation are to recite the texts aloud together. The congregation's role is limited to short responses (for the litanies, versicles, Divine Praises) and to the occasional "Amen."

The priest should follow this pattern, and limit the congregation's role to a few responses of this sort. Catholics have difficulties reciting lengthy texts together. Each layman also thinks the version of the prayer *he* remembers is the "correct" version anyway, and will recite it no matter what.[75] Handing out the texts, moreover, and insisting that the congregation recite them with the priest, undercuts the priest's role, and smacks of the *Novus Ordo* idea that the people must recite each and every word of a prayer for it to "work."

The priest should remove his maniple for these prayers, and for longer devotions, perhaps even his chasuble. The prayers, remember, are not part of the Mass.

For the same reason, the priest should employ only brief texts — no longer than the Leonine Prayers, say. Moral theologians, after all, say that a layman's obligation to assist at Mass on a Sunday or Holy Day is fulfilled once the priest has finished the Last Gospel. Pope Benedict XIV and Saint Alphonsus, moreover, teach that a public Low Mass —

---

[73] For the U.S., *Enchiridion Precum: Altar Prayers*, (New York: Benziger 1941); *Altar Manual Compiled from New and Approved Sources*, (New York: Kennedy 1953). Similar collections, no doubt, likewise exist for other nations.

[74] In most countries, this consisted of a versicle and Collect. In the U.S., however, it was customary to use parts of a longer prayer for the Church and government composed by Archbishop Carroll. The passages usually employed are the ones which refer specifically to the government.

[75] Witness the confusion which inevitably occurred in places where the congregation recited the Saint Michael Prayer together. Everyone followed his own version. The babble of tongues which resulted often sounded like something out of a prayer meeting for *Novus Ordo* charismatics.

not counting the sermon and distributing Holy Communion — should normally not take much more than a half an hour. This limit should be observed, as Regatillo noted, "lest those hearing Mass be wearied."[76] In the matter of these prayers, let us therefore exercise the same prudent restraint and concern for "weaker brethren" that is found in the writings of the Church's most eminent theologians.

* * * * *

Traditional Catholics tend to be pessimists. This is natural enough, given the terrible events which have unfolded in both the Church and modern society since the 1960s. The various factions in the Traditional Movement may never agree about the Pope, the validity of the modern sacraments, or interpretations of Canon Law, to be sure. But the one thing we'd agree on in an instant would be our common motto: Expect and believe the worst, and you'll never be disappointed.

This pessimism carries over into our prayers. Time and again, Traditional priests or writers will recommend this prayer or that in order to end one evil or another in the Conciliar Church or in modern society. But the evil whose end we pray for seems to continue anyway. We see no concrete result for the recommended prayer. And we trudge grimly on to pray that yet *another* evil end, secretly suspecting, perhaps, that God will never allow us to see any visible fruit from *that* prayer either.

The recent developments in Russia should be cause for a little less gloom and a little more optimism about our prayers. We Traditional Catholics, after all, are the ones who kept right on saying the Leonine Prayers for our persecuted brethren in Russia. *We* may not have understood exactly what the Church's intention was for these prayers, but God certainly did. And in His providence He granted His Church's petition and our own.

Here, then, is something we Traditional Catholics can point to as some welcome good news — and as a concrete confirmation of the power of the Church's prayer.

(*Sacerdotium* 5, Autumn 1992).

---

[76] Eduardus F. Regatillo SJ and M. Zalba SJ, *Theolgiae Moralis Summa*, (Madrid: BAC 1954), 3:194. "*Si publice celebratur, curandum ne Missa semihoram multum excedat, ne audientes taedio afficantur.*"

APPENDIX

Prayer to Saint Michael from Exorcism against Satan and the Apostate Angels (Approved 18 May, 1890)

NOTE: In 1902 the Congregation of Rites issued a decree approving a new version of the prayer. The passages indicated in **bold face** below were removed.

O glorious Archangel St Michael, Prince of the heavenly host, defend us in battle, and in the struggle which is ours against the Principalities and Powers, against the rulers of this world of darkness, against spirits of evil in high places. (Eph 6.) Come to the aid of men, whom God created immortal, made in His own image and likeness, and redeemed at a great price from the tyranny of the devil. (Wis 2, 1 Cor 6.)

Fight this day the battle of the Lord, together with the holy angels, as already thou hast fought the leader of the proud angels, Lucifer, and his apostate host, who were powerless to resist thee, nor was there place for them any longer in Heaven, But that cruel, that ancient serpent, who is called the devil or Satan, who seduces the whole world, was cast into the abyss with all his angels. (Apoc 12.)

Behold, this primeval enemy and slayer of man has taken courage. Transformed into an angel of light, he wanders about with all the multitude of wicked spirits, invading the earth in order to blot out the name of God and of His Christ, to seize upon, slay and cast into eternal perdition souls destined for the crown of eternal glory. This wicked dragon pours out, as a most impure flood, the venom of his malice on men of depraved mind and corrupt heart, the spirit of lying, of impiety, of blasphemy, and the pestilent breath of impurity, and of every vice and iniquity.

These most crafty enemies have filled and inebriated with gall and bitterness the Church, the spouse of the Immaculate Lamb, and have laid impious hands on her most sacred possessions.

In the Holy Place itself, where has been set up the See of the most holy Peter and the Chair of Truth for the light of the world, they have raised the throne of their abominable impiety, with the iniquitous design that when the Pastor has been struck, the sheep may be scattered.

Arise then, O invincible prince, bring help against the attacks of the lost spirits to the people of God, and bring them the victory.

The Church venerates thee as protector and patron; **in thee holy Church glories as her defense against the malicious powers of this world and of hell**; to thee has God entrusted the souls of men to be established in heavenly beatitude.

Oh, pray to the God of peace that He may put Satan under our feet, so far conquered that he may no longer be able to hold men in captivity and harm the Church. Offer our prayers in the sight of the Most High, so that they may quickly conciliate the mercies of the Lord; and beating down the dragon, the ancient serpent, who is the devil and Satan, do thou again make him captive in the abyss, that he may no longer seduce the nations.

BIBLIOGRAPHY

ALTAR MANUAL COMPILED FROM NEW AND APPROVED SOURCES. New York: Kennedy 1953.
"AN INTERESTING STORY," *The Maryfaithful* (Sept–Oct 1978). 19.
BERS. "*Die Gebete nach der hl. Messe,*" *Theol-Prakt. Quartalschrift* 87 (1934). 161–163.
BESTE, UDALRICUS, OSB. *Introductio in Codicem.* Collegeville: Saint John's 1946.
BOUSCAREN, T. LINCOLN SJ & Adam C. Ellis SJ. *Canon Law: A Text and Commentary.* Milwaukee: Bruce 1946.
BRENNAN, RICHARD E. "The Leonine Prayers," *American Ecclesiastical Review* 125 (1951). 85–94.
CAPPELLO, FELIX M., SJ. *Summa Juris Canonici.* 4th edition. Rome: Gregorian 1945.
CICOGNANI, AMLETO GIOVANNI. *Canon Law.* 2nd revised edition, translated by Joseph M. O'Hara. Westminster MD: Newman 1934.
CODEVILLA, GIOVANNI. "Commentary on the New Soviet Law on Freedom of Conscience and Religious Organizations," *Religion in Communist Lands* 19 (Summer 1991). 119–145.
CONTE A CORONATA, MATTHAEUS, OFMCap. *Institutiones Juris Canonici.* Rome: Marietti: 1950.
DURAND, ARTHUR H. "Satan's Hundred Year War," *The Remnant* (15 January 1984). 9–10.
ENCHIRIDION INDULGENTIARUM: PRECES ET PIA OPERA OMNIUM CHRISTIFIDELIUM. Vatican: Polyglot Press 1950.
ENCHIRIDION PRECUM: ALTAR PRAYERS. New York: Benziger 1941.
GIUFFRÉ, GARY. "Exile of the Pope-Elect, Part VII: Warnings from Heaven Suppressed," *Sangre de Cristo Newsnotes* 69–70 (1991). 3–11.
JARRY, E. "Les États Pontificaux." In *Tu es Petrus: Encyclopédie Populaire sur la Papauté,* edited by G. Jacquemet. Paris: Bloud 1934. 551–617.
LANZA, ANTONIUS. *Theologia Moralis.* Rome: Marietti 1949.
LAW OF THE UNION OF SOVIET SOCIALIST REPUBLICS: *On Freedom of Conscience and Religious Organizations,* 1 October 1990, Pravda, 9

October 1990. 4. Translated in *The Current Digest of the Soviet Press* 42.40 (1990). 6–8, 31.

LEBBE, BEDE, OSB. *The Mass: A Historical Commentary.* Westminster MD: Newman 1949.

MAHONEY, E.J. *Priests' Problems*, edited by L.L. McReavy. New York: Benziger 1958.

MCHUGH, JOHN A., OP and Charles J. Callan OP. *Moral Theology: A Complete Course.* New York: Wagner 1929.

MERKELBACH, BENEDICTUS H., OP. *Summa Theologiae Moralis.* Paris: Desclée 1946.

O'CONNELL, J. *The Celebration of Mass: A Study of the Rubrics of the Roman Missal.* Milwaukee: Bruce 1941.

OCHOA, XAVERIUS, editor. *Leges Ecclesiae post Codicem Juris Canonici.* Rome: Polyglot 1969.

PALAZZINI, PETRUS. *Dictionarium Morale et Canonicum.* Rome: Catholic Book Agency 1962.

PARSONS, WILFRED SJ. *The Pope and Italy.* New York: America Press 1929.

PIUS IX. Encyclical *Cum Sancta Mater Ecclesia*, 27 April 1859.

_____. Encyclical *Qui Nuper*, 18 June 1859.

PIUS XI. Allocution *Indictam ante*, 30 June 1930, *Acta Apostolicae Sedis* 22 (1930). 296–303.

PONTIFICIA COMMISSIO PRO RUSSIA. Decree *Cum Summus*, 11 July 1930, *Acta Apostolicae Sedis* 22 (1930). 366.

PRÜMMER, DOMINIC M. OP. *Manuale Theologiae Moralis.* 10th edition. Barcelona: Herder 1946.

REGATILLO, EDUARDUS F. SJ. *Institutiones Juris Canonici.* 5th edition. Santander: Sal Terrae 1956.

_____ and M. Zalba SJ. *Theolgiae Moralis Summa.* Madrid: BAC 1954.

RITUALE ROMANUM. 6th edition *post typicam*. Ratisbon: Pustet 1898.

SACRORUM RITUUM CONGREGATIO [S.R.C.]. Decree *Iam Inde ab Anno*, 6 January 1884, *Acta Sanctae Sedis* 16 (1884). 249–250.

_____. Decree Mechlin., 31 August 1867, 3157, in *Decreta Authentica*.

_____. *Decreta Authentica Congregationis Sacrorum Rituum.* Rome: Polyglot Press 1898.

S.C. DE PROPAGANDA FIDE. *Ex audientia Sanctissimi* 18 May 1890, *Acta Sanctae Sedis* 23 (1890–91). 747.

_____. "Exorcismus in satanam et angelos apostaticos iussu Leonis XIII P.M. editus," *Acta Sanctae Sedis* 23 (1890–91). 743–746.

S.C. RITUUM. Decree *A Nonnullis Locorum*, 9 March 1960. Ochoa 2895.

_____. Indult *Excellentissimus*, 22 July 1955. Ochoa 2513.

S.C. RITUUM (CONSILIUM). Instruction *Inter Oecumenici* on the orderly carrying out of the Constitution on the Liturgy, 26 September 1964, *Documents on the Liturgy, 1963-1979: Conciliar, Papal, and Curial Texts*, translated, compiled and arranged by International Committee on English in the Liturgy. Collegeville MN: Liturgical Press, 1982. 293–391

SAINT MICHAEL AND THE ANGELS, compiled from Approved Sources. Rockford IL: TAN 1988.

SCHNÜRER, GUSTAV. "States of the Church." *The Catholic Encyclopedia*, edited by Charles G. Habermann et al. New York: Encylopedia Press 1912. 14:257–268.

ST. JOHN, AMBROSE [translator]. *The Raccolta or Collection of Indulgenced Prayers and Good Works*. 11th edition. London: Burns Oates 1930.

VOGL, CARL. *Begone Satan: A Soul-Stirring Account of Diabolical Possession in Iowa*, translated by Celestine Kapsner OSB. Saint Cloud MN: 1935. Reprinted Rockford IL: TAN Books 1973.

WERNZ, F.X., SJ and P. Vidal SJ. *Jus Canonicum*. Rome: Gregorian 1938.

WUEST, JOSEPH, CSSR. *Matters Liturgical: The Collectio Rerum Liturgicarum*, translated and revised by Thomas W. Mullaney CSsR. New York: Pustet 1925. New edition rearranged and enlarged by William T. Barry CSsR. New York: Pustet 1956.

Chapter 8
The *Motu* Mass Trap
(2007)

by Rev. Anthony Cekada

Ratzinger "liberates" the '62 Missal. Welcome to his rainbow...

A "mark of identity... a form of encounter...particularly suited to them....." A "sacrality which attracts many people."

- **Benedict XVI**, on his reasons for instituting the *Motu Mass*

"Legitimate diversity and different sensibilities, worthy of respect... Stimulated by the Spirit who makes all charismata come together in unity."

- **John Paul II**, on the Traditional Mass, to the Fraternity of Saint Peter

"Everything in their system is explained by inner impulses or needs."

- **Pope Saint Pius X**, on modernists and the sacraments, *Pascendi*

On July 7, 2007, Benedict XVI issued *Summorum Pontificum*, his long-anticipated *Motu Proprio* allowing a more widespread use of the 1962 version of the traditional Latin Mass. His action came as no surprise. As a Cardinal, Joseph Ratzinger had already spoken favorably about the old Mass many times.

Here are some salient provisions of the *Motu Proprio* and his accompanying letter:

- The New Mass of Paul VI is the "ordinary" expression of the "law of prayer" (*lex orandi*), while the John XXIII version of the old Mass is the "extraordinary" expression. They are "two uses of the one Roman Rite." (*Motu Proprio*, ¶1)
- Any priest can celebrate the Mass of "Blessed John XXIII" privately.

(¶2)
- In parishes where there is a stable group of faithful "attached to the previous liturgical tradition," the pastor should accede to their requests for a celebration of the '62 Mass. (¶5.1)
- Such celebrations can take place on weekdays, "while on Sundays and feastdays there may be one such celebration." (¶5.2)
- Scripture readings can be proclaimed in the vernacular. (¶6)
- The older rite may also be used, when requested, for weddings and funerals (¶5.3), and the pastor may allow using the older rites for administering other sacraments as well. (¶9.1)
- The diocesan bishop may set up a "personal parish" for such celebrations. (¶10)
- The New Mass and the old are not "two Rites," but a two-fold use of "one and the same rite."(Letter to Bishops)
- The old Missal was "never juridically abrogated, and consequently, in principle, was always permitted."
- The two rites are "mutually enriching."
- New saints and new Prefaces from the New Missal "can and should be inserted into the old."
- There is "no contradiction" between the two rites.
- Priests from communities that adhere to the former usage "cannot, as a matter of principle, exclude celebrating according to the new books."

So, now that the *"Motu Mass"* has finally arrived, what should we make of it? Here are some preliminary considerations.

I. Positive Aspects

1. An Admission of Failure

As a seminarian in the 1960s, I lived through the liturgical revolution on the inside, and since then I have read commentaries on the reform by those who directed it — Bugnini, Jungmann, Braga, Wagner, Patino, Botte, Vaggagini, Brandolini, and many others.

In those days and for these men, there was never *any* question of allowing the pre-Vatican II Mass to survive, even on a restricted basis. The new rite of Mass in the 1970 Missal of Paul VI was to become the Mass of the Roman Rite, period, and it was to be a great step forward for the Church.

This was the intention of Paul VI, himself. In November 1969, shortly before his New Mass was to be introduced in churches throughout the world, he developed this theme in two General Audiences:

> "[The liturgical reform] is a step forward for [the Church's] genuine tradition. It is a clear sign of faithfulness and vitality... It is not a fad, a fleeting or optional experiment, the invention of some dilettante... This reform puts an end to uncertainties, arguments and arbitrary abuses. It summons us back to that uniformity of rites and attitudes that is proper to the Catholic Church."...

> "[T]he fundamental outline of the Mass is still the traditional one, not only theologically but also spiritually. Indeed, if the rite is carried out as it ought to be, the spiritual aspect will be found to have greater richness."...

> "Let us then not speak of a 'new Mass,' but of a 'new age' in the life of the Church."

The new age is now over. During four decades of "greater richness," ordinations in the U.S. declined by 72%, seminary enrollment by 90%, seminaries by 66%, teaching sisters by 94%, Catholic school enrollment by 55%, and Mass attendance by about 60%.

In the 1990s, a new generation of clergy started to turn away from the rite of Paul VI and look longingly towards the Tridentine Missal. Graduates of garden-variety diocesan seminaries sought out old-style vestments, took courses on the pre-Vatican II rubrics, celebrated the Traditional Mass on the sly, and generally, hoped for something more Catholic than was to be found in the new rite.

If the New Mass had been a success, there would be none of this. The *Motu* Mass is an admission that the *Novus Ordo* was a failure.

2. Removing the Stigma

From 1964 to 1984, the modernist hierarchy treated those who wanted the old Mass as outcasts, crackpots, and troglodytes. The 1984 Indult and then the establishment of the *Ecclesia Dei* commission in 1988, however, removed some of the stigma from promoting the "Latin Mass."

Ratzinger's *Motu* Mass will further "legitimize" pre-Vatican II liturgical practices in the eyes of many.

3. A Cause of Division in the Enemy Camp

Despite the elaborate safeguards Ratzinger tried to lay down, *Motu* Mass will inevitably cause conflict among adherents to Vatican II.

I don't know about other parts of the world, but I can probably predict how this will play out in suburban America, where the majority of *Novus Ordo* Catholics now reside. There, in churches architecturally indistinguishable from chain restaurants and bank branches, committees of "empowered" and aggressive laywomen, both salaried and volunteer, together with the occasional liberated "women religious," now dictate parish policies and practices. They and their fellow suburbanites like the easy-going Mass and religion of Vatican II just as it is.

Should a neo-con pastor (typically: "Father Bob,"— late 30s, overweight, and in his second career) announce that, thanks to the *Motu Proprio*, he will be bringing out all the old liturgical gear that he's bought on eBay and start celebrating the old Mass in Latin at 10am on Sundays, a parish-wide insurrection, complete with protests to the bishop and a full media campaign, would be organized by the women's soviet.

Multiply this by a few parishes per diocese, and you can see the strife the *Motu* Mass could cause among the enemy. A divided house cannot stand, and divisions that advance the decomposition of the new religion can only speed the restoration of the old — *quod Deus det*!

4. Warning Flares for Committed Trads

Most long-time Traditionalists detest any tinkering with the Mass. Ratzinger, however, hints at some changes that might be in store for them at their local *Motu* Mass: new saints' feasts, new Prefaces, and vernacular readings — whether even the Bugnini lectionary can be used is left unclear.

Great! Fooling around like this with the old Mass will make old-timers very uneasy, alert them to Ratzinger's game (one hopes), and perhaps even start them on the road to thinking that modernists like Ratzinger are the *problem*, not the solution, for real Catholics.

5. Rubbing Priests' Noses in the New Mass

Since 1988 John Paul II and Ratzinger have approved a great number of quasi-traditionalist religious communities (Fraternity of Saint Peter, Institute of Christ the King, the Good Shepherd Institute, etc.) that are allowed to use the '62 Missal and other pre-Vatican II rites. These have insulated many clergy who detested the New Mass from being forced to celebrate it.

No longer. Ratzinger sends them a rocket: "Needless to say, in order to experience full communion, the **priests of the communities adhering to the former usage cannot, as a matter of principle, exclude celebrating according to the new books.** The total exclusion of the new rite would not in fact be consistent with the recognition of its value and holiness."

Again, great! The more that priests in these institutes are personally confronted with the evil of the New Mass, the sooner they will realize the irreconcilable contradictions of their own position.

6. An Introduction to the Real Issues

Although the John XXIII Mass that Ratzinger authorizes is a stripped version of the integral traditional liturgy, it still retains enough of the old to demonstrate that, in comparison, the New Mass of Paul VI represented an entirely new religion — "man-centered," as one of its creators, Father Martin Patino, proudly proclaimed.

For many Catholics, the road to becoming Traditionalists began when they encountered a traditional Latin Mass for the first time and compared it with the neo-Protestant rite celebrated in their parishes. With the *Motu* Mass, the possibility of such encounters multiplies exponentially.

This will no doubt lead many sincere and thoughtful souls to look beyond the liturgical question to the larger *doctrinal* issue — the heresies of Vatican II and the post-Conciliar popes — and eventually embrace the only logical position for a faithful Catholic: Sedevacantism.

II. Negative Aspects

1. Co-opted by Modernist Subjectivism

Because they still think in the old Catholic religious categories, Traditionalists who promoted the *Motu* Mass will consider its approval a resounding defeat for Modernism.

But in fact, something different has occurred: with the *Motu* Mass,

the modernists will now co-opt unsuspecting "trads" into their *own* subjectivist program.

Pope Saint Pius X condemned Modernism because (among other things) it spurned dogma and exalted the "religious sense" of the individual believer. And the Vatican pronouncements that authorize the use of the Traditional Mass — from the 1984 Indult onwards — all do so on the basis of slippery and subjective modernist categories like "different sensibilities," "feelings," "legitimate diversity," "enjoyment," various "charismata," "cultural expressions," "attachment," etc.[1]

Ratzinger now repeatedly sounds this theme: "attachment," "affection," "culture," "personal familiarity," "mark of identity," "dear to them," "attraction," "form of encounter," and "sacrality which attracts."

Everything is reduced to the subjective.

Let the Traditionalists who promoted it say what they will. For Ratzinger, the *Motu* Mass makes them merely one more color in his Vatican II rainbow.

2. A Side Chapel in an Ecumenical Church

As we have repeatedly pointed out elsewhere, Joseph Ratzinger's personal contribution to the longlist of Vatican II errors is his "Frankenchurch" heresy. For him, the Church is a "communion" — a type of ecumenical, One-World Church to which Catholics, schismatics and heretics all belong, each possessing "elements" of the Church of Christ either "fully" or "partially." According to his *Catechism*, all are part of one big happy "People of God."

Under this roof, some enjoy Lutheran chorales, guitar Masses, Gregorian chant, communion in the hand, altar girls, lay Eucharistic ministers, Hindu and African "inculturated" liturgies and Mariachi

---

[1] The 1984 Indult: Catholics who are "attached" to the Tridentine Mass. John Paul II's letter *Ecclesia Dei* (1988): The old Mass is part of a "richness for the Church of a diversity of charisms, traditions of spirituality and apostolate, which also constitutes the beauty of unity in variety; of that blended 'harmony' which the earthly Church raises up to Heaven under the impulse of the Holy Spirit... Respect must be shown for the feelings of all those who are attached to the Latin liturgical tradition." John Paul II, 1990 address to the Benedictines of Le Barroux: The Traditional Mass is permitted because the Church "respects and fosters the qualities and talents of the various races and nations... This concession is meant to facilitate the ecclesial union of persons who feel attached to these liturgical forms." Cardinal Mayer, 1991 letter to the U.S. bishops: "diversity" and respect for "feelings." Cardinal Ratzinger, 1998 address in Rome to Traditionalists: "Different spiritual and theological emphases... that richness which pertained to the same single Catholic faith." Cardinal Castrillon-Hoyos, May 2007: "ritual expression enjoyed by some... this sensibility." See also John Paul II, address to Fraternity of Saint Peter. October 1998.

music. Others (in "partial communion" with Ratzinger) enjoy somber Orthodox chanting, rock music, priestesses, Anglican smells and bells, Canons with the Words of Consecration missing, "accept Jesus as your perrrzonal savior" altar calls, and *Filioqu*e-free Creeds.

It is therefore hardly surprising that Ratzinger would offer Traditionalists the *Motu* Mass, and with it a large and comfy side chapel in his ecumenical church. Just one more option...

And in fact, Father Nicola Bux, a Vatican official who was involved in drafting the *Motu Proprio*, called it just that: an "'extension' of options."

And of course, there is a price to be paid.

According to Ratzinger's *Motu Proprio* and accompanying letter, the *Novus Ordo* — the ecumenical, Protestant, modernist sacrilege that destroyed the Catholic faith throughout the world — is the "**ordinary** expression of the law of prayer of the Catholic Church." Your *Motu* Mass — the true Mass, you may like to call it — is merely "extraordinary." The new and the old are merely two uses of **the same Roman Rite**.

If you accept the *Motu* Mass, you buy into all this, and become a paid-up member of Ratzinger's One-World Ecumenical Church.

3. Catholic Rituals, Modernist Doctrines

For decades, Traditionalists rallied to the cry, "It's the Mass that matters!"

But ultimately this is just a slogan. You can get to heaven without the Catholic Mass, but you *can't* get to heaven without the Catholic faith.

Ratzinger will now give you the Mass — but the Faith? Will those who accept his generous offer be free to condemn the *Novus Ordo*, the Vatican II errors, and the false teachings of the post-Conciliar popes?

To find out, one need only look at the Fraternity of Saint Peter, the Institute of Christ the King and the other organizations already celebrating the old Mass under the auspices of the Vatican's *Ecclesia Dei* Commission. The most their clergy dared to do was offer the occasional polite criticism about "deficiencies" or "ambiguities" in the new religion. They are now all sold men.

Their principal concern now, like that of the Anglican High Church wing, will be to maintain the externals of Catholicism, especially its worship. But the heart of Catholicism — the Faith — is gone.

So while a neo-con priest who offers a *Motu* Mass may now find it very thrilling to chant the ancient Collects with their "negative" language about hell, divine retribution, Jews, pagans, heretics and the like, he should remember that Vatican II abolished the *doctrinal* presuppositions on which this language was based.[2]

For the good Father and his congregation, the *lex orandi* which they observe (the Traditional Mass) has no connection whatsoever with their official *lex credendi* (the Vatican II religion).

From its 19th-century beginnings, Modernism sought to create a religion that is divorced from dogma, but that nevertheless satisfies man's "religious sense." It is ironic that this self-contradicting and dogma-free religion is now fully realized in Ratzinger's *Motu* Mass.

4. Non-Priests Offering Invalid Masses

"Once there are no more valid priests, they'll permit the Latin Mass."

This was the prediction made in the mid-1970s by the Capuchin Father Carl Pulvermacher, an older Traditionalist priest who worked with SSPX and was an editor of their U.S. publication *The Angelus*.

It was also prophetic. In 1968, the modernists formulated a new Rite of Episcopal Consecration that is invalid — it cannot create a real bishop.[3] Someone who is not a real bishop, of course, cannot ordain a real priest, and all the Masses — traditional Latin or *Novus Ordo* — offered by an invalidly ordained priest are likewise invalid.

So nearly 40 years later, when, thanks to the post-Vatican II Rite of Episcopal Consecration, there are few validly ordained priests left, the modernist Ratzinger (himself invalidly consecrated in the new rite) permits the Traditional Mass.

As a result of the *Motu Proprio*, therefore, traditional Latin Masses will start to be celebrated widely throughout the world: chant and Palestrina will echo in magnificently appointed churches, cloth-of-gold vestments will glisten, clouds of incense will fill Baroque apses, preachers in lace will proclaim the return of the sacred, solemn-faced clerics will officiate with as much rubrical perfection as the truncated

---

[2] Indeed, when word of the *Motu Proprio* first started to circulate, the Jews registered protests against the restoration of the old prayers for their conversion. And why not? Didn't Vatican II already assure them of their victory?

[3] See "Absolutely Null and Utterly Void," "Why the New Bishops are Not True Bishops," and "Still Null and Still Void," in *"The Anti-Modernist Reader: Volume 3"* and on www.traditionalmass.org. The reformers completely changed the essential sacramental form — the one sentence in the rite containing what is necessary and sufficient to consecrate a true bishop. In the process, they removed an essential idea: the power of Holy Orders that a bishop receives. If a sacramental form is changed in such a way as to remove an essential idea, the form becomes invalid.

rites of John XXIII will allow.

But the *Motu* Mass will all be an empty show. Without real bishops, no real priests; without real priests, no Real Presence; without the Real Presence, no God to receive and adore — only bread...

III. Say No to the *Motu*...

In the long run, the *Motu* Mass will contribute to the steady decline of post-Conciliar religion and the eventual death of Vatican II — Ratzinger's devil-baby, for which Limbo was never an option. At all this, we can only rejoice.

In the short term, however, many gullible Traditionalists will be lured to the *Motu* Mass because of convenience or the prospect of "belonging to something bigger."

But the negative aspects of actually assisting at the *Motu* are pure poison. Here are two key points to remember:

1. In most cases, your local *Motu* Mass will be **invalid**, because the priest who offers it will have been ordained by an invalidly consecrated bishop. Even some Indult parishioners already avoid the Masses of FSSP priests for this reason.
2. The *Motu* Mass is **part of a false religion**. Sure, you have your "approved" Latin Mass and perhaps even your *Baltimore Catechism*. But your co-religionists in the Church of Vatican II also have their Mass and *their* Catechism, all "approved" as well.

By assisting at the *Motu* Mass, you become part of it all and affirm that the differences between you and the folks down the road at Saint Teilhard's are merely cosmetic — "legitimate diversity and different sensibilities, worthy of respect... stimulated by the Spirit," as John Paul II said to the Fraternity of Saint Peter about their apostolate of offering the old Mass.

But if as a faithful Catholic, you're disgusted at the thought of compromising with heresy and becoming one more color in the modernists' liturgical and doctrinal rainbow, you have only one choice:

Say no to the *Motu*!

Chapter 9

The Pius X and John XXIII Missals Compared

(1984)

by Most Rev. Daniel L. Dolan

An overview of some of the differences.

Note: In 1982, as part of his program to strike a compromise with John Paul II and Ratzinger, Archbishop Lefebvre and the Society of Saint Pius X attempted to impose the Missal of John XXIII on the American priests of the Society. They refused, and this was one of the issues that precipitated their expulsion from SSPX in April 1983.

Missal of Saint Pius X	**Missal of John XXIII**
1. Promulgated by a canonized saint who condemned Modernism, and composed with the collaboration of absolutely orthodox priests both learned and pious.	**1.** Promulgated by a pope who admitted that he was suspect of Modernism, the same pope who called Vatican II to "consecrate ecumenism" and open up the windows of the Church to "renewal". Composed under the direction of Ferdinando Antonelli, who signed the document promulgating the New Mass, and under the direction of Annibale Bugnini, the "Great Architect" of the New Mass, notorious modernist and suspected Freemason.
2. Based upon sound traditional Catholic principles which were employed many times by the popes in the past. This missal was used by the Church from 1914 until the ascendancy of the modernist "Liturgical Movement" in the 1950's.	**2.** Based upon the principles of the modernist "Liturgical Movement" often condemned in the past by the Roman Pontiffs, this missal was a transitional work. According to Father Bugnini it was a "compromise" until the liturgy could be made "a new city in which the man of our age can live and feel at ease." It was used for only four years.
3. "Do not innovate anything; remain content with Tradition." (Pope Benedict XIV)	**3.** "it is a bridge which opens the way to a promising future." (Annibale Bugnini)

Prayers at the Foot of the Altar
4. Always said.

Prayers at the Foot of the Altar
4. Omitted on (1) The Purification after the Procession, (2) Ash Wednesday after the distribution of ashes, (3) Holy Saturday, (4) Palm Sunday after the Procession, (5) the four Rogation Days after the Procession, and (6) certain other Masses according the new rubrics of the Roman Pontifical.

The Collect
5. On days of lower rank, in addition to the Collect of the day, the Collects of Our Lady, Our Lady and All the Saints, Against the Persecutors of the Church, For the Pope, or For the Faithful Departed, etc. are recited.

The Collect
5. All these Collects are abolished.

6. The commemorations of a lower ranking feast of a saint or a Sunday are made according to the rubrics.

6. The commemorations of a lower ranking feast of a saint or a Sunday are either abolished or strictly curtailed, so that on an ordinary Sunday most saints' feasts entirely disappear.

The Lessons on Ember Days
7. Always recited.

The Lessons on Ember Days
7. The bulk of the Lessons are optional.

The Epistle
8. Always read by the celebrant at Solemn Mass as specifically mandated by Pope Saint Pius V.

The Epistle
8. The celebrant at Solemn Mass sits over on the side and listens instead, just as he does at the New Mass.

The Sequence
9. The *Dies Irae* must always be sung at a Requiem High Mass.

The Sequence
9. The *Dies Irae* at a daily Requiem High Mass is optional.

The Gospel
10. Always read by the celebrant at Solemn Mass as specifically mandated by Pope Saint Pius V.

The Gospel
10. The celebrant at Solemn Mass listens instead

The Creed
11. Recited on many feasts according to the rubrics.

The Creed
11. Suppressed on many feasts (Doctors of the Church, Saint Mary Magdalene, the Angels, etc.)

The Canon of the Mass
12. Unchanged since the time of Pope Saint Gregory the Great.

The Canon of the Mass
12. The name of Saint Joseph is inserted; thus the Canon is no longer the "unchanging rule" of worship.

The Communion of the People
13. The *Confiteor, Misereatur,* and *Indulgentiam* are always said before Holy Communion.

The Benedicamus Domino
14. Recited in place of *Ite Missa Est* on Sundays and Weekdays of Advent and Lent, Vigils, Votive Masses, etc.

The Last Gospel
15. Either the beginning of Saint John's Gospel or the proper Last Gospel of an occuring feast ends every Mass.

Changes in Feasts
16.
Saint Peter's Chair in Rome
Finding of the Holy Cross
Saint John Before the Latin Gate
Apparition of Saint Michael
Saint Leo II
Saint Anacletus
Saint Peter in Chains
Finding of Saint Stephen
Commem. of Saint Vitalis
Saint Philomena (by indult)
Saint Joseph, Patron of the Universal Church
Circumcision of Our Lord
Saint Peter's Chair at Antioch
Most Holy Rosary of the BVM
Saint George
Our Lady of Mount Carmel
Saint Alexius
Ss. Cyriacus, Largus & Smaragdus
Impression of Stigmata of Saint Francis
Ss. Eustace and Companions
Our Lady of Ransom
Saint Thomas a Becket
Saint Sylvester
Seven Sorrows of Our Lady

The Communion of the People
13. Abolished.

The Benedicamus Domino
14. Abolished, except when there is a procession after Mass.

The Last Gospel
15. The proper Last Gospel is abolished with one exception. No Last Gospel at all is recited for: (1) the Third Mass of Christmas, (2) Palm Sunday, (3) Holy Thursday, (4) Holy Saturday, (5) any Mass followed by a procession, (6) Requiem Masses followed by the Absolution, and (7) certain other Masses according to the new rubrics of the Roman Pontifical.

Changes in Feasts
16.
Abolished
Abolished
Abolished
Abolished
Abolished
Abolished
Abolished
Abolished
Abolished
Abolished
Changed to Saint Joseph the Worker

Changed to Octave Day of Christmas
Changed to Saint Peter's Chair
Changed to our Lady of the Rosary
Downgraded
Downgraded
Downgraded
Downgraded
Downgraded
Downgraded
Downgraded
Downgraded
Downgraded
Downgraded

Octaves of Feasts	*Octaves of Feasts*
17.	**17.**
Epiphany (7th Century)	Abolished
Corpus Christi (1294)	Abolished
Ascension (8th Century)	Abolished
Sacred Heart (1928)	Abolished
Immaculate Conception (1693)	Abolished
Assumption (ca. 850)	Abolished
Saint John Baptist (8th Century)	Abolished
Ss. Peter and Paul (7th Century)	Abolished
All Saints (ca. 1480)	Abolished
Nativity of Our Lady (1245)	Abolished
Saint Stephen (8th Century)	Abolished
Saint John the Evangelist (8th Century)	Abolished
Holy Innocents (8th Century)	Abolished
Dedication of a Church (8th Century)	Abolished

Vigils of Feasts	*Vigils of Feasts*
18.	**18.**
Epiphany	Abolished
Saint Matthias	Abolished
Saint James	Abolished
Saint Bartholomew	Abolished
Saint Matthew	Abolished
All Saints	Abolished
Saint Andrew	Abolished
Immaculate Conception	Abolished
Saint Thomas	Abolished

Miscellaneous Rubrics

19. Three tones of voice are used by the celebrant: audible, secret, and audible only to those at the altar.

20. When the celebrant is at the Epistle or Gospel side of the altar, he always bows to the cross at the center of the altar whenever he mentions the Holy Name.

The Holy Week Rites

21. Contains the Holy Week rites mandated by Pope Saint Pius V.

Miscellaneous Rubrics

19. Third tone of voice is abolished.

20. Abolished.

The Holy Week Rites

21. Radically altered to such a degree that they are no longer the Holy Week rites of the Tridentine Missal. These rites, in fact, needed only cosmetic changes to fit the pattern of the New Mass in 1969.

FINAL NOTES:

1. The Communion of the People: Some priests, who claim to adhere to the changes of John XXIII on the grounds of "papal authority" nevertheless refuse to suppress the *Confiteor, Misereatur* and *Indulgentiam* before the Communion of the People, as prescribed by John XXIII.
2. The Last Gospel: Father Bugnini expressed the wish "of many" that the practice of reciting the Last Gospel be severely curtailed or suppressed altogether. He only had to wait for a few years.
3. Changes in Feasts: Note the modernist prejudice against the cult of the saints and against feasts which refer to papal prerogatives or apparitions approved by the Church. During Lent, the John XXIII Missal suppresses most of the Masses of the saints.

Chapter 10

The Pius XII Reforms: More on the "Legal" Issue

(2006)

by Rev. Anthony Cekada

Despite the Bugnini connection, shouldn't we just obey "the last true pope"?

In April 2006 I posted a short article on the Internet that explained briefly why rejecting the Pius XII Holy Week reforms and adhering to the previous liturgical practices was not really "illegal," arbitrary, nor a case of "picking and choosing" à la SSPX.

I pointed out that, by applying the general principles for the interpretation of ecclesiastical laws, the laws imposing the reforms could no longer be considered binding because: (1) They lacked one of the essential qualities of a law, stability (or perpetuity); and (2) They became harmful (*nociva*) because of a change of circumstances, and hence automatically ceased to bind.

To support the factual claims for each argument, I quoted extensively from a 1955 work by Father Annibale Bugnini, who was not only involved in formulating the Pius XII reforms, but also the person most directly responsible for the creation of the *Novus Ordo* in 1969.

Bugnini repeatedly described the reforms as provisional or as steps leading to measures that would be even more far-reaching (read: the *Novus Ordo*).

One reader sent me some additional questions that I have answered below.

1. **"Stability" and the Legislator's Intention.**

"Thank you for your article on the Pius XII Holy Week changes. This is a question I have had some difficulty with lately, with respect to how we can reject the liturgical laws of a true pope."

"In your first point, on the transitory nature of the reforms, all of the quotes

you gave were from Bugnini. But since a law is an act by a legislator, isn't it the legislator's intent that is relevant, and not the man who merely drafted the law or advised the legislator?"

The various stages of the reforms were outlined beforehand (at least in a general sense) in a 340-page typeset document called the *Memoria sulla riforma liturgica*, which was presented to Pius XII in 1948.

The *Memoria* bears one signature, that of Father Ferdinando Antonelli OFM, who in the last sentence of the document graciously thanks "the Rev. Father Bugnini CM, a member of the Commission, for the help he gave me in the revision of the drafts." Some 21 years later, Father Antonelli would also sign the April 3, 1969, decree promulgating Paul VI's *Novus Ordo Missae*.

The *Memoria* states specifically that the "complete and general revision" it envisions "cannot be put into practice in a few days" and must be carried out in "successive phases" (¶334). The reform will begin with the Breviary, followed by the Missal, the Martyrology, and the rest of the liturgical books. (¶339). These will be approved at each stage by the pope (¶340). The process will culminate with the promulgation of a "Code of Liturgical Law" that will be gradually prepared during the work of the Reform and "should guarantee its stability."(¶341: *garantire la stabilità*).

The *Memoria* deferred to "the Commission's second stage of work" (¶316) such possibilities as introducing a *Novus Ordo*-style multi-year cycle of Scripture readings (¶258), using the vernacular (¶314), fostering "participation" (¶314), introducing concelebration (¶314), or changing the "internal structure of the Mass itself" (¶314).

In practice, however, only a few points from the first stage (the Breviary) were introduced. Changes in the Missal were limited for the time being to the new Holy Week.

The "Code of Liturgical Law" that the *Memoria* said was to "guarantee the stability" of the proposed reform, obviously, was never issued.

The provisions of the 1955 Decree promulgating the new rubrics for the Breviary underscored the transitory nature of the reforms as well: Although the Decree introduced numerous rubrical changes, it specified that the liturgical books then in force must continue to be used "until further provision is made" and that "no change whatever is [to be] made in arranging whatever editions may be made of the Roman Breviary and Missal."

From all this, it is absolutely clear that Pius XII himself regarded the 1950s liturgical legislation as transitory — temporary steps leading to something else.

And in the practical order, moreover, the changes **were** transitory. The last batch (1958) stayed in full force only until 1960, when John XXIII issued a new set, intended to tide everyone over till Vatican II overhauled everything.

All the foregoing is more than sufficient to establish that the laws introducing the Pius XII reforms lacked the essential quality of stability (or perpetuity), and for that reason must be considered no longer binding.

2. "Cessation" and Changed Circumstances?

"As to the second point, I don't understand what the changed circumstances are. If the circumstances are the modernists' intentions that this be the first step to a massive destruction of the Church, then the circumstances didn't in fact change. It already existed at the time the law was passed. And to say that these evil intentions can be attributed to the law itself would seem to say the devil slipped one past the Holy Ghost and used the Church's authority for evil."

The changed circumstances that render the 1950s legislation harmful are not simply the modernists' intentions, but principally the **fact** of the promulgation of the New Mass — a rite which all Traditionalists regard as evil, harmful to the Catholic faith, sacrilegious and grossly irreverent, if not outright invalid.

Now, among the principles and precedents introduced in the Pius XII liturgical changes, we discover the following elements that were subsequently incorporated across the board into the New Mass:

1. Liturgy must follow the "pastoral" principle to educate the faithful.
2. Vernacular may be an integral part of the liturgy.
3. Reduction of the priest's role.
4. Lay participation must ideally be vocal.
5. New liturgical roles may be introduced.
6. Prayers and ceremonies may be changed to accommodate modern "needs."
7. "Needless duplications" must be eliminated.
8. The *Ordo Missae* itself may be changed, or parts eliminated.
9. The Creed need not be recited on more solemn occasions.

10. The priest "presides" passively at the bench when Scripture is read.
11. Certain liturgical functions must be conducted "facing the people."
12. Emphasis on the saints must be reduced.
13. Liturgical texts or practices that could offend heretics, schismatics or Jews should be modified.
14. Liturgical expressions of reverence for the Blessed Sacrament may be "simplified" or reduced.

The 1950s liturgical legislation introduced these things here and there, and on a limited basis. Taken individually, none was evil in itself.

But 50 years later, we recognize that these principles and precedents were the foot in the door to the eventual destruction of the Mass. In the very document promulgating the *Novus Ordo*, in fact, Paul VI himself points to the Pius XII legislation as the beginning of the process.

Continuing to follow these practices promotes the modernist lie that the New Mass was merely an organic development of the true Catholic liturgy. You can hardly criticize the New Mass's vernacular, passive presider and ceremonies facing the people if you engage in the very same practices every year when Holy Week rolls around.

3. Indefectibility of Church?

"What becomes of the indefectibility of the Church and the guidance of the Holy Ghost if we assert that a heretic has used the authority of a true pope to promulgate a liturgy that is harmful to the Church?"

The application of laws promulgating the liturgical changes **became** harmful after the passage of time because of the changed circumstances, as explained in 2.

Canonists and moral theologians (e.g., Cocchi, Michels, Noldin, Wernz-Vidal, Vermeersch, Regatillo, Zalba) commonly teach that a human law can become harmful (*nociva, noxia*) due to changed circumstances after the passage of time. In such a case it automatically ceases to bind.

One cannot therefore maintain that the application of this principle contradicts the teaching of dogmatic theology that the Church is infallible when she promulgates universal disciplinary laws.

4. Are You "Pope-Sifting"?

"How is this distinguishable from the SSPX's "pope sifting"? If we don't draw the line between true popes and false popes, then where do we draw it? It seems we could hardly criticize the SSPX for picking and choosing what they accept from their "pope". Even more frighteningly, must we make the same judgments about earlier popes? What about the liturgical laws of Saint Pius X? Saint Pius V?"

The phrase "pope-sifting" originated with Father Franz Schmidberger's statement that one must sift (*cribler*) the teachings of Vatican II and the post-Conciliar popes in order to separate what is Catholic from what is not Catholic.

The essence of pope-sifting consists in the **ongoing act of private judgment exercised over each teaching and law that emanates from a living Roman Pontiff, coupled with refusal of submission to him.** SSPX has made this the fundamental operating principle for its apostolate.

For those who do not observe the Pius XII liturgical legislation, however, there is no living pope to "sift" or refuse submission to. We merely apply to these laws the same general principle we apply to all **other ecclesiastical** laws: If because of the post-Vatican II crisis, applying a particular law (e.g., restrictions on delegations for administering sacraments, dimissorial letters for ordinations, permissions for erecting churches, faculties for preaching, requirements for Imprimaturs, etc.) would now have some sort of harmful effect, we consider the law to be no longer binding.

Or put another way: If like SSPX you recognize someone as a living pope, he is your living lawgiver; you are bound to approach him to ask which laws apply to you and how to interpret them. If you are a sedevacantist, however, you have **no** living lawgiver to approach; when you have a question about whether a law applies or how to interpret it, your only recourse is to follow general principles the canonists have laid down.

5. Obedience to Lawful Authority?

"How do we reconcile this with obedience to lawful authority? It seems we are questioning the wisdom of the legislation instead of accepting the judgment of the Church on it."

The principles enunciated in points 1 (stability) and 2 (cessation of laws that become harmful) are found in approved commentaries on the Code of Canon Law.

If the application of these principles were indeed inconsistent with the virtue of obedience owed to lawful authority, these commentaries would never have received ecclesiastical approval.

* * * * *

That said, all the foregoing questions assume that the **sole** principle that must determine how Traditional priests perform the liturgy is the liturgical legislation of "the last true pope."

But this is not as simple as it sounds, because before a priest can maintain that the Pius XII legislation alone is legally binding, he must first demonstrate conclusively that John XXIII and Paul VI (at least before the end of 1964) were **not true popes**.

Until he does so, he must consider himself bound by all the John XXIII changes —"legally binding" is your principle, remember — as well as all the early Paul VI changes.

(Among the early Paul VI changes are the following: At Mass the priest never recites texts that the choir sings, bits of the Ordinary are sung or recited in English, the Secret is said aloud, the *"Per Ipsum"* at the end of the Canon is recited aloud, the *"Libera Nos"* is recited aloud, *"Corpus Christi/Amen"* is used for the people's communion, the Last Gospel is suppressed, Scripture readings are proclaimed in the vernacular alone and facing the people, lay lectors/commentators assist the priest, the *"Pater Noster"* is recited in English, etc.)

In the case of both Roncalli and early Montini, a putative legislator was "in possession." If observing the liturgical legislation of "the last true pope" is supposedly the golden norm for traditional Catholic worship, shouldn't Father then follow the "safer course" by chopping up the Mass and training the lectors, just in case?

Since the "last true pope" principle leads to other problems, what then?

The answer is simple: Follow the liturgical rites that existed before the modernists started their tinkering.

We Traditionalists endlessly reaffirm our determination to preserve the traditional Latin Mass and the Church's liturgical *tradition*. To my way of thinking, it makes no sense whatsoever to preserve the liturgical "tradition" of Holy Week ceremonies invented in 1955, transitional Breviary rubrics, and "reforms" that lasted for all of five years.

The Catholic liturgy we seek to restore should be the one redolent

of the fragrance of antiquity — not the one reeking with the scent of Bugnini.

(Internet, 10 July 2006).

Chapter 11

THE OTTAVIANI INTERVENTION: ITS ENDURING VALUE

(1992)

by Rev. Anthony Cekada

Background to the "charter" of Traditionalist resistance.

Note: *This article first appeared as the Preface to Father Cekada's new translation of the Ottaviani Intervention, TAN Books, 1992.*

> "It is rather strong to claim that the New Mass is contrary to the Council of Trent but, displeasing as it is, it is true."

Thus spoke Alfredo Cardinal Ottaviani. Under three popes, he served as head of the Holy Office, the Vatican tribunal responsible for uprooting heresy and protecting the purity of the Catholic faith. Before him in September, 1969, lay the document you are about to read – a study which contends that the New Order of Mass promulgated in April, 1969, poses a serious threat to the integrity of the Catholic faith. Such a charge will strike most Catholics as exceedingly odd. While the Mass they assist at each Sunday may seem a bit boring now and again (or even more like entertainment than prayer on occasion), what would prompt a distinguished cardinal to call it contrary to one of the General Councils of the Catholic Church? A partial answer to the question, at least, is to be found in the story of The Ottaviani Intervention.

For centuries, the rite of the Mass was fixed, stable, otherworldly, uniform throughout the world and unsurpassed in beauty. The core of the Mass, the Roman Canon, had remained essentially unchanged at least since the days of Saint Ambrose (4th century). Other prayers in the Mass were similarly ancient. In response to Protestant attacks on the Mass, the Council of Trent (1545-63) reiterated and defined the Church's teaching on Christ's Real Presence in the Eucharist and on the sacrificial character of the Mass. Shortly thereafter, in 1570,

Pope Saint Pius V promulgated a Missal which codified the Church's already-existing liturgical tradition.

The Mass of Saint Pius V (often called the "Tridentine Mass") continued to be used until the Second Vatican Council (1962-5) opened the door to a whole series of sweeping changes in the Mass. In 1963, Pope Paul VI established an entity known as *Consilium* (The Committee for Implementing the Constitution on the Sacred Liturgy) which he entrusted with the duty of carrying out the liturgical reform mandated by Vatican II. *Consilium* formulated a new Order of Mass — the framework of prayers and ritual gestures employed each time Mass is celebrated — which Paul VI duly promulgated on 3 April 1969.

Conservatives—they would later be referred to as Traditionalists — viewed the New Order of Mass (*Novus Ordo Missae*) with alarm. They had endured five years of continuous liturgical change, each stage of which appeared to bring the Mass closer to Protestantism and closer to the teaching of the progressive theologians who sought to subvert the Church from within. In the New Order of Mass, Protestantism and the new theology seemed to have triumphed.

Origins of the Intervention

In the conservative camp were two members of the Roman aristocracy, Vittoria Cristina Guerrini and Aemilia Pediconi. Both were friends of Cardinal Ottaviani (then retired from his post as Prefect of the Holy Office), and both had wide connections at the Vatican and in other ecclesiastical circles. The ladies used their contacts to bring together a small group of conservative theologians, liturgists, and pastors who would prepare a study of the contents of the New Order of Mass. Cardinal Ottaviani agreed — it is unclear at exactly what point — to revise the study and to present it to Paul VI.

The group met a number of times in April and May 1969. The task of preparing a suitable text fell to a Dominican theologian and philosopher, Father M.L. Guérard des Lauriers, then a professor at the Pontifical Lateran University in Rome. Working from his notes in French, Father Guérard dictated a text to Madame Guerrini, who simultaneously translated it into Italian.

The result was the Short Critical Study of the New Order of Mass (*Breve*

Esame Critico del Novus Ordo Missae), now known in English-speaking countries as The Ottaviani Intervention. At the request of Archbishop Marcel Lefebvre, then recently retired from his position as Superior General of the Holy Ghost Fathers, Father Guérard translated the text into French.

Cardinal Ottaviani, for his part, composed a covering letter to Paul VI which supported the Study's conclusions. The organizers hoped to have a large number of high-ranking ecclesiastics sign it along with the cardinal. Archbishop Lefebvre spoke of 600 bishops. Had such been the case, it is conceivable that the Study would have moved Paul VI to modify substantially or even rescind the New Order of Mass.

From May through September 1969, the organizers lined up at least a dozen cardinals to sign, among them, Arcadio Cardinal Larraona, former head of the Sacred Congregation of Rites. Cardinal Ottaviani spent several days examining the Critical Study and signed the covering letter on 13 September 1969.

The following day, however, a French Traditionalist priest compromised the project by publishing the Critical Study, even though it was not supposed to have been made public until a month after the group of cardinals presented it to Paul VI. His action appears to have scared off most of the signers.

Antonio Cardinal Bacci, however, remained undeterred. The cardinal was a famous Latinist, and during this time served on the Vatican Congregations for Religious, Causes of Saints, and Catholic Education. In 1967, Cardinal Bacci had written a laudatory preface to a book which charged that the liturgical reform had betrayed the Faith of the Council of Trent, and that the head of *Consilium*, Cardinal Lercaro, was "Luther resurrected."

Such a prelate did not scare easily. Cardinal Bacci signed the letter on 28 September, and the following day both the letter and the Critical Study were presented to Paul VI.

Content of the Intervention

The central contention of The Ottaviani Intervention is that the New Order of Mass teems with dangerous errors in doctrine and represents an attack against the Catholic teaching on the Mass defined by the Council of Trent. The authors of the Intervention stated that their intention was not to present an exhaustive treatment of all the problems the New Mass posed, but rather to point out those deviations from Catholic doctrine and practice which are most typical of the New Mass. Among these, the Intervention lists the following:

1. A new definition of the Mass as an "assembly" rather than as a sacrifice offered to God.
2. Omissions of elements emphasizing the Catholic teaching (utterly repudiated by Protestants) that the Mass makes satisfaction for sins.
3. The reduction of the priest's role to a position approximating that of a Protestant minister.
4. Implicit denials of Christ's Real Presence and the doctrine of Transubstantiation.
5. The change of the Consecration from a sacramental action into a mere narrative retelling of the story of the Last Supper.
6. The fragmenting of the Church's unity of belief through the introduction of countless options.
7. Ambiguous language and equivocation throughout the rite which compromise the Church's doctrines.

The Intervention leveled these charges against two texts: (1) the New Order of Mass itself, and (2) the 1969 General Instruction on the Roman Missal, a 341-paragraph document which set forth not only the rubrical directions for performing the new rite, but also the theological principles on which it was based.

The General Instruction would be a particular bone of contention during the controversy which would follow.

Vatican Reaction

Once the conservative Catholic press spread the story of the Intervention throughout the world, a major scramble ensued at the Vatican.

Though Paul VI had received a copy of the General Instruction in 1968 and had personally approved every detail of the New Order of Mass, he sent the Intervention to the Sacred Congregation for the Doctrine of the Faith on 22 October 1969, with word that they should determine whether or not the criticisms were justified.

―――――――――― CHAPTER 11 ――――――――――

On 12 November 1969, the Congregation replied with a letter to the Vatican Secretary of State. In his memoirs, the Secretary of *Consilium*, Monsignor Annibale Bugnini, assured readers that the General Instruction (which the Intervention had subjected to particularly severe criticism) was found to conform to the Church's teaching, but he quotes only one sentence from the Congregation's letter, rather than reproducing the entire text.

Monsignor Bugnini's reticence here is somewhat out of character. Elsewhere in his memoirs (a work nearly a thousand pages long), he quoted at great length documents which defended the orthodoxy of the new rite. Had the Congregation for the Doctrine of the Faith stated that all the Intervention's criticisms were utterly unfounded, one can be sure that Monsignor Bugnini would have reproduced the full text of the reply.

The members of *Consilium* met in Rome in early November. "Some difficulty," they noted, "emerged over certain points of The General Instruction on the Roman Missal, in particular over Article 7 [the new definition of the Mass]" — an understatement, to be sure, as some in the press were starting to refer to the *Novus Ordo* as the "heretical Mass." On 18 November 1969, *Consilium* issued a stiffly-worded Declaration "clarifying" the General Instruction. *Consilium* attempted to handle the Intervention's doctrinal objections to the *Novus Ordo* by claiming the General Instruction was not intended to be a doctrinal statement but merely a pastoral or rubrical instruction — a contention others who defended the New Mass would later repeat in good faith. Tactically, this was a clever move — a document not intended as a doctrinal statement could hardly misstate doctrine.

Well before the dispute provoked by The Ottaviani Intervention, however, members of the 13-man *Consilium* subcommittee directly responsible for creating the New Order of Mass were telling a different story. Father Bugnini and the Reverend Peter Coughlan had already stated that the Instruction would treat of "theological principles," constitute a "full theological... exposition" of the new rite, describe the New Mass "from a doctrinal point of view," or serve as an "introduction of a doctrinal character."

The 1969 General Instruction, therefore, was clearly intended to be a statement of the theological and doctrinal principles behind the New

Order of Mass. *Consilium*'s 18 November 1969 declaration was little better than a lie.

In a lengthy speech to a general audience on 19 November 1969, Paul VI likewise sought to quell fears over the orthodoxy of the New Order of Mass. Viewed against the new rite as actually promulgated, his words, one is forced to say, have an aura of unreality about them. He assured his hearers that the substance of the Mass had not been altered and that the new rite affirmed the Church's traditional teachings just as unfailingly as the old rite did—but he limited himself to this general statement and provided no specific examples from the rite itself.

Paul VI also stated that the new rite "puts an end to uncertainty" and "summons us back to that uniformity of rites and attitudes that is proper to the Catholic Church." But as a cursory reading of the General Instruction will show (or even a visit to an unfamiliar parish on a Sunday), the Mass Paul VI promulgated allows endless options and adaptations, the very opposite of a "uniformity of rites and attitudes."

Cardinal Ottaviani himself never received a written reply to his letter to Paul VI. In late November, the cardinal checked into a hospital during another bout with the eye disease that periodically left him blind. In his diary he noted that his audience with Paul VI which followed on 2 December was: "A bit rough at the beginning, due to the recollections of my letter and Bacci's on the New Mass."

As a result of this encounter, Cardinal Ottaviani would henceforth remain silent in the face of any public discussion about his position on the New Mass. His diary entry for 8 January 1970 reads: "In Germany, little stories about my declarations on the New Mass." This is followed by one word: "Silence..." Emilio Cavaterra, who wrote a book based on Ottaviani's diaries, said of this entry that one can almost see the cardinal making a gesture to show that his lips are sealed.

With this in mind, we turn to the attempt made in the following month to undermine the Intervention's impact by trying to disassociate it from Cardinal Ottaviani.

An Ottaviani Retraction?

In February 1970, a French clergyman, Dom Gerard Lafond, published a defense of the New Order of Mass entitled *Note Doctrinale sur le nouvel Ordo Missae*. Among other things, the Note claimed that Cardinal Ottaviani had been the author of certain passages in the New Order of Mass, that these passages were the same ones attacked in the Critical Study, that the cardinal had not approved the Critical Study, and that it is probable that its contents were withheld from him. No proof was given to substantiate these allegations.

The following month, Dom Lafond published the facsimile of a letter Cardinal Ottaviani was alleged to have written to him on 17 February 1970. In this letter, the cardinal is said to have stated that: (1) he examined the *Note Doctrinale*, (2) he not only approved of it but congratulated Dom Lafond on the dignity of its expression, (3) he did not authorize the publication of his letter to Paul VI, and (4) his hesitations over the *Novus Ordo* have been put to rest by the discourses Paul VI gave on 19 and 26 November.

We have spoken of the 17 February letter as something Cardinal Ottaviani is alleged to have written. Is there any reason to suspect the letter's authenticity?

First, it seems somewhat strange that the cardinal would have approved of the *Note Doctrinale*. The work, after all, contained statements which in effect were calumnies against him.

Second, the 17 February letter leaves the impression that the Intervention had been published without the cardinal's authorization. This too seems somewhat strange for on two separate occasions (in October 1969 and again after the 17 February letter was published) the cardinal did in fact personally authorize two different individuals to publish the Intervention.

Third, in his book on Ottaviani's diaries, Emilio Cavaterra says nothing about the 17 February letter. Had the letter been authentic, it would have provided Cavaterra, who sought to explain away the cardinal's hesitations about the New Mass, with an ideal opportunity to show that Ottaviani's worries had been put to rest.

Cavaterra, moreover, quotes from his interview with Monsignor Gilberto Agustoni, the cardinal's secretary, who likewise tried to distance Ottaviani from the Intervention. Monsignor Agustoni, too, is silent about the letter, which, had it been authentic, would have supported the monsignor's contention that the cardinal always maintained "a positive attitude towards the liturgical reform."

Fourth, there is the matter of Monsignor Agustoni himself. He himself had signed the *Note Doctrinale*. It would have been in his interest to secure the cardinal's approval as well. A number of Traditionalist writers pointed this out in 1970, and noted that, since Cardinal Ottaviani was blind by this time, it would have been child's play for Monsignor Agustoni to have tricked the cardinal into signing the 17 February letter. At first blush the charge seems far-fetched. Since 1970, however, some interesting facts about Msgr. Agustoni have come to light. Consider the following:

- Monsignor Agustoni was a member of *Consilium*, and also had been responsible (together with Benno Cardinal Gut, Monsignor Paul Phillipe and Monsignor Annibale Bugnini) for approving the final version of the new Eucharistic Prayers the Intervention had denounced as compromising Catholic teaching.
- Monsignor Agustoni by this time also served on the Sacred Congregation for Divine Worship, the Vatican body responsible for implementing the liturgical reform. He had been appointed to the post on 12 September 1969, the day before Cardinal Ottaviani signed the letter to Paul VI approving of the contents of the Intervention.
- Among the 12 members of Study Group 10, the section of *Consilium* directly responsible for creating the New Order of Mass, we find a certain Father Luigi Agustoni — the brother of none other than Monsignor Gilberto Agustoni.
- And finally (as they say), the clincher: On 24 May 1966, three members of *Consilium* sent Paul VI a lengthy and detailed memorandum proposing a New Order of Mass which was nearly identical to the one he would promulgate in 1969. This proposed *Ordo Missae* contained all the elements which the Intervention would denounce in 1969. This memorandum was prepared by Monsignor Bugnini, Monsignor Anton Hänggi — and Monsignor Gilberto Agustoni.

Monsignor Agustoni, therefore, had much to gain by attempting to disassociate Cardinal Ottaviani from the Intervention. In light of this, it becomes much less difficult to imagine a blind cardinal signing a letter whose actual contents have been misrepresented by his secretary.

─── CHAPTER 11 ───

Stranger things, after all, have occurred in the history of the Vatican.

While the foregoing facts were unknown in 1970, a public dispute over the authenticity of the 17 February letter erupted nevertheless. Jean Madiran, the editor of the respected French journal *Itinéraires*, publicly accused Monsignor Agustoni of obtaining the cardinal's signature by fraud. Shortly thereafter, Monsignor Agustoni relinquished his position as the cardinal's secretary.

Whatever one may care to surmise from the foregoing, two points are clear: (1) No claim has ever been made that the other signatory of the letter to Paul VI, Cardinal Bacci, ever retracted or modified his position. (2) The Vatican itself ignored the affair of the 17 February letter, and treated the Intervention's charges as grave enough to warrant yet another response.

A Climate of Suspicion

When Paul VI promulgated the New Order of Mass in April 1969, the rest of the new Missal (the part containing the variable prayers proper to each Sunday and feast) had yet to be completed. Paul VI's Apostolic Constitution *Missale Romanum* had set 30 November 1969, the First Sunday of Advent, as the date when the new Missal would become obligatory.

But the controversy The Ottaviani Intervention started forced the Vatican to delay publication until the objections could be addressed—objections which, as one liturgist said, "engendered a climate of suspicion regarding the theological foundations of the New Order of Mass." A lengthy and permanent defense of the New Mass was needed, or else the chorus of protest would never die down.

The Congregation for Divine Worship asked Paul VI to write a Motu Proprio defending the orthodoxy and legitimacy of the New Mass. He eventually suggested adding an explanatory Foreword (*Proemium*) to the new Missal. On 14 February 1970, Paul VI met with Father Bugnini and decided that the Foreword should defend the new Missal's conformity to Tradition and should demonstrate that the doctrine of the New Mass was identical to that of the old.

An Ephemeral Document

The result when the Missal finally appeared in March 1970 was a new 8-page Foreword to the General Instruction. At first reading, it sounds nearly "Tridentine" — one would expect, since the liturgists claimed it "guarantees the doctrinal orthodoxy of the New Order of Mass."

The author of the Foreword, however, was faced with an impossible task: superimposing a traditional theology of the Mass on a rite composed with entirely different principles in mind. The teachings the Foreword expresses, hence, are contradicted by elements of the new rite itself. Here are some examples:

- The Foreword states that the New Mass "constantly" expresses the Council of Trent's teaching on the sacrificial nature of the Mass. To support this contention, however, the Foreword was able to cite only two phrases in the new rite: one in Eucharistic Prayer III and the other in Eucharistic Prayer IV — hardly, it must be said, a "constant" expression of the teaching of the Council of Trent. One is left to draw the reasonable conclusion, moreover, that when Eucharistic Prayer II is used, the New Order of Mass does not express the sacrificial character of the Mass — precisely one of the points which The Ottaviani Intervention makes.
- The Foreword states that the New Mass proclaims belief in the Real Presence and Transubstantiation by "the spirit and expression of reverence in which the Eucharistic liturgy is carried out." While this is an edifying thought, one has but to look to the new rite itself to see that most of the old external expressions of reverence for the Sacrament are gone. As the Intervention pointed out, all but three genuflections are abolished, the Blessed Sacrament is relegated to a hiding place outside the nave of the Church, kneeling for communion is eliminated, and just about every other mark of belief in the Real Presence has been removed.
- In an attempt to rebut the Intervention's charge that the New Mass contradicts Catholic teaching on the priesthood, the Foreword referred readers to the new Preface for the Mass of Chrism. This Mass, however, is celebrated but once a year, and then only by the diocesan bishop. And when we examine the text the Foreword cites, we discover that, far from reaffirming the traditional understanding of the priesthood, this Preface leaves the clear impression that the ordained priesthood arises out of the "priesthood of believers," a thoroughly Protestant concept.

CHAPTER 11

Other examples could be given. Conservative defenders of the *Novus Ordo* often cite this document as proof that the new rite reflects the Church's constant teaching on the nature of the Mass. Their confidence, alas, is misplaced. Suffice it to say that the lofty thoughts and traditional sentiments expressed in the Foreword are almost inevitably brought low by the reality of the new rite. The English liturgist Father Crichton, an enthusiast for the reforms, perhaps best summed up the Foreword when he called it "a controversial statement, intended to rebut the criticisms of the new Order, and in the nature of the case a very ephemeral document."

The Cleverness of the Revisers

As a direct result of the Intervention's criticisms of the 1969 *General Instruction*, the new Missal published in March 1970 contained not only the new Foreword but also a revised General Instruction. Since *Consilium* maintained all along, however, that there was nothing wrong with the Instruction in the first place, the changes were introduced with some verbal legerdemain.

This came in a document called a "Presentation" — a statement so convoluted that it could have come out of the Ministry of Truth in George Orwell's *1984*. Its line of reasoning — if such it can be called — ran roughly as follows:

- Some points in the Instruction "did not come across clearly because of the difficulty of keeping all the contents in mind."
- Complaints against the new rite "were based on a prejudice against anything new; these were not worth considering because they are groundless."
- Consilium itself, after all, had examined the Instruction and "found no reason for changing the arrangement of the material and no errors in doctrine."
- Nevertheless, "to overcome problems," the decision was made "to supplement or rewrite the text of the General Instruction in some places."
- And finally, "these emendations are in fact few."

Naturally, the passages affected — the list covered 16 pages — were the ones the Intervention had criticized the most strongly. Father Crichton tartly noted: "The procedure is obvious: every time there is an incriminated expression, what may be called for short a 'Tridentine' phrase is put beside it." We cite a few examples which illustrate the revisers' method:

- When the Intervention criticized the new definition of Mass as "assembly," Consilium replied that the passage was not a definition, but merely a simple description of the Mass. The disputed passage in the Instruction, therefore, was slightly recast to reflect the new position. Moreover, rather than speaking of "the Lord's Supper or Mass," the revised definition transposed the terms and spoke of "the Mass or Lord's Supper." As well, where the original definition spoke of the Mass merely as a memorial, the new version adds the phrase "or eucharistic sacrifice."
- In an attempt to deal with the Intervention's attack on the original Instruction for omitting the mention of Transubstantiation, the revised version speaks of Christ as being present "substantially and permanently under the eucharistic elements." Together with this phrase, however, the revised Instruction added other "presences" of Christ: in the assembly, in Scripture, and in the minister. Thus these are made to appear equivalent to Christ's substantial presence. The word Transubstantiation — a red flag for Protestants — is still not employed.
- The Intervention pointed out how the priest's role was reduced to that of a mere "president of the assembly." In one paragraph in the revised Instruction, the notion that the priest acts "in the person of Christ" has been restored. This still does not remove the false notion, implied elsewhere in the Instruction, that the people "offer" or "celebrate" the Mass. In other passages, moreover, the priest continues to be referred to as a "president" or "one who presides."

Many souls found the addition of a handful of traditional terms reassuring. Others have demonstrated, however, that the revisions do not remedy the defects of the original Instruction.

In arriving at an assessment of the New Order of Mass, what weight should we give to the changes in the General Instruction?

Father Crichton's observation provides us with a clue: in each passage cited above, the revisers merely introduced a "Tridentine" term as an equivalent to a new term. Since the Instruction presents the terms as equivalent, it is reasonable to conclude that one is free to regard the

Mass as either:

1. A propitiatory sacrifice, offered by an ordained priest, in which Christ becomes present under the appearances of bread and wine through Transubstantiation; or
2. An assembly-supper, co-celebrated by the congregation and its president, during which Christ is present in the people, the Scripture readings, and in the bread and wine.

The first position is the doctrine of the Council of Trent; the second, the position of Protestantism and neo-Modernism. Subsequently, it would be the latter position — the Mass as "assembly-supper" — which would pervade the writings of the overwhelming majority of modern liturgists, and which would provide the theoretical justification for countless aberrations and abuses.

Is it stretching the plain meaning of the 1970 Instruction to claim that, even with all its traditional-sounding phrases, it still leads us away from the teaching of the Council of Trent and towards Protestantism? For an answer we turn to an article written five years later by a member of *Consilium*, the Rev. Emil Joseph Lengeling:

> "In the 1969 General Instruction on the Missal, an ecumenically-oriented sacramental theology for the celebration of Mass emerged... Despite the new 1970 edition forced by reactionary attacks — but which avoided the worst, thanks to the cleverness of the revisers — it leads us... out of the dead end of the post-Tridentine theories of sacrifice, and corresponds to the agreements signaled by many of last year's interfaith documents."

A Theoretical Exercise

We have spoken at some length of the General Instruction on the Roman Missal because the arguments advanced against the New Order of Mass in the Intervention and elsewhere centered on this document. But as is often pointed out, the Instruction is not the rite itself, but merely a general explanation of its underlying theological principles.

The New Order of Mass is found in the official liturgical books published by the Church in Latin, the most important being the Missale Romanum itself. In 1970, the new Missal appeared with its rubrics — directions for the priest who celebrates the new rite — set out in brief Latin sentences. Latin versions of the other books necessary for the complete celebration of the new rite followed shortly thereafter.

But even if one sets aside the defects of the General Instruction, the New Order of Mass still gives rise to concerns on doctrinal grounds. The practical details for offering the New Mass (and celebrating the sacraments) are set out in thousands of pages of vernacular translations. These provide for countless options, the celebration of Mass *ad populum* (facing the people), the almost exclusive use of the vernacular, the distribution of communion in the hand, communion under both species, and the use of altar girls, Eucharistic ministers, and extraordinary ministers of communion, among other novelties. The doctrinal questions thus become: How does the New Mass differ in practice from the old, and what sort of theology does it embody?

Here are some points to consider:

- The pre-1970 Missal's prayers, rubrics, and overall structure express a concept of the Mass as a propitiatory sacrifice offered to God. The priest offers the sacrifice of the Mass on behalf of the people, acting *in persona Christi* (in the person of Christ). The language used throughout the old rite clearly articulates these doctrines.
- The New Order of Mass, however, reduces the emphasis on the sacrificial nature of the Mass and the priesthood. It places more emphasis on the communal aspects of the celebration, aligning more closely with Protestant theology. The priest is often referred to as the "presider" over the assembly, and the language used throughout the rite tends to be more ambiguous regarding the sacrificial nature of the Mass.
- The changes in the rubrics and prayers, such as the introduction of the "General Intercessions" and the reduction of the Offertory prayers, further shift the focus away from the sacrificial nature of the Mass.
- The New Order of Mass allows for a greater degree of participation by the laity, including roles previously reserved for the clergy, which also aligns more closely with Protestant practices.

Conclusion

The Ottaviani Intervention remains a significant document in the history of the Roman Catholic Church. It highlights the concerns of Traditionalists regarding the theological implications of the liturgical reforms introduced by the Second Vatican Council. Despite the Vatican's attempts to address these concerns, the debate over the New Order of Mass continues to this day.

The Intervention's criticisms of the New Order of Mass and the General Instruction on the Roman Missal raise important questions about the direction of liturgical reform and its impact on Catholic doctrine. The document serves as a reminder of the importance of preserving the integrity of Catholic teaching in the face of change.

As the Church continues to navigate the challenges of modernity, the lessons of The Ottaviani Intervention remain relevant. The balance between Tradition and innovation, and the need to safeguard the core doctrines of the faith, are issues that continue to resonate within the Catholic community.

Citations and Footnotes:

1. *"Avertissement,"* in Cardinaux Ottaviani et Bacci, *Bref Examen Critique du Nouvel "Ordo Missae"*, new edition with Italian text, edited and translated into French by M.L. Guérard des Lauriers OP (Vailly-sur-Sauldre, France: *Editions Sainte Jeanne d'Arc* 1983), 5.
2. *"Avertissement,"* 5-6.
3. *"Avertissement,"* 7. Guérard lost his position at the Lateran as a result of his involvement in the project. He later taught at Lefebvre's seminary in Ecóne, Switzerland.
4. *"Avertissement,"* 7.
5. Based on an account by one of the organizers, Dr. Elizabeth Gerstner, a résumé of which is provided in Michael Davies, *Pope Paul's New Mass* (Dickinson TX: Angelus Press 1980), 483-4.
6. The work was Tito Casini, *La Tunica Stracciata* (Rome: 1967).
7. Apostolic *Constitution Missale Romanum* had set 30 November 1969, the First Sunday of Advent, as the date when the new Missal would become obligatory.
8. Bugnini, *La Riforma*, 285.
9. "The work *Short Critical Study...* contains many statements which are superficial, exaggerated, inexact, impassioned and false." Quoted Bugnini, *La Riforma*, 285.
10. Bugnini, *La Riforma*, 193.
11. SC Divine Worship, *Presentation Edita Instructione,* May 1970, DOL 1371.

12. [Annibale Bugnini CM], "*Decima Session Plenaria 'Consili'*" *Notitiae* 4 (1968), 181.
13. Annibale Bugnini CM, in a report to the Medellin Conference of the Latin American Episcopate, 30 August 1968, *Revista Ecclesiastica Brasiliera* 28 (1968), 628.
14. [Annibale Bugnini CM], "*Ordo Missae et Institutio Generalis*" *Notitiae* 5 (1969), 151, 153. In his 1983 memoirs (*La Riforma Liturgica*, 382-3), Monsignor Bugnini repeats the passage word for word and without attribution.
15. Peter Coughlan, *The New Mass: A Pastoral Guide* (Washington: Corpus 1969), 32.

Chapter 12

Una Cum: Mass 'in Union with our Pope'?

Most Rev. Donald J. Sanborn

Naming the post-Vatican II "popes" in the Canon of the Mass.

Introduction

In the many discussions which have taken place over the past fifteen years about the vacancy of the papal see since the time of the Vatican II "popes," there has always been a "bottom line" which occurs in the *Te Igitur* of the Mass, which is the first prayer of the Canon. It is the passage in this prayer which requires the priest to pray for the reigning pope and bishop of the diocese in which the Mass is offered. If you pick up your missal, and turn to the Canon, you will see the phrase we are presently talking about: *"... which in the first place we offer up to Thee for Thy holy Catholic Church, that it may please Thee to grant her peace, to protect, unite and govern throughout the world, together with Thy servant N. our Pope, N. our Bishop, and all true believers and professors of the Catholic and Apostolic Faith."* In Latin the phrase *together with* is rendered by *una cum*. Because the rubrics instruct the priest to leave out the name of the pope or bishop if the see is vacant, i.e., when a pope dies and the new pope is not elected, the mention or non-mention of the name by the priest is a litmus test for the priest's position about John Paul II and the New Church. If he thinks that John Paul II is the true Pope, successor of Saint Peter, then he must place his name in the Canon. If, on the other hand, he does not hold him to be a true Pope, but a false one, then the priest must not mention his name in the Canon. So, this little phrase in the Mass, *una cum*, says it all: *is he or isn't he the Pope?*

The position of the Society of Saint Pius X is quite clear: *he is*, and if you do not agree, then get out. If I am not mistaken, they take an omission of the name to be a schismatic act. This they maintain despite the fact that they seem to admit a gray area in the speculative order; many of them openly speak about doubt concerning John Paul II's papacy. Father Schmidberger even stated that the Fraternity was not in communion with the Conciliar Church which identifies itself with the *Novus Ordo Missae*. How such non-communion would not include John Paul II is mysterious. How can they be so emphatic about breaking communion with the conciliarists, and yet at the same time insist that priests declare themselves in communion with the *head* of the conciliarists?

Actions speak louder than words, and the appearance of the odious name in the Canon of the Mass is an action which clearly states that the Fraternity is in communion with the Conciliar Church.

What if, however, you are not in communion with the New Church, but the only Traditional Mass available to you is one in which a public declaration of communion with the Heresiarch is made? Is it licit to attend such a Mass?

In the course of the discussion, I will first examine the import of the *una cum* phrase, as there are varying theories, as is evident from the accompanying article in *Forum*. Next I will cite texts from diverse authors indicating that the mention of the reigning pope's name is an explicit declaration of ecclesial communion. From here I will examine the ecclesiological problems of being in communion with John Paul II, and the liturgical problems which arise therefrom, and finally draw some moral conclusions from the principles stated. Afterwards I will respond to objections.

Import of the *Una Cum* Phrase

To my knowledge, there are three differing opinions of how this phrase should be understood. The first is to take *una* as an adjective, modifying *Ecclesia*, thus rendering the meaning to be "one with" or "united with." The basis for this opinion is the fact that the Roman Pontiff is the principle of unity of the Catholic Church as a whole, and the local bishop the principle of unity of the particular Church. The second is to take *una* as an adverb modifying *offerimus*. "We offer...together with etc." The reason for this opinion is that the Mass is an ecclesial act, offered not merely by a particular priest, but by the whole Church, in the name of which the priest is functioning. Since the Roman Pontiff is the head and principle of unity of the whole Church, it is fitting that his name be mentioned as the principal offerer. The third interpretation is to take the *una cum* phrase as an appositional link with *Ecclesia*, by which it would mean essentially *including*: "...which we offer Thee for Thy holy Catholic Church, *which includes*..."

Which is the correct way to accept *una cum*? I think that the *third* way is correct. Convincing proof to me is the fact that in medieval times, the name of the king was often inserted in this place, as well as that of the pope and bishop, which name is incompatible with the first two meanings of *una cum*, but not with the third. For the king is neither the principle of unity of the Church, nor is he in any way a principal or extraordinary offerer of the Mass. In these matters, he does not differ from the peasant in the pew. He is, however, a prominent member of the Mystical Body, as are pope and bishop, and does deserve special mention as such in the Mass and at other times in the sacred liturgy. The *una cum* phrase also appears in the *Exsultet* of Holy Saturday where the names of the pope and local bishop are to be inserted and, prior to 1918, the name of the Austrian Emperor. In this context the names are clearly there as prominent members of the Mystical Body.

Such a conclusion, however, does not deny the fact that the Roman Pontiff is the principle of unity of the Roman Catholic Church, nor that the Mass is an ecclesial act. To the contrary, both of these truths must be asserted about both the Church and the Mass.

A Declaration of Ecclesial Communion

Praying for someone *as pope* and *as bishop of the diocese* is different from merely mentioning the name of your favorite aunt, or even that of the king or emperor. It is more, much more, than a mere friendly gesture of praying for someone. Rather, the mentioning of these names of pope and bishop "and particularly that of the pope" has always been taken by the Church to be a sign of recognition of communion with the Roman Pontiff. Conversely, the deliberate failure to mention these names, and particularly that of the pope, has always been interpreted by the Catholic Church to be a declaration of non-communion with the Roman Pontiff. Submission to the Roman Pontiff is the foundation of the relation of the communion among the members of the Mystical Body, which is the same thing as the Roman Catholic Church. (Cf. *Sacerdotium* V, "Communion"). The mentioning of the name of the pope in the Mass, therefore, has always been commonly taken as a token of recognition of and submission to the power of the reigning pontiff; its omission has been taken as a sign of lack of recognition of and of submission to the reigning pontiff. Thus, the eastern schismatics omitted the name in their Masses, and, when they returned to the unity of the Catholic Church, would resume the mention of the name, and purposely omitted any name which was obnoxious to the Catholic Church, such as that of the schismatic patriarch.

I adduce the following texts in proof of the foregoing:

Pope Benedict XIV

"But whatever can be said about this controverted point of ecclesiastical learning, it is sufficient for us to be able to affirm that the commemoration of the Roman Pontiff in the Mass as well as the prayers said for him in the Sacrifice are considered to be, and are a certain declarative sign, by which the same Pontiff is recognized as the head of the Church, the Vicar of Christ, and the Successor of Saint Peter, and becomes of profession of a mind and will firmly adhering to Catholic unity; as Christian Lupus correctly indicates, writing on the councils (*Tom.* 4. *Editionis Bruxell.* pag. 422): *This commemoration is the supreme and most distinguished kind of communion.*" Nor is this any less proven by the authority of Ivo Flaviniacensis (in *Chronicle*, p. 228) where it reads: '*Let him know that he separates himself from the communion of the whole world, whoever does not mention the name of the Pope in the Canon, for whatever reason of dissension;*' nor [by the authority of] the well-known Alcuin, who, in his book *De Divinis Officiis* (chap. 12) wrote this: "*It is certain, as Blessed Pelagius teaches, that those who, for whatever reason of dissension, do not observe the custom of mentioning the name of the Apostolic Pontiff in the sacred mysteries, are separated from the communion of the whole world.*" This fact is further proven by a more severe statement of the Supreme Pontiff Pelagius II, who held the Apostolic throne in the 6th century of the Church, and who in his letter contained in the *Labbeana Collectio Conciliorum* (Tome 5, col 794 sq. and col 810) left this in writing concerning our subject: "*I am shocked at your separation from the whole Church, which I cannot tolerate; for when blessed Augustine, mindful of Our Lord's words which placed the foundation of the Church in Apostolic Sees, says that he is in schism whosoever shall separate himself from the authority of or communion with those who preside in these same Sees, and who does not publicly profess that there is no other Church than that which is established in the pontifical roots of the Apostolic Sees, how can you not esteem yourselves to be cut off from the communion of the whole world, if you withhold the mention of my name in the sacred mysteries, as is the custom, in whom, though unworthy, you see at the present time the strength of the Apostolic See through the succession of the episcopate?"*

It is clear from this text that the mentioning of the name of the reigning pope is not a mere friendly gesture, but rather a test of communion with the Roman Catholic Church, and that failure to mention the name of the reigning pope is a sure sign of schism from the one, true Church.

R. P. Pierre Le Brun

"*UNA CUM FAMULO TUO....with our Pope N. your servant.* Saint Paul recommends to us that we pray for our pastors. We name in particular and in the first place the bishop of the first See, who alone is called because of honor and distinction the Holy Father, *our Pope*, that is, our Father. It is quite fitting that in praying for the unity of the Church, we also pray for him who is the center of communion, who presides over this Church, as Saint Irenaeus says, with which every other Church must agree. "He presides as Vicar of Jesus Christ, as the successor of Saint Peter, upon which the Church has been established."

"*ET ANTISTITE NOSTRO N. ...& our Prelate N.*" After the Pope we mention the bishop who governs the local diocese. For since the successor of Saint Peter is the center of unity of all the Churches of the world, the bishop is the center of unity of his flock, who form with him one Church, as Saint Cyprian says. This union of the faithful with the bishop makes a particular Church, like the union of all the faithful and of all the bishops together make the universal Church, as the same holy Doctor also states."

Dom Ernest Graf, O.S.B.

"Let us note in the first place that the priest speaks in the plural.

Like the Sacrifice of the Cross, the Eucharistic Sacrifice is a universal one. The Mass is the act of the Church, accomplished on behalf of the Church – that is, for the pastors and the sheep and the lambs entrusted to their care. Hence we make explicit mention of the Pope, the universal shepherd, of the diocesan bishop, and finally of all those who profess the Catholic and Apostolic Faith."[1]

Father William J. O'Shea, S.S., D.D.

"There is one official who symbolizes and represents the unity of the Church in each diocese, and who has been placed there by the Holy Spirit to rule the Church of God: that is the bishop. Originally only the local bishop was mentioned: *papa* once meant any bishop, but was later restricted to the pope. Outside Rome the words *'et antistite nostro N.'* were added to avoid confusion; our Canon now prays both for the symbol and center of unity in the Church at large and in each diocese in particular. *'Et omnibus...fidei cultoribus'* is an ancient addition which refers not to the faithful but to the other bishops throughout the world, who are real *'cultores fidei'*: 'maintainers of the catholic, apostolic and orthodox faith.' The faith is designated by its ancient titles: it is catholic, for the whole world; apostolic, coming from them and resting upon their teaching; orthodox, the *true* faith.[2]

F. Lucius Ferraris

"First the priest offers the sacrifice for the Church, then in particular for the Pontiff, in accordance with an extremely old custom of the Churches, for the purpose of signifying the unity of the Church and the communion of the members with the head."

All of the authors speak similarly. It is, therefore, accurate to say that the mention of the name of the reigning pope is a declaration of ecclesial communion with him as *head of the Catholic Church*, and not merely as a private Catholic.

An Ecclesiological Nightmare

The obvious question which poses itself now is: *is it licit to declare*

---

[1] DOM ERNEST GRAF, O.S.B., *The Priest at the Altar*, (New York: Joseph F. Wagner, 1926) p. 181.
[2] WILLIAM J. O'SHEA, S.S., D.D., *The Worship of the Church* (Westminster, Maryland: The Newman Press, 1958) p. 393.

CHAPTER 12

oneself in communion with John Paul II as head of the Roman Catholic Church? I declare emphatically no, since to do so is an explicit recognition of the new religion as the Catholic faith, and of the New Church as the Catholic Church. For *where Peter is, there is the Church*. The notions of pope and Catholic Church are intrinsically inseparable, and to be united to one is to be united to the other; to be separated from one is to be separated from the other.

To hold, however, that the new religion is the Catholic faith and the New Church is the Catholic Church is to implicitly assert that Vatican II, including its heresies on religious liberty, ecumenism, and the Church, is the ordinary magisterium of the Catholic Church (declared to be such by Paul VI), that the New Mass and sacraments are Catholic and not sinful to accept, that the 1983 Code of Canon Law is a heresy-free and sin-free Catholic document.

Thus, the mentioning of John Paul II's name in the Canon of the Mass is to approve of the entire Vatican II reform as Catholic and to accept the entire New Church hierarchy as the Catholic hierarchy. It is to declare that the new religion is the way of salvation, and that every Catholic can accept it in perfectly good conscience, nay, *must* accept it under pain of grave disobedience or even schism. This fact becomes evident when we hear the rest of Saint Ambrose's well-known ecclesiological axiom: Where Peter is, there is the Church: '*and where is the Church is, there is no death, but life eternal.*'[3] If, therefore, John Paul II is the Pope, then the Church of which he is the head is the Roman Catholic Church, and the hierarchy with which he is in communion is the Catholic hierarchy. It would then follow that their ordinary magisterium (e.g., Vatican II) is infallible, their rites and sacraments are both valid and Catholic and therefore entirely acceptable, and that their general laws (e.g., 1983 Code) do not prescribe anything sinful. For where the Church is, there is eternal life, and the Catholic would need not trouble his conscience about the doctrines, rites, sacraments and practices of the *Novus Ordo* church.

I would sooner accept death than admit these things about the John Paul II church.

But the loathsome name in the Canon is an implicit admission of the

---
[3] *Enarratio in Ps. 40*, no. 30.

legitimacy of the reform and of the New Church; it is like the tiny grain of incense offered to the Emperor. It is therefore not licit to mention the name of John Paul II in the Canon.

The Society of Saint Pius X attempts to avoid the ecclesiological problem which the mentioning of the name causes by asserting the impossible ecclesiology to which they adhere. They do recognize John Paul II as pope and his church as the Catholic Church and his hierarchy as the Catholic hierarchy, but say, at the same time, that the faithful must sift the acts of the hierarchy in order to distinguish what is Catholic from what is non-Catholic.

This theory strips the Church of its essential role as infallible mother and teacher of the human race, and transfers this dignity to the 'sifter,' in this case the Society of Saint Pius X. It separates the three things which Saint Ambrose so aptly linked together: pope, Church, and eternal life. If the doctrines, sacraments and laws of the pope and of the Church have to be sifted, lest something non-Catholic, sinful, or poisonous be given to the faithful, then eternal life is not something intimately linked with the Church.

If the Church needs a sifter, then why have the Church? Of what use is it? The purpose of the Church is to bring men *infallibly* to their ultimate supernatural end of eternal life. It accomplishes this *infallibly* by its three essential functions of teaching, ruling and sanctifying. The effect of its act of teaching is its doctrine; the effect of its act of ruling is its laws, and the effect of its act of sanctifying is eternal life by means of its sacraments and the Holy Sacrifice of the Mass.

If the Church can err in these matters, so much so that a sifter is necessary, then she can err in her essential mission, which is to bring men to eternal salvation. But if she can err in this mission, that is, if we could go to hell by following her and believing her, then for what purpose does she exist?

This is why Saint Ambrose has linked eternal life to pope and Church, since they are linked inexorably together in the divine constitution of the Catholic Church.

The priest who is saying the Traditional Mass in defiance of the orders of John Paul II and the local *Novus Ordo* hierarch is doing so because the New Mass and sacraments are evil, the new doctrines are erroneous, and the new practices of the *Novus Ordo* church are sinful. He must necessarily conclude that they do not proceed from the Church, since the general doctrine and practice of the Church cannot be evil, erroneous or sinful. From this he must conclude that John Paul II cannot be the pope, since, if he were, the author of the evil, erroneous and sinful doctrines and practices would be the Church. But this is *de fide* impossible. *Ergo.*

Pope, Church and eternal life are three inseparable entities: when one is removed, the other two immediately perish.

Communion with Heretics

Another problem with the *una cum* declaration is that it is a sin against the profession of the Faith.

As much as it is necessary for the Catholic priest to mention the name of the reigning pontiff as a sign of his communion with him and the Catholic Church as a whole, it is equally necessary for him to *avoid* mentioning the name of anyone who is not in communion with the Catholic Church. When schismatics were reconciled to the Catholic Church, they had to omit, as part of their sign of adherence, the names of their schismatic Patriarchs from the Canon of the Mass. In his *Bibliotheca*, Father Ferraris cites the case of a schismatic bishop who was reconciled to Rome. The papal legates reassure the pope that, during the course of the Mass, no name was mentioned which was odious to the Catholic faith:

> "Finally the legates of [Pope] Hormisda recount to the Pope with these words what happened to them during the reconciliation of the bishop of the city of Troili Scampina: *We confess*, they said, that it would be hard to find in another people so much devotion to Your Holiness, so much praise to God, so many tears and so much joy. Nearly all the people received us into the city, both the men and the women with candles, and the soldiers with crosses. Masses were celebrated, and no name which is loathsome to religion was mentioned but only that of Your Holiness."

He also mentions that it is licit to pray for the conversion of infidels, heretics and schismatics in the *Memento* of the living, since it is a private and not a public prayer, thereby implying that it would not be licit to mention them publicly:

> "The priest should be warned however [with Azor. lib X, cap. 22, *quæst.* 3,] that he can correctly pray in the *Memento* for the conversion of infidels, heretics and schismatics, since this is a private and not public prayer."[4]

Benedict XIV himself ordered the Italo-Greeks to mention the name of the Pope and local bishop, lest there be any suspicion of schism among them, and furthermore forbade from mentioning the name of a schismatic Patriarch:

> "The second part of the same warning follows in which, as was noted above, the Greek priest is enjoined, during the Mass, after he has prayed for the Roman Pontiff, to pray also for his own bishop, and for his Patriarch, provided that they be Catholic; for if one or the other or both were a schismatic or a heretic, he would not be permitted to make a mention of them."[5]

Pope Benedict, in fact, makes frequent warning of the necessity not to mention the name of anyone who is a schismatic or a heretic:

> "...but let him carefully avoid making mention of the names of schismatics or heretics."

> "Nor is he [the Greek priest] generally prohibited, in the often cited Monitum, from making mention of the Patriarch, but only in the case where the Metropolitans or Patriarchs should be schismatics or heretics..."[6]

He then cites three cases in which priests were specifically forbidden by the Holy Office to mention the name of schismatic prelates, in 1673, 1674 and 1732 respectively. The one in 1673 is of special interest, since the priest's motive in mentioning the name of the schismatic was to attract the schismatics to the Catholic Church. The answer was it is *absolutely forbidden*. Put that in your ecumenical pipe and smoke it.

Pope Benedict states that the reason for this prohibition is that heretics and schismatics are excommunicates, and it is not licit to pray publicly for excommunicates: *'The Sacred Canons of the*

---

[4] *op. cit.,* p. 51.
[5] *op. cit.,* p. 18.
[6] *ibid.,* p. 22.

Church prohibit praying for excommunicates...And although there is nothing wrong with praying for their conversion, this must not be done by pronouncing their names in the solemn prayer of the Sacrifice. This observance is in accordance with the traditional discipline...'[7] He furthermore quotes Saint Thomas: *'One can pray for excommunicates, although not in those prayers which are offered for the members of the Church.'*[8]

Oddly, neither Pope Benedict nor Saint Robert Bellarmine see any problem in mentioning the name of an infidel ruler (e.g., the Turkish Sultan of Constantinople). Saint Robert, whom Pope Benedict follows, states that it is tolerable since there is nothing proper to the nature of the Mass which prohibits it to be offered for infidels, and that they know of no Church law which condemns the practice. Both are clear, however, that they are not referring to *heretical* or *schismatical* rulers, but only the unbaptized, for the heretical and schismatical are excommunicated, and are therefore subject to exclusion by the laws of the Church. Thus, heretical and schismatical rulers fall under the same prohibitions as heretical and schismatical Patriarchs. Since there is no law prohibiting the mention of infidels, however, it seems to Pope Benedict and Saint Robert that it can be done. The former, however, qualifies his opinion by saying, *'However, leaving these assertions to their probability...,'* and goes on to say that it is a moot point in any case, since none of the Greek Catholics mention the name of the Turk in the Mass.[9]

"But, John Paul II is a Heretic"

Now that we have established that heretical and schismatical prelates must not be mentioned in the Mass, it remains only to assert the minor: John Paul II is a heretic. Therefore, he must not be mentioned in the Canon of the Mass.

The fact that he is a heretic I must leave to other books and articles to prove. This task has been accomplished already in diverse times, publications, and languages. Suffice it to say that he has, both *by word* and *by deed* manifested an adherence to heresy.

---

[7] *ibid.*, p. 23.
[8] In 4 Sent. dist. 18. quest. 2. art. 1.
[9] POPE BENEDICT XIV, *op. cit.*, pp. 27 & 28.

The glaring objection to this minor premise of the argumentation is that John Paul II is not formal in his heresy, and therefore does not incur an excommunication. Therefore, he may still be licitly mentioned in the Mass.

I respond to this objection in the following manner: (1) there is strong evidence that he is formal in his adherence to heresy; (2) the law of the Church presumes guilt (i.e., formality) in the public profession of heresy until the contrary be proven; (3) it is the practice of the Church to treat all those who publicly adhere to heresy as formal heretics in the external forum, whether or not, in the internal forum, they be morally guilty of their heresy; (4) to recognize John Paul II as a member of the Catholic Church ruins the theological basis of resistance to the changes. Now let us examine each of these responses individually.

1. **There is strong evidence that John Paul II is formal in his adherence to heresy.**

Formal heresy is distinguished against material heresy. The former involves stubbornness against the teaching authority of the Catholic Church; the latter lacks this stubbornness. The only manner in which a person may lack stubbornness, or *pertinacity* as the canonists call it, is through ignorance of the fact that the opinion to which he adheres is contrary to divine and Catholic faith. For the other motives of adhering to false opinion, such as pride, vainglory, a spirit of contradiction, etc., all constitute a sufficient bad will to qualify the heresy as pertinacious and formal.

John Paul II, however, cannot be reasonably excused on the title of ignorance, even culpable ignorance. He received his seminary education in one of the finest institutions of the Church, the *Angelicum*, under the tutelage of one of this century's best theologians, Garrigou-Lagrange. Nor is John Paul II a brainless dolt. He speaks many foreign languages fluently, and he could never have risen to the heights of bishop, "cardinal" and "pope" unless he possessed a sharp intellect. To the contrary, he is one of these post-World War II avant-garde theologians like de Chardin, de Lubac and Rahner, who set out to overthrow the tradition of the Catholic Church and replace it with what we have today. He was a liberal seminarian, a liberal young priest, a liberal bishop, and liberal phony cardinal, and now is a liberal phony pope.

He is not some do-gooder Catholic-at-heart who has, through no fault of his own, stumbled into Modernism along the way. Rather he is one of the great *Novus Ordo* theoreticians, the choice of none other than Cardinal König, who was among the most modernistic prelates in the whole world.

The pertinacity of a John Paul II and of clergy like him can be seen in their *hatred* for the pre-Vatican II Church. In this consists their bad will, for in hating the pre-Vatican II Church, they are hating *the Church*.

Another strong argument in favor of his pertinacity is that lack of formality on his part does not assign a sufficient cause for the destruction which has been wrought in the Church. The devastation which surrounds us is not the work of a disorganized group of ignorant Catholic clergy 'who don't know any better,' but the effect of a diabolical conspiracy of the gates of hell against the Church. *An enemy hath done this*. To say that the spearheads of this noxious reform, John XXIII, Paul VI, and John Paul II, are not conscious parties to the overthrow of the traditional Faith is to posit an effect without a sufficient cause. It is impossible. It would be comparable to Our Lord's saying in the parable of the wheat and the cockle, 'The sowers just made an honest mistake.' The *Novus Ordo* religion is so radically different from Catholic faith, that no person in his right mind, regardless of education, could fail to recognize the difference. The pertinacious modernist simply replies: *vive la différence*.

Nor am I saying here that John Paul II must necessarily be one of the plotters. Sufficient for formal heresy is any type of *mala voluntas*: pride, curiosity, self-aggrandizement. Only ignorance excuses.

Furthermore, John Paul II has been sufficiently told that his new religion is a substantial departure from the pre-Vatican II religion. He does not live in a cave. Yet he continues to adhere to and implement this new religion.

The question of John Paul II's pertinacity is admittedly a judgment call, but to paint him as a material heretic is to me the same thing as saying that Robespierre was only a material terrorist. He meant well.

2. **The law of the Church presumes pertinacity unless the contrary be proven.**

The presumption of the law is against John Paul II:

> "The very commission of any act which signifies heresy, e.g., the statement of some doctrine contrary or contradictory to a revealed and defined dogma, gives sufficient ground for juridical presumption of heretical depravity."[10]

Not only has John Paul II made statements of doctrine contrary to revealed and defined dogma (e.g., non-Catholic religions are means of salvation, contradictory to *outside the Church there is no salvation*), but he has also explicitly declared himself to be in communion with 'in the same Church as' schismatics and heretics. He has, furthermore, compounded these abominable statements with acts which confirm his adherence to heresy, such as *communicatio in sacris* and ecumenical services with everything that walks on two legs. It is not, therefore, the law or the spirit of the Church to automatically exonerate the guilt of someone publicly spewing heresy, but rather to presume it. The guilty party must come forward and prove his innocence:

> "There may however be circumstances which excuse the person either from all responsibility, or else from grave responsibility. These excusing circumstances have to be proved in the external forum, and the burden of proof is on the person whose action has given rise to the imputation of heresy. In the absence of such proof, all such excuses are presumed not to exist. When satisfactory proof is offered, the juridical presumption will yield to fact, and the person will be pronounced innocent of heresy, and not liable to censure."[11]

3. **It is the practice of the Church to treat all those who publicly adhere to heresy as formal heretics in the external forum.**

This is the most important point. In my article on communion (*Sacerdotium* V), I pointed out that the Church makes no judgment about the interior dispositions of those who adhere to heresy, but rather treats them as formal heretics. If the Church did not do this, its very divine constitution as the congregation of the faithful

---

[10] ERIC F. MACKENZIE, A.M., S.T.L., J.C.L. REV., *The Delict of Heresy*, (Washington, D.C.: The Catholic University of America, 1932) p. 35. (Cf. Canon 2200 § 2)
[11] *ibid.*

(*congregatio fidelium*) would be eroded; the unity of Faith would not survive as one of its four marks. If only those excommunicated by name were considered to be outside the Church 'the heresiarchs like Luther' and the rest were considered to be in good conscience and therefore Catholics, the Church would have lost in the first few years of its existence the sacred Deposit of Faith. It is precisely because membership in the Church is strictly dependent upon the profession of the orthodox Faith that the Church has her mark of unity of Faith.

For this reason, regardless of our 'hunches' about culpability of his heresy, it is necessary that we treat him as a heretic and as an excommunicate. For heresy incurs an automatic excommunication; in normal times it is authority which confirms the automatic excommunication with a declaratory sentence. When the authority itself falls into the heresy, and fails to excommunicate itself, so to speak, and other heretics who are deserving of it, the faithful of the Church must observe the *reality* of his self-severance from the Church, even if it is not established *legally*. For law is a reflection of reality, and reality does not cease to be reality because authority fails to enshrine it by law. When heretics occupy the places of authority, heresy becomes the law, and orthodoxy becomes heresy. This legalization of heresy does not debilitate the Catholic faithful, but rather places a heavy burden upon them to bear witness to the wickedness of the law, and to its logical consequence, the *non-authority* of the apparent authority.

For there are some who argue that, since John Paul II is not excommunicated by a declaratory sentence, that we are free to regard him as a Catholic.

Not so. The declaratory sentence which follows an automatic excommunication is merely a legal recognition of something which already exists. If this were not true, the automatic excommunication would be meaningless. The excommunicated person is already severed from the Church; the declaratory sentence merely legally ascertains both the fact of the delict and the guilt of the party who has committed it. Once the declaratory sentence is handed down, all in the Church, including the guilty party, are required to *observe* the excommunication.

In the present crisis of the Church, during which we are deprived of authority, a declaratory sentence of excommunication is impossible. This lamentable fact, however, does not and cannot mean that the Church becomes an absolute free-for-all, for the Church would be essentially defective if it did not maintain its unity of Faith. This unity of Faith is that by which it is constituted; it is that by which it is recognized as the one true Church of Christ.

Catholics then must recognize the heresy as heresy in the would-be authority, presume guilt (pertinacity) unless there is evidence to the contrary, and hold as excluded from the ranks of the Church those who profess adherence to the Vatican II religion. It is true that there are many cases of non-pertinacious adherence to the new religion among the lay people, and even perhaps among priests, but this particular lack of guilt is determined on a case-by-case basis, whereas the presumption of guilt is required by the general law.

Hence most (nearly all) Traditional priests of all persuasions do not require a formal abjuration nor an absolution from excommunication of *Novus Ordites* returning to the traditional Faith, for the reason that the priests perceive in them a lack of pertinacity in their adherence to the *Novus Ordo*. On the other hand, I know of no Traditional priest who considers a Hans Küng to be a Catholic, since pertinacity is presumed in his case. So should it be presumed in the case of John Paul II, since (a) the law requires it, and (b) ignorance is the only viable excuse from pertinacity, and ignorance is virtually impossible in John Paul II, nor is there evidence of it.

Nonetheless, it is important to recall that there is no substitute for the authority of the Church, and even the collective spurning of John Paul II by Catholics does not equal the same thing as the declaratory sentence of authority. For until someone is excommunicated by declaratory sentence, it would be legitimate for any Catholic to say, "I think that there is evidence to say that he is not pertinacious in his heresy, and therefore not excommunicated." This is true since a presumption always yields to fact, and since John Paul II's pertinacity is not an established legal fact, the fact of his excommunication is likewise not legally established.

In any case, the certitude about John Paul II's non-papacy does not arise from arguments of his pertinacity in heresy, but rather from serious ecclesiological arguments, namely, that it is impossible that the authority which he claims to have "the very authority of Christ" prescribe for the Church what John Paul II has prescribed. If the authority of the Church, which is the authority of Christ, can give us official teaching of heresy, heretical sacramental rites, and sinful laws, then the Church would be defectible. But this is *de fide* impossible. Therefore, it is impossible, by the very nature of the Church, that John Paul II be the Pope.

4. **To recognize John Paul II as a member of the Catholic Church ruins the theological basis of resistance to the changes.**

This is where the *una cum* question becomes so critical. From the reasoning which I have just presented, it is evident that ecclesial communion with John Paul II as pope means one of two things:

a. that the reforms of Vatican II are Catholic, since they come from the indefectible Catholic Church;
b. that the Church has defected, since heresy and sin has come from the official teaching and laws of the Catholic Church.

Since (b) is against the Faith, only (a) is even considerable. If one admits (a), namely that the reforms of Vatican II are Catholic, then the whole motive of adherence to Tradition and resistance to the reforms is exploded. What possible motive could there be to retain the Traditional Mass, nostalgia excepted, if the New Mass is a Catholic Mass? The *una cum* Traditional Mass, therefore, is either *objectively* schismatic (altar against altar, as in the case of the Society of Saint Pius X) or it is said under the auspices of the *Novus Ordo* hierarchy for nostalgic purposes (e.g., the Indult Mass and the Saint Peter group). The *una cum* Traditional Mass is, in all cases, an implicit recognition of the Vatican II religion as the Catholic religion, and as the Conciliar Church as the Roman Catholic Church. But such a recognition is *in odium religionis (in hatred of the Faith)*. Therefore, to mention John Paul II's name in the Mass is, objectively, *in odium religionis*.

Here let me pause, after having made this rather withering criticism, in order to reassure the reader that I am not saying that every single priest who mentions John Paul II in the Canon is guilty of *formal* schism or of *formally* positing acts *in odium religionis*. I have been very careful to use the word "objectively" in all cases in order to emphasize that it is quite easy for an *una cum* priest to be in good conscience about this matter. At the same time, everyone knows that the morality of an act is not determined objectively from the mistaken good conscience of the individual, but rather from the object itself. It is about this object that we are concerned in this article, and I am not recommending that anyone be burned at the stake.

And while we are on the subject, I should bring up something which has often been thrown up to me by critics: "*You, Father Sanborn, were once una cum!*" Yes, it is true, I was. Let me explain. I began adhering to the vacancy of the Apostolic See back in 1973 at Écône, at a time when a third of the seminarians openly thought similarly. In 1979, Archbishop Lefebvre began his *una cum* campaign and concomitant persecution. I went to see him in Switzerland in January of 1980 for an entirely different matter, at which time he insisted that I become *una cum*. I reluctantly accepted to do so because, at the time, I labored under the notion that the vacancy of the Apostolic See was a *matter of opinion*, and that a probable argument could be made for both sides. I thought, erroneously, that the *una cum* or *sede plena* position was a legitimate theological opinion. I thus accepted to be *una cum* because of the principle that one can act on a probable opinion even though one might be convinced that the opposite opinion is more probable.[12] Even in my *sede plena* days, however, I always felt in my heart that the *sede vacante* position made much more sense. So, I was *una cum* in all good, though uncomfortable, conscience from 1980 to 1983. I simply did not see the intrinsic and essential connection between John Paul II's papacy and the legitimation of the New Church; I did not see the necessary logical link between the rejection of the New Religion and John Paul II's claim to papal authority.

I now realize this link, and therefore realize that if John Paul II's papal authority is "a matter of theological opinion," then the non-Catholicism of the New Religion and of the New Church is also "a matter of theological opinion." For one cannot separate Pope and Church. *Where Peter is, there is the Church.* To make, therefore, the identity of *Peter* a matter of opinion is to make the identity of the Church a matter of opinion. *Where true Peter is, there is the true Church; where there is a false Peter, there is a false church.* But not: *where*

---

[12] Before the Thomists have a hemorrhage, let me point out quickly that one of the *Princeps Thomistarum* of this century, Hugon, says that it is legitimate to do such a thing. "*Non repugnat ut intellectus adhaereat uni opinioni, dum alteram existimat probabiliorem.*"*Cursus Philosophiae Thomisticae* Logica Maior, Tract. III., q. 1.

there is a false Peter, there is the true Church, nor where there is true Peter, there is a false church. This is impossible, for the Pope is the principle of unity of the Catholic Church, as we have already seen; the identity of the Catholic Church, therefore, is inseparable from the identity of the Roman Pontiff. You cannot separate Pope and Church.

In Persona Ecclesiae

In my article entitled "Communion" (*Sacerdotium* V), I spoke about the problem of validly ordained priests saying Masses which were liturgically Catholic but outside the Catholic Church. This is the case of the Greek schismatics, Old Catholics (in some cases valid), even High Church Anglicans who have gotten themselves validly ordained in one way or another.

I pointed out, by citing authorities on the matter, that for validity, it is necessary that the minister be acting *in the person of Christ* at the altar, but for the catholicity of the Mass, he must at the same time be acting *in the person of the Church*. Saint Thomas Aquinas explains the distinction:

> "And because the consecration of the Eucharist is an act which flows from the power of orders, those who are separated from the Church through heresy or schism or excommunication, can indeed consecrate the Eucharist which, when consecrated by them, contains the true body and blood of Christ: they nevertheless do not do this rightly, but rather sin when they do it. They therefore do not receive the fruit of the sacrifice, which is a spiritual sacrifice."

> "The priest at Mass indeed speaks in the prayers in the person of the Church, in whose unity he remains; but in consecrating the sacrament he speaks as in the person of Christ, Whose place he holds by the power of orders. Consequently, if a priest separated from the unity of the Church celebrates Mass, not having lost the power of Order, he consecrates Christ's true body and blood; but because he is severed from the unity of the Church, his prayers have no efficacy."[13]

Some saints and popes had some stronger words about schismatic Masses:

Pope Pelagius I: "One body of Christ establishes the fact that there is one Church. An altar which is divided from the unity [of the Church]

---
[13] IIIa q. 82 a. 7, corpus & ad 3um.

cannot gather together the true body of Christ."[14]

Saint Cyprian: "The schismatic dares to set up an altar and to profane the truth of the divine Victim by means of false sacrifices."[15] (He also wanted returning schismatic priests to be reduced to the lay state, referring to them as those who against the unique and divine altar attempted to offer outside [of the Church] sacrilegious and false sacrifices."[16]

Saint Augustine: "Outside of the Catholic Church the true sacrifice cannot be found."[17]

St. Leo the Great: "Elsewhere [that is, outside the Church] there is neither an approved priesthood nor true sacrifices."[18]

Saint Jerome: "God hates the sacrifices of these [i.e., heretics] and pushes them away from Himself, and whenever they come together in the name of the Lord, He abhors their stench, and holds his nose..."[19]

Father Cappello explains this distinction clearly:

> "Priests who are cut off from the Church, although they validly sacrifice *in the name of Christ*, nevertheless do not offer the sacrifice *as ministers of the Church nor in the person of the Church*. For the priest has the power to pray, to intercede and to offer in the name of the Church by virtue of his commission from the Church, and with regard to this, the Church can deprive the priest who is cut off from sacrificing in its name."[20]

From these texts, it is clear that the validity of the Mass is not sufficient that it be a *Catholic* Mass, but rather another very important factor is necessary: *the fact that the priest act* in the person of the Church, *that is, that he be commissioned by the Church to pray in its name*.

This factor creates a terrible problem for the *una cum* Traditional Mass. If the priest is saying that John Paul II is the Pope, and that he

---

[14] *Ep. ad Joan. Patr.*, P.L. 69, 412.
[15] *De Unitate Ecclesiae*, c. 17. P.L. 4, 513.
[16] Ep. 72, c. 2. P.L. 3, 1048-1049.
[17] cf. PROSPERUM AQUITANUM, *Sent.*, sent. 15 P.L. 51, 430.
[18] Ep. LXXX *Ad Anatolium*, cap. 2.
[19] *In Amos*, V: 22, P.L. 25, 1033-1034.
[20] CAPPELLO, FELIX M. S. I.., *Tractatus Canonico-moralis de Sacramentis*, (Turin: Marietti), 1962, I, p. 462.

is in communion with him, he is necessarily saying that the Church of which John Paul II is the head is the Roman Catholic Church. In order that the Mass which the priest is saying, therefore, be deemed a *Catholic* Mass, it is necessary that the priest be commissioned by John Paul II to say the Mass *in the person of the Church*.

Without this commission, without this authorization from him who has the care of Christ's whole flock, from him who has the commission from Christ to teach, rule, and to sanctify, the Mass becomes a non-Catholic Mass. The Catholic priest must be acting as the agent of his bishop, who has the care of the diocesan flock, who, in turn must be acting as an agent of the Pope who has care of the whole flock. The Pope, in turn, must be acting as an agent of Christ, of whom he is the Vicar. This is the very constitution of the Catholic Church; it is this tight link of agency and authority which makes the Church Catholic.

If the priest, therefore, is acting without the authorization of the diocesan bishop, he is then acting without the authorization of the Pope, and his Mass and sacraments are cut off from both Christ and His Church. His Mass is not Catholic, nor are his sacraments, for he is not acting *in the person of the Church*.

How does the Traditional priest today act *in the person of the Church*, when there is no authority to authorize him to say Mass?

He does so by carrying on the mission of the Catholic Church, which is the sanctification of souls. Thus, it is perfectly legitimate and necessary for priests to say Mass, preach, and distribute the sacraments, as they are authorized by the Church to do so through the principle of *epikeia*. This principle, however, cannot possibly be invoked if the superior is present; one cannot invoke *epikeia* against a present, acting, and ruling superior. It simply does not make sense, since *epikeia* is essentially an estimation of the mind of the lawmaker in his absence.[21]

But the *una cum* Mass puts the lawmaker in Rome, and his personal representative in the local chancery, and thus destroys the entire moral underpinning of the extraordinary apostolates which are carried on by Traditional priests.

---

[21] "*Epikeia non potest licite adhiberi: (a) Si superior, qui dispensationem legis concedere valet, facile adiri queat.*" Prümmer, Manuale *Theologiae Moralis* I, no. 231 ff. q.v.

Thus, the *una cum* Mass ends up as an objectively schismatic Mass no matter how you slice it:

a. If, for the sake of argument, John Paul II were the Pope, the unauthorized (i.e., non-indult) Traditional Mass is schismatic, since it is not said in the person of the Church.
b. If John Paul II is not the Pope, then the una cum Mass is schismatic since it is said in union with, under the auspices of, a false pope and a false church.

In neither case does the priest have any business saying it.

The only situation in which it would be licit to carry on an extensive, habitual, "unauthorized" apostolate is in a case similar to our own, in which there is a long-term absence of authority. The authorization for saying Mass, preaching, and administering the sacraments would then be *per modum actus*, that is, in the individual acts themselves, and would not be a habitual authority. The authorization would be from the Church itself (*Ecclesia supplet*, that is, the Church supplies jurisdiction in the absence of the competent authority).

The Society of Saint Pius X is excommunicated by the person they say to be the Vicar of Christ on earth. They cannot invoke against his supposed authority the very authority of the Church (that is, they cannot invoke the principle of *Ecclesia supplet*), since he supposedly possesses the fullness of the authority of the Church. To do so is schismatic, and that is exactly what John Paul II considers the Society of Saint Pius X to be: schismatic.

Conclusions of the Speculative Order

The speculative conclusions from the foregoing are the following:

- The *una cum* phrase is a declaration of ecclesial communion with the reigning Roman Pontiff and local diocesan bishop.
- This declaration of communion is particularly significant, since the Roman Pontiff is the *principle of unity* of the entire Roman Catholic Church, and the local bishop, subordinately, is the principle of unity of the particular Church or diocese.
- Because the Roman Pontiff and local bishop constitute the principle of unity of the Church, the mentioning of their name in the Canon is an ecclesiological declaration, namely that the Church of which they are the head is none other than the Roman

Catholic Church.
- Because of the principle of *outside the Church there is no salvation*, it follows that union with and submission to the Roman Pontiff and the local bishop constitute an *absolute condition* of eternal salvation.
- Because of the principle of the indefectibility of the Roman Catholic Church, and of the infallibility of its ordinary magisterium and its general laws, it follows that the ordinary magisterium of the Roman Pontiff is free from error and the general laws which he promulgates cannot prescribe anything sinful.
- Because of the principle that the Holy Sacrifice of the Mass is by nature an ecclesial act, that is, an act of the whole Church, it follows that in order for it to qualify as a *Catholic* Mass, it must be offered *in the person of the Church*, that is, the priest must be authorized by the Church to sacrifice in its name.
- This authorization must be obtained from the duly constituted authority of the Catholic Church, that is, the Pope and local bishop. They have the power to withdraw this commission from a priest, in which case, should he say Mass, he would not be offering it *in the person of the Church*.
- The principle of *Ecclesia supplet*, by which a priest obtains authorization to act in the Church's name (*in the person of the Church*) in extraordinary circumstances cannot be invoked *against* the very authority which grants it. This would be an absurdity.
- Nor can the authorization of the Church be presumed by the principle of *epikeia*, if the authority of the Church is present and functioning, since *epikeia* presumes the absence of the authority. Thus, *epikeia* cannot be invoked against the present and ruling authority. This too would be an absurdity, and would lead to anarchy in any institution.

Now let us plug John Paul II, *as pope*, into the above principles:

- The Church of which he is the head is the Roman Catholic Church.
- The dogmatic and moral teachings of Vatican II, termed ordinary magisterium by Paul VI, deserve the assent of faith (cf. Vatican I), and the reforms of Vatican II, while perhaps not ideal, are Catholic and non-sinful.
- Only those priests who are authorized by John Paul II (and the local bishop in communion with him) can be deemed to be saying *Catholic* Masses.

- Masses offered by priests unauthorized by him and the local bishop are not Catholic Masses, since they are not offered *in the person of the Church*. Rather they are schismatic Masses, and fall under the severe condemnations of the Popes and Fathers mentioned in this article.

Now let us plug John Paul II, *as non-pope*, into these principles:

- The church of which he is the head is not the Roman Catholic Church.
- Neither Vatican II nor its reforms deserve the assent of faith or obedience, but rather should be rejected and ignored by Catholics.
- Masses offered in union with John Paul II are non-Catholic Masses, since they are offered *in the person of a heretical church*.
- Catholic priests may rightfully invoke the principles of *Ecclesia supplet* and *epikeia* as reasonable authorization of their apostolates, due to the absence of authority, and thus rightfully claim that their Masses and sacraments are authorized by the Catholic Church and are *in the person of the Church*.

Conclusions of the Moral Order

The following moral conclusions flow from what has been said:

I. *If John Paul II were the Pope:*

a. the only Traditional Mass which could be licitly attended would be one authorized by him, namely an Indult Mass, or a Mass offered by a priest of the Fraternity of Saint Peter.
b. it would be gravely sinful to attend a Mass which was not authorized by him, e.g., the Mass of a priest of the Society of Saint Pius X or of a non-una cum priest, since these would be schismatic Masses. The confessions and marriages would be invalid.

II. *If John Paul II is not the Pope:*

a. it would be objectively gravely illicit to attend a Mass which was *together with Thy servant John Paul our Pope* since (1) it would be an explicit declaration of union with a false, non-Catholic church and religion (*Where Peter is, there is the Church*) and (2) it would be active participation in a Mass which was not offered *in the person of the Church*, in a Mass which would be, *objectively*, schismatic.

A Neither-Nor Ecclesiological Twilight Zone

The position of the Society of Saint Pius X is odd in this sense: on the one hand they insist that John Paul II is Pope, but on the other hand they carry on an extensive apostolate, including the consecration of bishops, in absolute defiance of his condemnation, as if he did not exist.

It puts them in a "damned if you do and damned if you don't" ecclesiological[22] position. For if you regard John Paul II to be the Pope, their apostolate is obviously off-limits, for the reasons stated above, viz., because it would not be *in the person of the Church*. On the other hand, if you say that John Paul II is not the Pope, then their apostolate becomes off-limits, since it involves both an adherence to a false religion and church, as well as attendance at Masses which are not offered *in the person of the Church*.

They are, therefore, in a *neither-nor* ecclesiological Twilight Zone which has to be resolved some day. The recent discussions about their claims to jurisdiction are a symptom of this radically impossible ecclesiology which they are asserting.

It must never be forgotten that they are still looking forward to an absorption by John Paul II into the New Church fold; they are still looking for the side chapel in the modernist cathedral. This was plainly stated in 1988, that is, that the negotiations with 'Rome' would continue, and that perhaps in five years (1993) the whole problem would be resolved.

This desire to be reinstated by John Paul II is an important point to remember, for it means that the Society of Saint Pius X belongs *by explicit desire* to John Paul II's New Church, and their *una cum* Masses are an expression of this desire. Whether all of the adherents of the Society of Saint Pius X will go along with the reconciliation remains to be seen. Bishop Williamson said to *Monde et Vie* last August (1992) that he thinks that the next pope will be an anti-pope. The Mother of All Battles might then be fought out in the Society of Saint Pius X.

---

[22] The word ecclesiological means "pertaining to the theology of the Church."

Chapter 12

Answers to Objections

Objection I. *The priest who is una cum is in good conscience and does not want to be part of anything which is non-Catholic. Therefore, he is not formally schismatic. Therefore, his Mass is not schismatic.*

Answer. That most priests who are *una cum* are in good conscience, *I admit*. That they are therefore not formally schismatic, *I admit*. That therefore their Masses are not schismatic, *I deny*. The Mass is an *ecclesial* act, and its 'ecclesiality,' its very catholicity, does not depend on the formality or materiality of the schism of the priest. The priest's good or bad conscience does not in any way affect the object of the act of the *una cum* statement, which is both to declare communion with John Paul II *as pope*, and to place the Mass under the auspices of something other than the Roman Catholic Church. By analogy, a priest may, through inadvertence, throw away a consecrated host into the sacristy trash can. Others around him who know that the host is consecrated cannot consent to or participate in the priest's action, even though the priest did it in good conscience. Everyone knows that the objective morality of an act does not flow from the intention of the agent but from the object itself.

Objection II. *Anyone who has not been officially excommunicated (by declaratory or condemnatory sentence) may still be mentioned in the Canon of the Mass. But John Paul II has never been officially excommunicated. Therefore, he may still be mentioned in the Canon of the Mass.*

Answer. Anyone who has not been officially excommunicated (by declaratory or condemnatory sentence) may still be mentioned in the Canon of the Mass, *I distinguish*, in normal times, *I admit*, in times when the Apostolic See and apparently all episcopal sees are possessed by heretics, *I deny*. As I said earlier, heresy becomes the law when heretics gain positions of "authority." Catholics in such a case cannot permit the Church to become an absolute anarchy and hold harmless the wholesale abandonment of the Faith throughout the world. By analogy, the New Mass has never been officially condemned by the Church. Yet Catholics by the instinct of their faith uncompromisingly reject it. Thus one could just as easily say, "The Church has never officially condemned the New Mass, so therefore we are free to accept it." No, the firmness of Catholics against the New Mass, the new sacraments, the new doctrines of Vatican II, in short the whole new religion, *must* ecclesiologically translate into a rejection of the authority of the "Popes" who promulgated it. If the new religion is defective, it *cannot* be from the Catholic Church. If it cannot be from the Catholic Church, then the Conciliar "Popes" *cannot* be said to have the authority of the Church. Otherwise, you end up with a defectible and defected Catholic Church. While it is true, therefore, that John Paul II has not been officially condemned, the situation in the Church is such that Catholics must bear witness to the heresy of the new religion, and therefore of his lack of authority. If Catholics let these Conciliar "Popes" pass as true Catholic Popes, then historically the Catholic Church will be said to have defected. Hence it is absolutely necessary that Catholics treat them as non-popes.

Objection III. *The mentioning of the name of John Paul II in the Mass is an evil, certainly, but it can be tolerated for the greater good of not depriving sacraments of a great many people.*

Answer. An evil may only be tolerated if its toleration does not entail the positing of an intrinsically evil act. But to mention John Paul II's name is intrinsically evil, for, as I have said, it involves the identification of the Roman Catholic Church with the New Church, the Roman Catholic faith with the new religion. To mention his name is objectively, really and truly in *odium religionis*, in hatred of the Faith. It is a *name loathsome to our Faith*. Since he is being mentioned *as pope*, it involves an identification of what Church you belong to. It is an intrinsically evil act, however, to declare yourself to be a member of a non-Catholic church, and in communion with a non-Catholic heresiarch sect-leader. I do realize, on the other hand, that what I am saying presents dire consequences for many, should they accept it. I do not see, however, how the *Te Igitur* of the Mass is not a true ecclesiological battlefield in which a profession of Faith must be made. The reason why there has been such a great proliferation of the *una cum* Mass is because Archbishop Lefebvre always sought to have the Traditional Mass under the auspices of the New Church. Only in 1976, when he declared the Vatican II Church to be a schismatic church, did he openly depart from this idea. Even then, however, he continued to seek to have the Society recognized by the schismatic church. Even now, despite the excommunication, the same Society seeks re-admission into this same schismatic church. If Archbishop Lefebvre had been as firm on the Church issue as he had been on the Mass, virtually no Traditional priest would be *una cum* today. You cannot have the Catholic Mass in a schismatic church, but that is exactly what the Society is attempting to do. Catholics must reject the New Church as much as they reject the New Mass. *Let us* not do evil things in order that good things come about. (cf. Romans III: 8)

Objection IV. *The lay people can attend the* una cum *Mass without necessarily consenting to the* una cum *phrase.*

Answer. Active participation in worship is consent to the worship, and one is presumed to consent to everything which is part of the worship. The name of John Paul II in the Mass is *exactly* the same thing as the presence of John Paul II in the sanctuary *as pope*. It is a sign, a declaration of ecclesial communion. Such external and public signs deserve external and public disapproval; active participation gives external consent. Furthermore, the presence of John Paul II's name *as pope, as principle of unity of the Church*, places the entire act of worship in the schismatic category, and not just the little phrase, since it places the entire act of worship *outside the Church*. But outside the Church there is no salvation.

Conclusion

It is evident, therefore, that the mention of John Paul II's name in the Canon (a) is an explicit declaration of ecclesial communion with a heresiarch; (b) is an explicit declaration of the identity of the Roman Catholic Church with the *Novus Ordo* Church, for *where Peter is, there is the Church*; (c) causes intrinsic and insoluble problems and 'ecclesiological nightmares' for the Traditional priest, since it places his Mass *outside* the Church and makes it schismatic, since he is setting up "altar against altar."

The only logical alternative for someone who recognizes John Paul II as pope is to place himself in the Fraternity of Saint Peter, or to say an Indult Mass.

Since the *una cum* phrase is a statement of communion, the following things are true:

- The *una cum* Mass is therefore the equivalent of having John Paul II in your sanctuary during the Mass, and of showing him the external signs of being the Pope, such as incensations, genuflections, etc. Of course you would have to give him Holy Communion, for if the Pope is not a member of the Catholic Church, then who is? *Where Peter is, there is the Church.*
- The *una cum* Mass is the equivalent of singing the *Oremus pro Pontifice*, a hymn sung to pray for the Pope: *Let us pray for our*

Holy Father John Paul. May God preserve him, and give him length of days, and make him blessed upon earth, and not deliver him into the hands of his enemies.

- The *una cum* Mass identifies John Paul II and the local *Novus Ordo* bishop with *all the orthodox and the maintainers of the Catholic and Apostolic Faith*. This is absurd. It is a lie. To lie in the Canon of the Holy Sacrifice of the Mass cannot be pleasing to God.

And if they are the orthodox, and the maintainers of the Catholic and Apostolic Faith, then, by God, let us be with them and not against them. But if they are not the orthodox, and the maintainers of the Catholic and Apostolic Faith, then, by God, let us be against them, and not with them.

Where Peter is, there is the Church:

where the Church is, there is eternal life.

(*Sacerdotium* 6, Winter 1993).

Footnotes

1. DOM ERNEST GRAF, O.S.B., *The Priest at the Altar*, (New York: Joseph F. Wagner, 1926) p. 181.
2. WILLIAM J.O'SHEA, S.S., D.D.,*The Worship of the Church* (Westminster, Maryland: The Newman Press, 1958) p. 393
3. *Enarratio in Ps.* 40, no. 30.
4. *op. cit.*, p. 51.
5. *op. cit.*, § 18.
6. *ibid.*, § 22.
7. *ibid.*, § 23.
8. In 4 Sent. dist. 18. quæst. 2. art. 1.
9. POPE BENEDICT XIV, *op. cit.*, §§ 27 & 28.
10. ERIC F. MACKENZIE, A.M., S.T.L., J.C.L. REV., *The Delict of Heresy*, (Washington, D.C.: The Catholic University of America, 1932) p. 35. (Cf. Canon 2200 § 2)
11. *ibid.*
12. Before the Thomists have a hemorrhage, let me point out quickly that one of the *Princeps Thomistarum* of this century, Hugon, says that it is legitimate to do such a thing. *"Non repugnat ut intellectus adhæreat uni opinioni, dum alteram existimat probabiliorem."* Cursus Philosophiæ Thomisticæ Logica Maior, Tract. III., q. 1.
13. IIIa q. 82 a. 7, corpus & ad 3um.
14. *Ep. ad Joan. Patr.*, P.L. 69, 412.

CHAPTER 12

15. *De Unitate Ecclesiæ*, c. 17. P.L. 4, 513.
16. Ep. 72, c. 2. P.L. 3, 1048-1049.
17. cf. PROSPERUM AQUITANUM, *Sent.*, sent. 15 P.L. 51, 430.
18. Ep. LXXX *Ad Anatolium*, cap. 2.
19. *In Amos*, V: 22, P.L. 25, 1033-1034.
20. CAPPELLO, FELIX M. S. I.., *Tractatus Canonico-moralis de Sacramentis*, (Turin: Marietti), 1962, I, p. 462.
21. "*Epikeia non potest licite adhiberi: (a) Si superior, qui dispensationem legis concedere valet, facile adiri queat.*" Prümmer, Manuale Theologiæ Moralis I, no. 231 ff. q.v.
22. the word *ecclesiological* means "pertaining to the theology of the Church."

Chapter 13

Dedicated to Patrick Henry Omlor

The Grain of Incense:

Sedevacantists and *Una Cum* Masses

By Rev. Anthony Cekada

Should we assist at Traditional Masses offered "together with Thy servant Benedict, our Pope"?

> "Do not allow your tongue to give utterance to what your heart knows is not true.... To say *Amen* is to subscribe to the truth."
>
> — **Saint Augustine**, on the Canon

> "Our charity is untruthful because it is not severe; and it is unpersuasive, because it is not truthful… Where there is no hatred of heresy, there is no holiness."
>
> — **Father Faber**, *The Precious Blood*

In our lives as Traditional Catholics, we make many judgments that must inevitably produce logical consequences in our actual religious practice. The earliest that I remember making occurred at about age 14. Guitar songs at Mass, I concluded, were irreverent. Thereafter, throughout eight years in the diocesan seminary, I never once opened my mouth to sing one.

For some questions, the practical course of action that follows from a judgement is self-evident: If the Paul VI rite for making priests and bishops is invalid, we should avoid the Masses these priests and bishops offer.

For other questions, how we must act may not be so obvious — or it may be dictated by instinct, because we cannot necessarily explain all the underlying principles.

For some sedevacantists, one issue in particular falls into the latter category: a traditional Latin Mass offered by a validly ordained priest who utters a phrase in the Canon referring to *Benedict, our Pope*. This practice is followed by all priests who offer the recently instituted Motu Masses, as well as by priests of the Society of Saint Pius X (SSPX), its affiliated organizations and the majority of "independent" Traditionalist priests.

These Masses are also sometimes referred to as "*una cum* Masses," from the Latin phrase in the Canon into which the name of a reigning pope is inserted: *una cum famulo tuo Papa nostro N.* (together with Thy servant N., our Pope)

Now, since a sedevacantist is a traditionalist who has concluded that Benedict XVI is a *heretic* and *not* a true pope, his first instinct is to seek out a traditional Latin Mass offered by a sedevacantist priest, and to *avoid* Traditional Masses where the priest refers to Benedict XVI as a pope. To act otherwise seems contradictory or somehow "feels" wrong for the sedevacantist, even though he may not necessarily be able to articulate any theological reasons or arguments for what he does.

He has read or heard the stories of countless early martyrs who chose horrible deaths, rather than offer even *one* grain of incense in tribute to the false, ecumenical religion of the Roman emperor. So better to avoid altogether the Masses of priests who, through the *una cum*, offer a grain of incense to the heresiarch Ratzinger and *his* false ecumenical religion...

In many parts of the world, however, the only traditional Latin Mass available may be one offered by a priest (Motu, SSPX or independent) who puts the false pope's name in the Canon. Faced with choosing this or nothing, a sedevacantist is then sometimes tempted to assist at the Mass anyway.

The temptation will be much greater now, since Ratzinger has permitted the *Motu Mass*. In some dioceses, older priests who were validly ordained have come out of retirement to offer Mass according to the

'62 Missal. Moreover, a substantial number of priests who were validly ordained in SSPX have defected to organizations like the Fraternity of Saint Peter and will also offer the *Motu* Mass. Such Masses will be valid. Why not simply overlook Benedict's name in the Canon, and "just go for the Mass"? It's just *one* grain of incense, after all...

Although various arguments have been offered to justify the assistance of sedevacantists at *una cum* Masses, none of them really seems to ring true.

The priests who offer these Masses assert in the Canon that Ratzinger is a *true* pope, while a sedevacantist (by definition) affirms the opposite. By actively assisting at such a Mass, a sedevacantist condones the assertion that the celebrant publicly makes in the name of all present — *Benedict*, **our** *Pope* — an assertion that the sedevacantist knows and believes to be false.

The inconsistency — a complete disconnect between belief and worship — should be obvious after about 10 seconds of reflection. The theoretical conclusion (Ratzinger is not a true pope), we sense, should dictate the practical conclusion (don't assist at Masses where the prayers say the opposite).

But what are the underlying *principles* that should dictate our course of action here? *Why* is it wrong for a sedevacantist to assist actively at a traditional Latin Mass in which the priest employs the phrase *Benedict our Pope* in the Canon?

Because I have written much over the years about sedevacantism, Canon Law and the sacred liturgy, I am now often asked this question. In this article I will answer it at some length, because I consider the issue crucial for the future of the Traditionalist Movement.

Moreover, there is a vast amount of material in the writings of popes, dogmatic theologians, canonists, moral theologians, Vatican decrees and liturgical scholars that, taken together, provides us with a very clear answer to this question.

Not everyone will have the patience to slog through a long article. I promise such readers that I will soon produce a brief summary of what follows, much as I offered a short résumé of my study on the

1968 Rite of Episcopal Consecration.

In either version, though, the structure of our inquiry will be fairly straightforward, and we will examine the following points:

I. The meaning of the *una cum* phrase in the Canon, both linguistically and theologically, and how that meaning must be applied to Ratzinger.
II. Whether the sedevacantist who actively participates in an *una cum* Mass likewise participates in the prayer that contains that phrase.
III. Why a sedevacantist should not actively participate in such a Mass.

In this, the long version of the article, we will also present various arguments that have been made to justify assisting at Masses where Ratzinger is offered his grain of incense, and demonstrate how these need to be taken with more than a grain of salt. We will conclude with a summary.

I. The Meaning of the Prayer.

THE PHRASE under discussion (*una cum famulo tuo Papa nostro N.*) appears in the opening prayer of the Canon (the *Te Igitur*) that commends the Sacrifice to God. It is indicated below in **bold**:

> "..which in the first place we offer up to Thee for Thy holy Catholic Church, that it may please Thee to grant her peace, to protect, unite and govern her throughout the world, **together with Thy servant N. our Pope**, N. our Bishop, and all true believers and professors of the Catholic and Apostolic Faith."

What does the clause in bold actually mean? And more specifically, what meaning results when the name of Benedict XVI is inserted into the phrase?

To answer these questions, we will look first to the linguistic meaning of the phrase, and then to its broader theological meaning in the context of the Canon of the Mass.

A. Linguistic Meaning

1. **Grammar.** In an article written in 1992, Father (now Bishop) Donald Sanborn noted that the rules of Latin grammar permitted at least

three possible antecedents for the phrase *una cum* (*together with*), each of which produced a slightly different meaning.[1] Subsequent writers have suggested additional readings and meanings.

Lest my readers' eyes immediately glaze over at the mere mention of Latin grammar, I will "translate" these grammatical differences into the meanings that the *una cum* phrase conveys if the name *Benedict* (Joseph Ratzinger) is introduced into it:

1. **Adjective** modifying Church = *one with*, or *united with*: "The heretic/false pope Ratzinger is *united* to the Catholic Church and vice versa."
2. **Adverb** modifying *we offer* = we offer *together with*: "The heretic/false pope Ratzinger jointly offers the Holy Sacrifice of the Mass *along with* the priest and the Church."
3. **Appositional link** with *Church* = *for* thy Church, *which includes*. "The heretic/false pope Ratzinger is among the members of the Church for whom the priest and the Church *intercede* through the offering of the Mass."
4. **Coordinating conjunction** with *Church, bishop, all true believers* = *and for* Thy servant, the pope: "The priest and the Church offer the Mass *for* the servant of God and heretic/false pope Ratzinger."

Some sedevacantists maintain that the fourth explanation is the only possible meaning for the *una cum* phrase. The petition, they contend, is thus nothing more than a prayer of intercession offered *for* — and they repeatedly emphasize the *for* — the welfare of various members of the Church, rather than some sort of expression of union with a false pope. Thus, the mere fact that a priest prays *for* Benedict by name in the Canon should not prevent a sedevacantist from assisting at his Mass. It's a good thing to pray for people, after all…

But this fourth meaning for *una cum* "translates" no better than the first three, because it still places Ratzinger (as its proponents admit) in a prayer offered for the *members of the Church*. And a sedevacantist must reject this fourth proposition as well as the other three, because Ratzinger's heresy removes him not simply from the papacy, but *from the very Church itself*.

The canonists and theologians cited to support the key principle in

---

[1] D. Sanborn, "*Una Cum*," *Sacerdotium* 6 (Winter 1993), 40–1

the sedevacantist case state that it is the *loss of membership in the Church* that produces the loss of the pontificate. Thus the dogmatic theologian Iragui says:

> "Theologians commonly concede that the Roman Pontiff, if he should fall into manifest heresy, **would no longer be a member of the Church**, and therefore could neither be called its visible head."[2]

So, no matter how you construe it grammatically, the phrase *together with Thy servant, Benedict, our Pope* still produces an affirmation that the heretic Ratzinger is not only a true pope, but also a member of the true Church.

And this proposition a sedevacantist firmly rejects.

2. **Terminology.** Obviously, a sedevacantist takes exception to applying the expression *our Pope* to Ratzinger. But another expression, *Thy servant*, poses a similar problem.

The Latin word that the Canon employs is *famulus*. This does not merely connote someone you employ to perform occasional tasks for you — the cleaning lady, the waiter, or (in California) your pool boy or personal trainer.

Rather, in ecclesiastical Latin its sense is *a servant of God; a Christian*.[3] In liturgical prayers, it is applied exclusively to members of the Church.[4] No heretic can be a *famulus*. He has abandoned the service of God in the household of the Faith.

Employed in the Canon with the name Benedict, the expression *famulus tuus*, like *una cum*, produces another affirmation that the heretic Ratzinger is a member of the Church.

Once again, this is a proposition that a sedevacantist rejects.

3. **Context.** There are two more terms in the context of the phrase that pose problems

---

[2] S. Iragui, *Manuale Theologiae Dogmaticae* (Madrid: Ediciones Studium 1959), 371. See also the quotes from Wernz-Vidal, Coronata, Saint Antoninus, Saint Robert Bellarmine, Badii, Beste and Regatillo in A. Cekada, *Traditionalists, Infallibility and the Pope*.
[3] M. Ellebracht, *Remarks on the Vocabulary of the Ancient Orations in the Missale Romanum* (Nijmegen: Dekker 1963), 30.
[4] For examples, see P. Bruylants, *Les Oraisons du Missel Romain* (Louvain: CDIL 1952) 1:236.

a. The designation of Ratzinger as *our Pope* occurs in a phrase linking him to — indeed placing him *before — all true believers and professors of the Catholic and Apostolic Faith*. (The Latin word is *orthodoxis*.)

While a few liturgical scholars maintained that the phrase refers to all Catholics, lay and clerical, most say that it refers to Catholic bishops. These are by definition *orthodoxi* and, in virtue of their office, what the Latin terms cultores (cultivators, protectors, promoters) of the Catholic and apostolic faith.

The sedevacantist knows that Ratzinger, if anything, is the opposite.

b. Saint Robert Bellarmine says that the three prayers that begin our Canon (*Te igitur*, the *Memento* of the Living, and *Communicantes* that contain the names of the saints) are but one prayer. The third, *Communicantes* (*In communion with*) joins "the mortals who are in the Church Militant" with "the saints who reign with Christ in heaven."[5]

And again, this poses the same problem: If Ratzinger is a heretic, he cannot be in communion with either the Church Militant or the Church Triumphant.

B. Theological Meaning in the Liturgy

Thus the linguistic considerations. But what of the far more important *theological* meaning that is attached to mentioning the pope by name in the most solemn prayer of the Catholic liturgy?

Here is how various popes and liturgical scholars have explained its significance.

1. Recognition of the Head of the Church. In a Bull addressed to

---

[5] *De Missa*, 6.21, in *De Controversiis Christianae Fidei* (Naples: Guiliano 1858) 3:565. "*Prima igitur oratio Canonis, quae incipit*: Te igitur clementissime Pater, *extenditur usque ad illud*: Hanc igitur oblationem.… [The intervening prayers] *non sunt diversae orationes, sed partes sunt primae orationis*.… Communicantes *non haberet ullum sensum, nisi continuaretur cum praecedentibus verbis*.… [This one continuous prayer] *continet nomina eorum, pro quibus offertur et inquorum honorem offertur sacrificium, id est, mortalium qui sunt in Ecclesia militanti, et etiam sanctorum, qui cum Christo regnant in coelis.*"

Eastern Rite Catholics, this was one of the meanings that Pope Benedict XIV (1740-1758) assigned to the mention of the pope's name in the Sacred Liturgy:

> "It suffices Us to be able to state that a commemoration of the supreme pontiff and prayers offered for [the pope] during the sacrifice of the Mass is considered, and really is, an affirmative indication which recognizes him as the head of the Church, the vicar of Christ, and the successor of blessed Peter,..."[6]

2. **Recognition of the Principle of Unity.** In his lengthy book on the Canon of the Mass, Father Gassner observed of the first prayer in the Canon:

> "The unity prayed for is specified with the addition of the names of the Pope and the Bishop as the principle of that unity."[7]

Further, according to a commentary by Father Thalhofer:

> "The petition is offered for those instruments through which God guides and governs the Church: first, the Pope as the head of the whole Church and the supreme bearer of ecclesiastical unity."[8]

One of Cardinal Schuster's observations lends additional support to this point. He says that older manuscripts of the Canon include only the petition that mentions the Pope, and not the petitions referring to the diocesan bishop and *all true believers*. Thus the expression *una cum* (together with) more clearly refers back to the word *Ecclesia* (Church).[9] We see this in a 9th-century Missal from the time of Charlemagne. Here the sense of the phrase is clearly:

> "for Thy holy Catholic **Church**, that it may please Thee to grant her peace, to protect, unite and govern her throughout the world, **united with** Thy servant N. our Pope."[10]

---

[6] Bull *Ex Quo* (1 March 1756), ¶12 in *S.D.N Benedicti Papae XIV Bullarium* (Malines: Hanicq 1827) 4:299. "*Nobis satis est affirmare posse,commemorationem Romani Pontificis in Missa, fusasque pro eodem in Sacrificio preces, censeri, et esse, declarativum quoddam signum, quo idem Pontifex tanquam Ecclesiae Caput, Vicarius Christi, et B. Petri Apostoli Successor agnoscitur.*"
[7] J. Gassner, *The Canon of the Mass: Its History, Theology, and Art* (St. Louis: Herder 1950), 225-6.
[8] V. Thalhofer, *Handbuch der Catholicshen Liturgie* (Freiburg: Herderische Verlagshandlung), 164. "*Die sichtbaren Organe, durch welche Gott die Kircheleitet und regiert und für welche daher zuerst gebete wird, sind der Papst als Oberhaupt der ganzen Kirche und oberster Träger der kirchlichen Einheit.*"
[9] I. Schuster, *The Sacramentary (Liber Sacramentorum)* (London: Burns Oates 1924), 1:273.
[10] H.A Wilson ed., *The Gregorian Sacramentary under Charles the Great, Edited from Three Mss. of the Ninth Century*, (London: 1915), 2.

3. **Profession of Communion with the Pope.** This was yet another meaning that Pope Benedict XIV attached to the practice of mentioning the name of the pope in the Mass.

> "[This commemoration of the pope is, moreover] the profession of a mind and will which firmly espouses Catholic unity. This was rightly noticed by Christianus Lupus in his work on the Councils: 'This commemoration is the chief and most glorious form of communion'..."[11]

We have mentioned Saint Robert Bellarmine's contention that what we now think of as the first *three* prayers of the Canon (*Te igitur, Memento* and *Communicantes*) should be thought of as one prayer expressing the idea of communion among the members of the Church.

Cardinal Schuster offered a reconstruction of an earlier version of the text of the Canon that reflected this. He maintained that the word that begins what is now the third prayer of the Canon (*communicantes*, meaning *in communion with*) was directly linked without any intervening prayer to the petition in the first prayer that mentioned the name of the pope.

The sense of the text that results is as follows:

> "which **we** offer unto Thee for thy Church... — **we who are in communion with** and one with Thy servant, our pope, and venerating first of all the glorious and blessed ever-virgin..."[12]

4. **Profession of Communion with the True Church.** This is the conclusion one draws from the teaching of Pope Pelagius I (556–61) in a letter of rebuke to schismatics:

> "How can you believe that you are not separated from communion with the universal church if you do not mention my name within the sacred mysteries, as the custom is?"[13]

And further, according to the commentary on the Mass by Canon Croegaert:

---

[11] Bull *Ex Quo,* ¶12, *Bullarium* 4:299. "*...ac professio fit animi et voluntatis Catholicae unitati firmiter adhaerentis; ut etiam recte advertit Christanus Lupus, super Conciliis scribens* [cite omitted] *Haec commemoratio est suprema et honoratissima Communionis species.*"
[12] *Sacramentary,* 1:275, 276–7. "*tibi offerimus pro Ecclesia tua... una cum famulo tuo Papa nostro communicantes sed et memoriam venerantes imprimis gloriosae.*"
[13] *Epistola* 5, PL 69:398. "*Quomodo vos ab universi orbis communione separatos esse non creditis, si mei inter sacra mysteria, secundum consuetudinem, cominis memoria reticetis?*"

"To pray for the Pope is to give witness that you live in communion with the Head of the true Church."[14]

5. **A Sign of Orthodoxy.** In a lengthy discussion of the first prayer of the Canon, Cardinal Schuster also states:

"The mention of the name of the Pope in the Canon is a proof of the orthodoxy of the offerer."[15]

6. **Authorized Intermediary with God.** Dom de Puniet offers this as yet another theological explanation:

"The first name after the universal Church to be commended to God is that of the ruling Pontiff, the visible pastor and the authorized intermediary with almighty God for the various members of his flock."[16]

C. Application to Ratzinger

The fundamental problem with applying the *linguistic* meanings of the *una cum* phrase to Ratzinger, as we noted in (A), is that they all place him within the Church, where, as a heretic, he cannot be.

However, when we apply the *theological* meanings given above (1–6) to the phrase: *together with Thy servant Benedict our Pope*, in the Canon, here is what results:

- The heretic/false pope Ratzinger is "the head of the Church, the vicar of Christ, and the successor of blessed Peter."
- The acknowledgment of the heretic/false pope Ratzinger in the Canon is "the chief and most glorious form of communion" with him, "the profession of a mind and will which firmly espouses Catholic unity."
- The inclusion of the name of the heretic/false pope Ratzinger in the Canon specifies him as "the principle of unity."
- Mentioning the name of the heretic/false pope Ratzinger in the Canon is a sign that you "are not separated from communion with the universal church."
- The mention of the name of the heretic/false Pope Ratzinger in the Canon "is a proof of the orthodoxy of the offerer."

---

[14] A. Croegaert, *Les Rites et les Priéres du Saint Sacrifice de la Messe* (Paris: Casterman n.d.) 2:106. "*Prier pour le Pape c'est témoigner qu'on vit en communion avec le Chef de la vraie Eglise.*"
[15] *Sacramentary* 1:276.
[16] *The Mass: Its Origin and History* (New York: Longmans 1930), 137.

- The heretic/false pope Ratzinger is the "ruling Pontiff, the visible pastor and the authorized intermediary with almighty God for the various members of his flock."

A sedevacantist would consider each of these propositions a theological horror or absurdity. Yet, these are what results when a priest professes in the Canon that he offers the Traditional Mass *una cum* — *together with Thy servant Benedict, our Pope*.

"pro ecclesia tua sancta catholica quam pacificare custodire adunare et regere digneris toto orbe terrarum una cum famulo tuo papa nostro illo. Memento domine…" A footnote indicates that one of the manuscripts adds the phrase *"et antistite nostro illo et omnibus orthodoxis atque catholicae et apostolicae fidei cultoribus,"* which appears in the Canon of the Missal of Pius V.

II. Your Participation and Assent

Thus far, we have discussed the meaning of what the priest says at the altar.

But what bearing, if any, does all the foregoing information have on the proverbial man in the pew — in this case, a sedevacantist who, for some reason or another, is trying to figure out whether or not he should assist at an *una cum* Mass that is offered in the traditional rite by a validly-ordained priest?

The innate human inclination to act in a way consistent with firmly-held convictions tells the sedevacantist that he should *not* assist at such a Mass. His presence implies consent.

On the other hand, it is the *priest* who utters the heretic's name. The sedevacantist *objects* to the practice. Can he *withhold* his consent from the phrase *together with Thy servant Benedict our Pope?* Some have argued— and rather insistently — that this is possible.[17]

But it is not, and the notion is completely ridiculous.

This theory falls into the category of what I call "lay theology error,"

---

[17] Not only that, but some even *recommend* that sedevacantists assist at *una cum* Masses as a sort of fast lane to fostering back-slapping mateyness among trads.

because it is based on underlying principles that virtually *any* priest, no matter how dim or poorly educated, would instinctively sense are completely wrong. Other examples in this category are Feeneyism, Liénartism, Sirio-papism, and condemnations of NFP [Natural Family Planning].

Here is why a Traditional Catholic priest will immediately sense a problem with the "withhold-consent" theory. He spends about one-and-three-quarter hours a day reciting the Church's official public prayers — the Divine Office and the Mass. All of these prayers, virtually without exception, are composed in the first-person plural: *We* pray, *we* offer, *we* beseech, etc.

The priest knows that these official prayers are phrased this way for a reason: He, the priest, prays them on behalf of and in union with Our Lord and His Church, including all its lay members — and moreover in the case of the Mass, united with the faithful who are present.

This is the nature of the Church's liturgical prayer. For the laymen so bold as to "disagree" with petitions the priest makes in the various prayers prescribed for Mass, there are no "opt-out" or Country Buffet provisions. It is all of one piece. As Paulina, our long-time cook, says about her menu: You have two choices: take it or leave it.

To understand why the very idea of an *una cum* opt-out is a liturgico-theological impossibility, we now turn to some specific points about how we assist at Mass, what our participation connotes, how the laity present cooperate with the priest in offering the Sacrifice, and specifically, how and why the laity give their assent to the prayers of the Canon in particular.

A. How You Actively Participate at Mass

Traditional Catholics tend to look upon a sacrament as primarily something the priest *gives* and the layman *receives*. The priest is active, the layman passive. The priest *confers* the sacrament; the lay recipient cooperates and *consents* to receive it.

This paradigm does not hold, though, for assistance at Mass. You are not meant merely to consent and to *receive* something passively (grace, Holy Communion, "credit" for fulfilling your Sunday obligation, etc.), but to *participate* and to *give* something. What are you meant to give? Active worship of God, because as a result of your baptism, you are both privileged and obliged to participate, according to your state, in offering up the Holy Sacrifice.

Please note the verb: participate.

Unfortunately, during and after Vatican II, the modernists appropriated this language, corrupted its real meaning, and used it to transform the Mass into an engine for doctrinal revolution throughout the world. Thus, they turned the priest into a president, the "assembly" into the primary agent of worship, and regimented "responses" into the only permissible indicator of participation, with all present pummeled into submission by microphones and speakers that project the Giant Amplified Voice.

Traditionalists, therefore, are understandably skittish about any talk of how they are supposed to assist or participate actively in offering the Holy Sacrifice. Nevertheless, active assistance and participation in the Mass, understood in the correct sense, is *required* of every Catholic.

At the Traditional Mass, how do members of the laity manifest their active assistance or participation in the Mass? There are several ways, and this list is by no means exhaustive.

1. By receiving Holy Communion during the Mass.
2. Serving Mass for the priest at the altar.
3. Singing in the choir.
4. Singing responses as a member of the congregation at High Mass, or singing hymns during Low Mass, where either practice is the custom.
5. Using a Missal to follow and pray privately the prayers of the Mass as the priest recites them at the altar.
6. Using a book of meditations or prayers that follows the actions of the Mass.
7. Reciting the Rosary, while looking at the sacred actions taking place at the altar.
8. Attentively following the actions of the priest at the altar while making the customary external signs of devotion appropriate to each part of the Mass (standing, sitting, kneeling, striking your breast, making Signs of the Cross, looking up at the Sacred Host, folding your hands, etc.)

9. Physical presence, accompanied by the intention to assist at Mass and fulfill the Sunday obligation, together with a certain degree of attention during the rite.

In one or more of the foregoing, of course, the Traditionalist reader will recognize the method he employs every Sunday when he goes to Mass. But whichever of these methods the layman chooses, it does in fact constitute a true and active participation in the Mass.

B. Active Participation = Your Approval

Apart from an exterior manifestation of piety within, what does such active participation in common worship connote in general?

The longer treatises on Canon Law and moral theology explain that active participation in a religious rite constitutes an *implicit approval of the rite and a sign of unity in religion*.

Joint participation (*communicatio*), says the Spanish canonist and theologian Regatillo, consists in "performing an act simultaneously with another person in such a way that both persons morally participate in the same action." In worship this occurs through "gestures, movements, or ceremonial signs" that are somehow determined by convention.[18] These, says Benedictine canonist Beste, connote "cooperation or common action with another in the prayers and functions of worship."[19]

The Dominican moral theologian Merkelbach says that active religious participation "is rightly considered a sign of religious unity." It constitutes "implicit approval of an exercise of worship."[20]

So even according to general principles of moral theology and Canon Law, a sedevacantist who actively assists at a Mass in which the priest employs the phrase *together with Thy servant Benedict our Pope* in the Canon is presumed to cooperate with and approve of what takes place.

---

[18] E.F. Regatillo, *Institutiones Iuris Canonici* (Santander: Sal Terrae 1956) 2:103. "*Communicatio in aliqua actione est positio illius cum alio, ita ut actio moraliter eadem ab utroque participetur... Edere gestus, motus, signa ceremoniarum, quae ex conventione determinata...*"

[19] U. Beste, *Introductio in Codicem* (Collegeville: Saint Johns 1946), c. 1258. "*cooperationem seu communem actionem cum alio in orationibus et functionibus cultus.*"

[20] B. Merkelbach, *Summa Theologiae Moralis* (Montreal: Desclée 1949) 1:753-54. "*recte existimaretur ut signum religiosae unitatis.*" "*implicita approbatio exercitii cultus.*"

C. You Join with the Action of the Celebrant

More than that, however, the laymen who actively assist at the Traditional Mass through one of the methods we have described above do not simply *approve* of what the priest does at the altar; they actually *join with him* in offering it.

Various popes and pre-Vatican II theologians have explained how and why:

- **Pope Innocent III (1198–1216):** "Not only do the priests offer the sacrifice, but also all the faithful: for what the priest does personally by virtue of his ministry, **the faithful do collectively by virtue of their intention.**"[21]
- **Maurice de la Taille SJ (1920):** "The Congregation who Assist at Mass, as Offerers…. Those who assist exert, in a greater degree than those who are not present, their native power to offer as members of the ecclesiastical body, in so far as they are more intimately united with the sacrifice by this outward expression of actual devotion. **By their presence they indicate that they ratify, as far as in them lies, the offering which is made in their name**, and hence by a special title **they make it their own and offer it.**"[22]
- **Henry Noldin SJ (1920):** "The special and accessory offerers are those faithful who unite themselves in some way by their actions to the priest offering the Mass…. In the second place are **those who are actually present at the Mass, who therefore participate by their will and their presence.**"[23]
- **Pope Pius XII (1947):** "The people **unite their hearts in praise, impetration, expiation and thanksgiving with the prayers or intention of the priest**, even of the High Priest himself, so that in the one and the same offering of the victim and according to a visible sacerdotal rite, they may be presented to God the Father."[24]
- **Felix Cappello SJ (1954):** "The special offerer (which many call the secondary and accessory offerer) is each and every member of the faithful who (as we have indicated above) **joins in offering**

---

[21] Innocent III, *De Sacro Altaris Mysterio*, 3.6. "*Non solum offerunt sacerdotes, sed et universi fideles: nam quod specialiter adimpletur ministerio sacerdotum, hoc universaliter agitur voto fidelium.*"
[22] M. de la Taille, The Mystery of Faith (London: Sheed & Ward 1950) 2:260.
[23] H. Noldin, *Summa Theologiae Moralis* (Innsbruch: Rauch 1920) 3:166. "*Offerentes speciales et accessorii sunt fideles, qui sacerdoti offerenti aliquo modo actu se adiungunt…. secundum locum obtinent, qui missae reipsa intersunt, qui ergo voluntate et praesentia sua participant.*"
[24] Pius XII, Encyclical *Mediator Dei* (20 November 1947), ¶93.

the sacrifice through some external assent [... which Suarez correctly describes as...] **'to assist by consenting and by morally cooperating'.**"[25]

The sedevacantist therefore does indeed manifest consent and moral cooperation with the action of the priest as he offers the sacrifice together with Thy servant Benedict our Pope.

D. You Participate in and Ratify the Canon

And still more to our point, the faithful who actively assist at the Traditional Mass ratify, assent to and participate in the prayers of the Canon that the priest recites, even though they do not vocally recite these prayers themselves.

For this point, we draw our proofs from two sources, the Fathers of the Church and Pius XII:

1. **The Church Fathers.** The theologians we have cited to demonstrate that the people join with the priest in offering the sacrifice point to the writings of the Fathers of the Church, who state explicitly that the faithful ratify and affirm the truth of the "prayer of thanksgiving" the celebrant recites, that is, the Canon:

    - **Saint John Chrysostom:** "The prayer wherein thanksgiving is made [the Canon] **is common to both** [that is, the priest and the people], it is not the priest alone, but the whole of the people who give thanks to God. For it is only when he [the priest] has taken up their words, **by which they have agreed that it is meetly and justly done**, that he begins the action of thanksgiving or Eucharist."[26]
    - **Saint Augustine:** "When you have heard the priest say: *Lift up your hearts* you reply *We have lifted them up to the Lord*. Take pains to answer truthfully, because you are answering in the presence of the action of God. Let it be so, as you say it is; **do**

---

[25] F. Cappello *Tractatus Canonico Moralis de Sacramentis* (Rome: Marietti 1954) 1:494. "*Offerens specialis — quem nonnulli vocant secundarium et accesorium – est omnis et solus fidelis, qui, ut supra innimus, sacrificio offerendo cooperatur per quendam concursum externum.... 'denique assistere consentiendo, ac moraliter cooperando...'.*"

[26] Saint John Chrysostom, Homily *In II Cor.*, 18.3, PG 61:527. "*Rursus ea oratio, qua Deo gratiae aguntur, utriusque communis est: neque enim ipse solus gratias agit, sed etiam plebs universa. Nam cum prius illorum vocem sumpsit, atque illi assenserunt id digne ac juste fieri, tum demum gratiarum actionem auspicatur.*"

not allow your tongue to give utterance to what your heart knows is not true.... To say *Amen* is to subscribe to the truth. In Latin *Amen* means *It is true.*"[27]

- **Saint Remigius of Auxerre:** "The *Amen*, which is answered by the whole church, means *it is true*. **The faithful therefore give this reply to this great mystery, as they do in all legitimate prayer, and they as it were subscribe to its truth by so replying.**"[28]

Although in the Traditional Mass the choir (at High Mass) or the altar boy (at Low Mass) now make these responses vocally, they do so not only as representatives of the whole Catholic Church, but also as representatives of the faithful present and devoutly assisting at Mass.

2. **Pope Pius XII.** In *Mediator Dei*, his great encyclical on the Sacred Liturgy, Pius XII treats at great length the role that the laity play in offering the Holy Sacrifice.

> "Moreover, **the rites and prayers of the Eucharistic sacrifice signify and show no less clearly that the oblation of the Victim is made by the priests in company with the people**. For not only does the sacred minister, after the offering of the bread and wine when he turns to the people, say the significant prayer: 'Pray brethren, that my sacrifice and yours may be acceptable to God the Father Almighty;' but also **the prayers by which the divine Victim is offered to God are generally expressed in the plural number: and in these it is indicated more than once that the people also participate in this august sacrifice inasmuch as they offer the same.**"[29]

He quotes several passages in the Canon to demonstrate this truth:

- "For whom we offer, or who offer up to Thee . . . We therefore beseech thee, O Lord, to be appeased and to receive this offering of our bounded duty, as also of Thy whole household."
- "We Thy servants, as also Thy whole people."
- "[We] do offer unto Thy most excellent majesty, of Thine own gifts

---

[27] Saint Augustine, Homily *de Sacramento Altaris ad Infantes*, 3, PL 46:836. "*...cum audieritis a Sacerdote: Sursum cor! Respondetis: 'Habemus ad Dominum.' Laborate, ut verum respondeatis. Quia apud acta Dei respondetis, sic sit, quomodo dicitis. Non lingua sonet, et conscientia neget... Ad hoc dicitis: Amen. Amen dicere suscribere est. Amen latine interpretatur Verum.*"

[28] Remigius of Auxerre, *De Celebratione Missae et Ejus Significatione*, PL 101: 1265. "*Amen autem, quod ab omni Ecclesia respondetur, interpretatur, verum. Hoc ergo ad tanti mysterii consummationem, sicut et in omni legitima oratione, et quasi subscribunt respondendo.*"

[29] *Mediator Dei*, ¶84.

bestowed upon us, a pure victim, a holy victim, a spotless victim."

The language of the first prayer of the Canon that the priest at an *una cum* Mass uses to make the common offering — "which we offer up to Thee... together with Thy servant Benedict, our Pope" — is not such, then, that a sedevacantist can "withhold consent" from it. Together with the priest at the altar, he joins in offering the grain of incense to Ratzinger.

III. Why You Should Not Participate

In the two previous sections we established that: (1) The various linguistic and theological meanings for the phrase *together with Thy servant Benedict, our Pope* all place Ratzinger within the Church and explicitly acknowledge him as a true pope, and (2) a layman who assists or actively participates at a Mass in which a priest employs that phrase in the Canon likewise participates in and ratifies the priest's affirmation that Ratzinger *is* a true pope.

For a sedevacantist to do so, obviously, would be inconsistent and contradictory. But would it actually be wrong?

The short answer is yes — and for a whole host of reasons. For the most part, however, they are merely the logical consequences of the underlying idea identified above in section II.B: that active participation in a religious rite constitutes an implicit *approval of the rite* and a *sign of unity in religion*.

Positively, the idea is summed up in the famous Latin adage *lex orandi, lex credendi* (the law of praying is the law of believing). Theologians and liturgical scholars have spent quite a bit of time exploring this interrelationship.

On the negative side, the same idea is also behind Church legislation prohibiting *communicatio in sacris* — active participation in common worship with heretics and schismatics. These laws and pronouncements explain the doctrinal and moral principles that make it wrong for a Catholic to participate in a rite that somehow compromises his faith — "lest faith either be lost or endangered," as an 1859 Decree from the Holy Office explains.

"For this reason, Saint John strictly commands: 'If any man come to you and bring not this doctrine, receive him not into the house nor say to him: *Ave*. For he that saith unto him: *Ave*, communicateth with his wicked works.' It is clear from these words that **whatever expresses anything equivalent to *Ave* is prohibited, such as liturgical actions that were instituted to signify ecclesiastical unity.** For this reason, we read that the Fathers of the Council of Carthage decreed it forbidden either to pray or sing with heretics."[30]

We will turn to these principles here in order to explain why it is wrong for a sedevacantist to assist actively at an *una cum* Mass.

A. A Pernicious Lie

It is best to begin with something obvious: the moral virtue of *truthfulness*, sometimes also called *truth* or *veracity*. By this virtue, we exhibit external signs (either words or deeds) that manifest to others what is in our mind.[31]

Opposed to this, obviously, is the sin of lying. We tend to think of lies only in terms of false statements we knowingly make in words, either in speech or writing. But *any* external sign, including our deeds or actions, can be a false statement and therefore a lie as well.[32]

In the case at hand, the sedevacantist believes Ratzinger is not a true pope. Yet when the sedevacantist participates actively in an *una cum* Mass, by that very fact he affirms the opposite of what is in his mind. In so doing, he *lies*, because he knows that what he affirms through his actions — his participation — is false.[33]

---

[30] SO Instruction *Communicatio*, 22 June 1859, in *Collectanea S. Cong. de Prop. Fide* 1:1176. "Unde S. Ioannes severe praecepit: *Si quis venit ad vos et hancdoctrinam non affert, nolite recipere eum in domum, nec ave dixeritis ei, qui enim dicit illi ave communicat operibus eius malignis.* (Ioan. 2. 10). *Evidentissime ex his verbis prohibitum iri infertur quidquid huiusmodi ave exprimit, prout sunt actiones liturgicae quae ad ecclesiasticam unitatem significandum institutae fuere. Quapropter a PP. Concilii Carthaginensi sancitum legimus cum haereticis nec orandum nec psallendum..."*

[31] Merkekbach 2:849. *"signa externa (verba aut facta) quibus mentem nostram manifestamus proximo."*

[32] Merkelbach 2:857. *"quocumque signo externo, sive verbo, sive scripto, sive gestu, sive facto;... mendacium stricte dictum quod fit verbis vel signis aequivalentibus..."*

[33] To commit the sin of lying, it is not necessary to have the *explicit* intention to deceive another. It suffices merely to *know* that something is false and *intend* to say it, for the effect proper to a false statement is to deceive. Merkelbach 2:857. *"Contra mentem, scil. quae procedit ex intentione falsum enuntiandi... In hacintentione implicite includitur intentio fallendi, quia effectus proprius falsae enuntiationis est ut alius fallatur; quod autem aliquis explicite intendat falsitatem in opinione alterius constituere, non pertinet ad speciem seu essentiam mendacii, sed ad quamdam perfectionem ejus."*

To the affirmation in the Canon that the heretic/imposter Ratzinger is "our Pope," the sedevacantist, through his participation, says beforehand that *It is right and just*, and afterwards *Amen, it is so*. He gives utterance, as Saint Augustine says, to what his heart knows is not true. And that is a lie — and a lie is always wrong.

And here we have not merely the proverbial "little white lie" about something trivial, but rather a *pernicious* lie, so called because of the particular harm it causes. The Dominican theologian Merkelbach explains:

> "The gravest of all lies is one that harms God in a matter concerning religion.... The pernicious lie is a **mortal sin by its very nature** due to the evil attached to it, either because of its matter, if it concerns religious doctrine... or because of its end, if it is uttered to the injury of God or to the notable harm of neighbor."[34]

And so, it is alongside this principle — "the gravest of all lies is one that harms God in a matter concerning religion" — that the sedevacantist must line up all the lies about Ratzinger that he affirms by participating in an *una cum* Mass: that the heretic/false pope Ratzinger is a member of the Church, head of the Church, successor of Saint Peter, principle of unity in the Church, sign of communion with Christ's Church, touchstone of orthodoxy, the authorized intermediary with God, and so on.

To participate in this is to ignore Saint Augustine's solemn warning to Catholics about the Canon: "Take pains to answer truthfully, because you are answering in the presence of the action of God. Let it be so, as you say it is."

B. A Profession of Communion with Heretics

"The Sacrifice of the Mass," says the theologian Merkelbach, is *directly offered only for members of the Church*."[35]

For this reason, the Church does not offer intercessory prayers for heretics and schismatics during the course of the Mass, nor can a heretic

---

[34] Merkekbach 2:859. "*specialis nocumenti inferendi; ... omnium autem gravissimum est mendacium quod nocet Deo in re religionis.... mendacium autem perniciosum est mortale ex genere suo propter malum adiunctum, sive ex parte materiae, si fiat in doctrina religionis,... sive ex parte finis, si dicatur iniuriam Dei aut in notabile detrimentum proximi.*"
[35] Merkelbach 2:696. "*Sacrificium missae directe offertur tantum pro membris Ecclesiae.*"

or a schismatic be mentioned by name in a liturgical prayer.[36] They are outside the communion of the Church.

This principle was strictly observed from the earliest days in the Church. Beginning in the 3rd century, the names of Catholics who were being prayed for (e.g., the pope, bishops, illustrious lay persons, benefactors) were written on pairs of little tablets called "diptychs," and the lists were read out at Mass. These lists played an important role in the liturgy and in the life of the Church:

> "The purpose and chief use of the diptychs was to retain Catholic communion both of the living with one another and of the living with the dead."[37]

> "To read the name of a living bishop in the diptychs was always a recognized sign of communion with him."[38]

Omitting someone's name from the diptychs, on the other hand, declared that a person was *outside* the communion of the Church:

> "The liturgical diptychs admitted only the names of persons in communion with the Church; **the names of heretics and of excommunicated members were never inserted.**"[39]

In an excellent article on the *una cum* problem written in 2002, Patrick Henry Omlor, one of the leading lights from the early days of the U.S. Traditionalist Movement, explains in detail how Pope Saint Hormisdas (514–23) not only refused to admit heretics to communion, but also broke communion with other ecclesiastics in the East who merely *recited the names* of heretics in their diptychs. The pontiff required the bishops of the world to sign a formulary called "The Rule of Faith."

> "The main object of the Rule of Faith of Pope Saint Hormisdas was to condemn the naming of heretics in the diptychs,... reportedly 2,500 bishops signed the Rule of Faith in order to become restored to communion with the Church. **Until they signed they were denied communion solely and specifically because they had persisted in naming heretics in their diptychs.**"[40]

---

[36] Once a year (on Good Friday) the Church offers a liturgical prayer for their conversion only, and it is recited outside of Mass. See Bruylants, 2:227.
[37] *Missale Mixtum*, PL 85:541, note. "*Finis est usus praecipuus dip- tychorum erat ut retineretur catholic communio tum vivorum inter se, tum vivorum et mortuorum.*"
[38] A. Fortescue, *The Formula of Hormisdas*, CTS 102 (London: Catholic Truth Society 1913), 12.
[39] R. Maere, "Diptych," *Catholic Encyclopedia* (New York: 1913) 5:23.
[40] Omlor, Patrick Henry, *Sedevacantists and the "Una Cum" Problem* (Veradale WA: Catholic Research Institute 2002), 8–9.

A sedevacantist who actively participates at a Mass in which the heretic Ratzinger is named in the Canon, therefore, acts against the ancient tradition of the Church and puts himself in communion with someone he knows is a heretic.

C. Recognizing the One-World, Ecumenical Church

In addition to this general problem relating to communion with heretics, there is a more specific danger to the Faith posed by the post-Vatican II teachings on the Church.

Creating a dogma-less, ecumenical super-church like this has been the goal of Masons, liberals and modernists ever since the early 19th century. We have repeatedly pointed out that Joseph Ratzinger's personal contribution to the long list of Vatican II errors is his Frankenchurch heresy. For him, the Church is a "communion" to which Catholics, schismatics and heretics all belong, each possessing "elements" of the Church of Christ either "fully" or "partially." According to his *Catechism*, all these belong to one and the same People of God.

Since the naming of Ratzinger is indeed a profession of communion with him,[41] it is likewise a profession of communion with the ecumenical, One-World church of which he professes to be the head — an institution which a sedevacantist, obviously, repudiates.

This, in turn, poses another problem...

D. Implicit Profession of a False Religion

Each Catholic is required to make a profession of faith — an external manifestation of faith through some appropriate sign.[42]

Negatively, this precept forbids a Catholic "to deny the faith exteriorly — whether expressly or tacitly, whether by word, sign or deed (e.g., silence) — or to profess or to simulate a false faith." This can occur:

> ...*indirectly and implicitly* if without the intention of denying the faith, one performs an action which is understood by others as a denial of the faith... by *actions*,... those who perform an action which either in itself or **from the circumstances signifies the profession of a false**

---

[41] See above, section III.B.
[42] Merkelbach 1:711. "*Confessio fidei est externa eius manifestatio per aliquod signum ad hoc idoneum.*"

religion."⁴³

And indeed this is why martyrs went to their deaths rather than place the grain of incense into the fire before the image of the false god. There was a time when all Traditionalists — not just sedevacantists — regarded the religion of Vatican II as nothing less than a false religion, set up in opposition to the Catholic Church. Thus, Archbishop Marcel Lefebvre's ringing declaration after his suspension by Paul VI in 1976:

> "That Conciliar Church is a schismatic Church, because it breaks with the Catholic Church that has always been. It has its new dogmas, its new priesthood, its new institutions, its new worship, all already condemned by the Church in many a document, official and definitive...
>
> "The Church that affirms such errors is at once schismatic and heretical. This Conciliar Church is, therefore, not Catholic."⁴⁴

Benedict XVI, of course, is now the head of this entity. For a sedevacantist to participate actively in a Mass offered "together with Thy servant Benedict, our Pope," is to affirm that the entity of which Ratzinger is the head is, before God, the Catholic Church.

Thus, even though he does not intend to deny the Faith directly, by his actions the sedevacantist denies it "indirectly and implicitly."⁴⁵

E. A Violation of Church Law

Decrees of the Holy See repeatedly forbade naming heretical or schismatic clergy in liturgical prayers.

Thus, a 1669 decree forbade a deacon to sing out the names of heretics in the liturgy,⁴⁶ and a 1673 decree forbade a priest to name the Patriarch of the Armenians (both a heretic and a schismatic) in the prayers of

---

⁴³ Merkelbach 1:712. "... *confitendi fidem prohibet, ullo unquam caso vel periculo etiam mortis, expresse vel tacite, verbo vel signo vel facto (silentio v.g.), fidem exterius negare vel falsam profiteri aut simulari.... Quod fieri potest... indrecte et implicite, si absque intentione negandi actionem ponit quae ab aliis ut negatio fidei habetur,... factis... qui ponunt actionem quae ex se vel ex circumstantiis significat professionem falsae religionis.*"
⁴⁴ "Reflections on Suspension *a Divinis*," 29 July 1976.
⁴⁵ See Merkelbach 1:712. "*indirecte et implicite.*"
⁴⁶ SO Decree *Mesopotamia*, 28 August 1669, *Fontes* 4:740. "*Se possa permettersi ai diaconi di proferire ad alta voce nell'Officio divino in chiesa i nomi di Dioscoro, Nestorio, Barsuma ed altri eresiarchi...R. Negative, facto verbo cum SSmo. Et Sanctitas Sua approbavit.*"

the Mass.[47]

The general prohibition against naming heretics and schismatics is repeated in the 1756 Bull of Pope Benedict XIV already cited above:

> "...'Therefore where commemorations are customarily made in the sacred liturgy, the Roman Pontiff should be first commemorated, then one's own Bishop and Patriarch, provided they are Catholic. But **if either or both of them are schismatics or heretics they should by no means be commemorated'.**"[48]

My personal favorite on ecumenical grounds is an account of a 1636 decree from the Sacred Congregation for the Propagation of the Faith. The Congregation not merely forbade singing an acclamation for the schismatic Patriarchs of Constantinople, but added that since the Patriarchs were also heretics, they deserved to be cursed instead.[49]

In any event, later authors, such as the theologian de la Taille, also speak of the general prohibition:

> "Hence were anyone to mention by name an infidel, a heretic, a schismatic, or an excommunicated person (whether a king, or a bishop, or any other) either in the prayer *Te igitur* or in our *commemoratio pro vivis*, **he would certainly violate the law of the Church.**"[50]

Please note that de la Taille explicitly says that naming a heretic in the first prayer of the Canon — the prayer we are discussing — is a violation of Church law. At an *una cum* Mass, the sedevacantist countenances this violation of Church law.

---

[47] I. Szal, *Communication of Catholics with Schismatics*, CUA Canon Law Studies 264, (Washington: CUA 1948), 182–3.
[48] *Ex Quo*, ¶9, *Bullarium* 11:296. He quotes the first admonition from the earlier *Euchologium*: "...'Cum igitur in sacra Liturgia commemorationes fieri soleant, oportet primum quidem Romani Pontificis commemorationem agi, deinde proprii Episcopi, et Patriarchae, dummodo Catholici sint. Quod si alter eorum, vel ambo sint schismatici, sive haeretici, eorum commemoratio nequaquam fiat'."
[49] Szal, 182. "The Sacred Congregation instructed the bishop to repel from his church the Greeks who sang these acclamations, if indeed he could effectively do so, for the Patriarchs of Constantinople were not only schismatics, but also heretics, and consequently were deserving rather of imprecation."
[50] De la Taille 2:317. He adds in a footnote: "Though there are not a few teachers who think otherwise, through not paying sufficient attention to the force and meaning of our liturgical prayer." De la Taille does not indicate who these authors are, or precisely what they would allow in the way of naming schismatics or heretics. From Szal (183), though, it seems that the most the *Holy See* occasionally tolerated was a prayer for a *lay* heretic or schismatic in his capacity as a head of state (King, President, etc.) — but never one for a heretical or schismatic *cleric*.

F. Participation in a Sin

More than that, de la Taille maintains that mentioning a heretic by name in any liturgical prayer is also a sin:

> "Moreover, since today neither in the *commemoratio pro vivis* nor in any other part of the Mass does the Church commend by name any living person except such a one as is considered to be in communion with her, **today it would also appear sinful to mention by name in any liturgical prayer whatever, an infidel, a heretic, a schismatic, or an excommunicated person.** This privation of the common suffrages of the Church is by no means confined to the *excommunicati vitandi* alone, as may be seen from the *Code of Canon Law* (can. 2262, parag. 1)."[51]

Nor would it be morally permissible to *assist* at a rite where this is done. In 1729 the Vatican Congregation for the Propagation of the Faith decreed:

> "... There is hardly any rite among the heterodox that is not stained with some error in faith... **especially where a commemoration is made of living Patriarchs and Bishops — schismatics and heretics — who are proclaimed** *preachers of the Catholic faith*. For this reason, any Catholics who come together under circumstances like this to celebrate a rite of prayer and worship **cannot excuse themselves from the sin of evil common worship, or at least, from the sin of pernicious scandal.**"[52]

By actively assisting at an *una cum* Mass, the sedevacantist participates in this sin — one made all the worse because it is committed seconds before the Spotless Victim is brought down upon the altar.

G. Offering Mass with Ratzinger

When we discussed the various grammatical meanings possible for the *una cum* phrase,[53] we noted that the second meaning was an adverb modifying the phrase *we offer* — i.e., we offer the sacrifice *joined to or in union with* our Pope.

---

[51] De la Taille 2:318.
[52] SC de Prop. Fide, Instruction (*Pro Mission. Orient.*), 1729, *Fontes* 7:4505. "*Id ex eo etiam confirmatur magis quod vix ullus sit ritus apud heterodoxos qui aliquo errore in materia fidei non maculetur:... vel denique commemoratio fit viventium Patriacharum, et Episcoporum, schismaticorum, et haereticorum, qui ut fidei catholicae praedicatores commendatur. Qua de re, qui in ea ritus et orationis et cultus celebratione conveniunt in his facti circumstansiis catholiciquique, reatu perversae communicationis, aut saltem perniciosi scandali purgari non possunt.*"
[53] See above, section I.A.1.

This is de la Taille's understanding of the phrase, and he gives it as another part of his explanation as to why the names of heretics and schismatics are excluded from the prayer:

> "... priests gradually became accustomed to commend no living person in these public suffrages of the Church, except such as could be reckoned among those with whom he was considered to be **offering the sacrifice**.... [n]ote also the saying of Saint Isidore: 'The third prayer [which comes after the announcing of the names in the diptychs] is said **for the offerers**...' The same is also clear from the actual formula found in our own Roman Canon at the end of the prayer *Te igitur*, the first prayer of the Canon, where the celebrant says: '**We offer**... together with our Pope N., and our Bishop N. (and our King N. and with all orthodox worshippers of the Catholic and apostolic faith.'... [T]he custom was to mention no names in the list of the living, except of those who were **plainly united with the priest in the offering of the sacrifice**."[54]

If therefore you actively participate in a Mass at which Ratzinger is named in the Canon, you are united to him as you participate in Sacrifice. It is as if the sly old heretic himself unexpectedly emerged from the sacristy in your local Traditionalist chapel to offer Mass for you and to give you Holy Communion.

H. Recognition of a Usurper

In prohibiting common worship with heretics and schismatics, one of the Church's motives was to deny recognition to those who had usurped or intruded themselves into Church offices.

Thus in 1791, after the revolutionary government of France established a schismatic Constitutional Church and appointed to diocesan sees and parishes bishops and priests of its choosing, Pope Pius VI forbade Catholics to assist at services conducted by these intruders:

> "Keep as far from you as possible all intrusion and schism.... Above all, avoid and condemn the sacrilegious intruders..... **Keep away from all intruders... do not hold communion with them, especially in divine worship.**"[55]

---

[54] De la Taille 2:316-7.
[55] Pius VI, Encyclical *Charitas* (13 April 1791), ¶¶29, 31, 32, in *Fontes* 2:474. "*Omnis a vobis invasionem, et schisma, quam longissime potestis, arcete.... sacrilegos invasores vitetis, ac reprobetis.... invasores omnes... ita devitate, ut nihil cum illis sit vobis commune, praesertim in divinis...*"

In 1753, when the Holy Office issued a prohibition against common worship with Greek heretics and schismatics, the first reason given was "especially because they commemorate the Patriarch of Constantinople."[56]

In addition to the other dangers to the Faith posed by worshipping with heretics and schismatics, Archbishop Francis Kenrick (Archbishop of Baltimore, 1851–1863) likewise pointed to the recognition of a usurper as another reason for avoiding such services:

> "It is not allowed to communicate *in divinis* with heretics or schismatics:...all admit it is wrong whenever it carries with it... the **recognition of a usurped office.**" [57]

By the fact that he assists at an *una cum* Mass, the sedevacantist recognizes as pope someone he would otherwise say is a usurper.

I. Sin of Scandal

Scandal is "any conduct that has at least the appearance of evil and that offers to a neighbor an occasion of spiritual ruin."[58] Scandal may be either *direct* or *indirect*. Indirect scandal occurs when someone "performs an action which has the appearance of evil that is only a probable occasion of sin to one's neighbor, such as bad example."[59]

The Church legislation that forbade Catholics to participate actively in worship with heretics and schismatics invariably mentioned scandal as one of the reasons for the prohibition. Heretics and schismatics would conclude that a Catholic who worshipped with them approved of their errors or rebellion.

Thus, the Congregation for the Propagation of the Faith warned in 1729:

> "When they see Catholics go to their churches, assist at their rites, and participate in their sacraments, should not one believe (or at least fear) that from this fact alone they would be more greatly confirmed

---

[56] Holy Office, Decree *Mission. Tenos In Peloponneseo* (10 May 1753), Fontes 4:804. "*Non licere: maxime cum Patriarchae Constantinopolitani commemorationem faciant.*"

[57] F. Kenrick, *Theologia Moralis* (Malines: Dessain 1861) 2:366. "*Haud tamen licet in divinis cum haereticis vel schismaticis communicare.... fatentur omnes nefas esse, quandocumque falsi dogmatis professionem, vel muneris usurpati agnitionem secum fert: quod plerumque contingit.*"

[58] McHugh and Callan, *Moral Theology* (New York: Wagner 1929) 1:1447.

[59] Merkelbach 2:960 "*Indirectum, quando quis actionem ponit minus rectam quae est solum probabilis occasio peccandi pro proximo, uti est pravum exemplum.*"

in their errors, and also be persuaded by this example that they are walking the straight path to salvation?

> "From this it follows that it is most difficult to avoid the danger of pernicious scandal to heretics and schismatics themselves. Wherefore, a Catholic cannot be safe in his conscience if he worships together with them this way."[60]

In the case at hand, when a sedevacantist who is known as such assists actively at an *una cum* Mass, those present will assume either that he consents to naming Benedict XVI as a true pope, or that he regards the practice of doing so as morally indifferent. They can then draw the general conclusion that the identity of the Roman Pontiff (Is Ratzinger a true pope or not?) or (in the case of SSPX) actual subjection to him is a matter of no practical consequence to a Catholic. ("Not even a sedevacantist acts as if it meant anything!")

Such, obviously, is an occasion of "spiritual ruin."

J. The "Resistance" Clergy

The foregoing nine sections apply to all *una cum* Masses, no matter what auspices they are offered under.

However, *una cum* Masses offered by priests of the Society of Saint Pius X, its affiliates, and many independent priests, pose an additional problem. On the one hand, these priests affirm in the Canon and in public pronouncements that they recognize Ratzinger as a true pope; on the other, they conduct their sacramental ministry independent from and without any subjection to either Benedict XVI or the diocesan bishops in union with him. They speak of their "resistance" to the pope — and for this reason, we shall here refer to them as the "resistance" clergy.

On the face of it, of course, the resistance position is incoherent. But more than that, it contradicts one of the very reasons why the Church inserted the *una cum* clause into the Canon in the first place: to express

---

[60] SC de Prop. Fide, Instruction (*Pro Mission. Orient.*), 1729, Fontes 7:4505. "*Cum vero videant ad eorum ecclesias accedere, eorum ritibus interesse, de eorum Sacramentis participare catholicos, an non credendum, aut saltem timendum erit, ne ex hoc ipso magis in suis erroribus confirmentur, ac se in recto salutis tramite ambulare sibi etiam hoc exemplo persuadeant? Ex quo sequitur difficillime vitari posse periculum scandali perniciosi schismaticis, et haereticis ipsis: ac proinde catholicum tutum in conscientia non esse, si cum iis in divinis in hac facti specie communicet.*"

the relationship that must exist between the Supreme Pontiff and those who exercise the sacramental ministry of the Church. As Cardinal Bona explained in his commentary on the *una cum*, "*The unity of the sacerdotal ministry descends from the throne of Peter.*"[61]

To be part of this ministry, a priest or bishop must have legitimate deputation (proper authorization) for *all* the sacraments he confers, because the sacraments belong to the Church. At the beginning of his five-volume treatise on the sacraments, Cappello explains:

> "Since the confection and administration of the sacraments is divinely committed to the ministry of the Church, it is self-evident that sacraments **can only be conferred by someone who has been legitimately deputed by that same Church.**"[62]

On the other hand, priests and bishops who *lack* this deputation commit sin when they confer the sacraments. In the case of the Mass, moreover, their prayers have no efficacy, because they do not offer it *in the person of the Church*.

Saint Thomas Aquinas says that, although priests separated from the unity of the Church validly consecrate the Eucharist:

> "they nevertheless do not do this rightly, but rather **sin when they do it.** They therefore do not receive the fruit of the sacrifice, which is a spiritual sacrifice...

> "... the sacrifice is offered wrongly outside the Church. Hence **outside the Church there can be no spiritual sacrifice that is a true sacrifice with the truth of its fruit...**

> "In the Mass, the priest pronounces the prayers **in the person of the Church**, in whose unity he remains. ... Consequently if a priest who is separated from the unity of the Church celebrates Mass, he consecrates Christ's true body and blood, because he has not lost the power of Holy Orders; but **because he is severed from the unity of**

---

[61] G. Card. Bona, *Le Saint Sacrifice de la Messe* (Paris: Vivès 1855) 2:261. "*c'est là en effet le pivot, le sceau de l'unité de l'Église.... C'est là un signe d'union entre les members et leur chef; car... celulà communie avec l'Église catholique qui communie avec le pape, et de la chaire de Pierre découle l'unité du ministère sacerdotal.*" See also: Benedict XIV (P. Lambertini), *De Sacrosancto Missae Sacrificio* (Prato: Aldina 1843) 3:79. "*Postquam oravit Sacerdos pro Ecclesia Catholica, orat pro summo Pontifice:* Unitas enim sacerdotalis, *ut ait s. Cyprianus,* a Petri Cathedra exorta est."
[62] *De Sacramentis* 1:49. "*Cum sacramentorum confectio et administratio Ecclesiae ministerio sit divinis commissa, sequitur manifeste, sacramenta conferri non posse nisi ab eo qui sit legitime deputatus ab ipsa Ecclesia.*"

the Church, his prayers have no efficacy."[63]

Please note the last statement: because a priest is severed from the unity of the Church, *"his prayers have no efficacy."*

Cappello sums up the point as regards the Mass:

> "Priests who are cut off from the Church, although they validly sacrifice *in the name of Christ*, nevertheless **do not offer the sacrifice as ministers of the Church nor in the person of the Church**. For the priest has the power to pray, to intercede and to offer in the name of the Church by virtue of his commission from the Church, and with regard to this, the Church can deprive the priest who is cut off from sacrificing in its name."[64]

Apart from valid ordination, then, some commission from the Church is required if the priest is to offer Mass *in persona Ecclesiae* — in the person not only of Christ, but also *in the person of His Church*.

I have explained elsewhere at some length why sedevacantist clergy — who do not, of course, recognize Paul VI and his successors as true popes — enjoy a legitimate deputation and mission for the sacraments they confer.[65]

But in light of all the foregoing, can a priest of the *resistance* persuasion (SSPX, its affiliates, and various independents) likewise claim to exercise his sacerdotal ministry "in the person of the Church" if he is not in fact subject to the man he regards as the Roman Pontiff?

Well, no — because once you plug the recognition of someone as pope into the standard principles of moral theology, dogmatic theology and Canon Law, the *una cum* Masses of resistance priests all come out as

---

[63] *Summa* III.82 7, corpus, ad 1, et 3. *"non tamen recte hoc faciunt, sed peccant facientes. Et ideo fructum sacrificii non percipiunt, quod est sacrificium spirituale.... quod non recte extra Ecclesiam sacrificium offertur. Unde extra Ecclesiam non potest esse spirituale sacrificium, quod est verum veritate fructus, ... sacerdos in Missa in orationibus quidem loquitur in persona Ecclesiae, in cuius unitate consistit. ... Et ideo, si sacerdos ab unitate Ecclesiae praecisus Missam celebret, quia potestatem ordinis non amittit, consecrat verum corpus et sanguinem Christi, sed quia est ab Ecclesiae unitate separatus, orationes eius efficaciam non habent."*

[64] *De Sacramentis*, 1:547. *"Sacerdotes praecisi, quamvis valide sacrificent nomine Christi tamen non offerunt sacrificium, ut Ecclesiae ministri et inpersona ipsius Ecclesiae. Sacerdos enim habet ex commissione Ecclesiae, ut nomine eius oret, intercedat ac offerat, et, quoad hoc, potest Ecclesia privare sacerdotem praecisum, ne suo nomine sacrificet."*

[65] See A. Cekada, "Canon Law and Common Sense," (1992) and "Traditional Priests, Legitimate Sacraments," (2003), on traditionalmass.org.

gravely illicit, if not schismatic.

1. **Gravely Illicit Masses.** The resisters have, over the years, recognized that they must offer some answer to the charge that they do not act *in persona Ecclesiae* in their sacramental ministry and that their ministrations are illicit as regards ecclesiastical law. In order to resolve the problem of legitimate deputation, the resisters therefore appealed to many of the same general canonical principles as sedevacantists do: *epikeia*, intrinsic cessation of law, obligation arising from reception of Holy Orders, and necessity (common need).

The most notable attempt to lay out these principles and make the case that they apply to SSPX and other resisters was a lengthy canonical study by "Hirpinus." This was first published in the SSPX magazine *Courier de Rome*, and later reprinted in *The Remnant*, under the title "On the Doctrine of Necessity: Does the 'State of Emergency' Really Exist?"[66]

However, such arguments, impressive and well documented though they may seem, are completely futile for one obvious reason. In Canon Law, the principles of *epikeia*, cessation, obligation of Orders, and necessity (common need) can only be invoked in the *absence of the legislator* and of the clergy to whom the legislator has committed the care of souls (*cura animarum*). And since the resistance clergy all *recognize* Ratzinger as pope, they necessarily recognize him as the Supreme Legislator as well.

So if there is a question about interpreting the "mind of the legislator" (for the resisters to invoke *epikeia*), the continued binding force of a law (to invoke cessation), priestly or episcopal duty (to interpret the obligations of Orders) or the need to supply for dereliction of duty on the part of clergy with the *cura animarum* (to invoke state of necessity, common need or "emergency"), all a resistant priest need do is contact Benedict XVI, his Supreme Legislator. Ratzinger will then interpret the law, determine whether it still binds, ascertain the resister's obligation, and give orders to deal with the emergency. (For 911, dial B16…)

The appeal to general canonical principles for the legitimate deputation to confer sacraments, then, is closed to the "resistance" priest. Without such deputation, his Mass is gravely illicit — he does not offer it *in*

---

[66] *Remnant*, June-July 2004

persona Ecclesiae — and for that reason, a sedevacantist should not actively participate in it.

2. **Sin of Schism.** The second major problem for the resistance clergy is that acknowledging someone to be the pope while at the same time obstinately refusing to obey him is virtually the textbook definition of the sin of schism.

Moral theologians place schism among "sins against public peace," specifically, against the peace of the Church. Schismatics are:

> "those who refuse to be subject to the Supreme Pontiff (with rebellion, such that they obstinately refuse to obey his commands) and 2) those who refuse to be in communion with those who are subject to him (in doctrine, worship, sacraments). From this it is obvious that schism is a most grave sin and mortal *ex toto genere*."[67]

That Ratzinger is not in *reality* a true pope does not excuse the resisters from schism. They profess he *is* a true pope and they resist him as such. Therein lies the malice of the act— just as a man who deliberately steps on an unconsecrated host, thinking it was consecrated, would be formally guilty of the sin of sacrilege.

> Canonists such as Szal and Wernz-Vidal[68] flesh out a bit more the teaching of moral theology on schism when they lay out four requirements for the ecclesiastical crime of schism. Although many independent *una cum* priests meet the criteria in varying degrees, SSPX does so exactly and nearly point-for-point. It is as if canonists in the 1920s and 1940s were granted prophetic visions of SSPX's entire apostolate, and then wrote a *Schism for Dummies* guide for it.

This can be seen by quoting Szal's criteria, and then interspersing some of the deeds of SSPX:
Szal: "1) One must withdraw directly (expressly) or indirectly (by means of one's actions) from obedience to the Roman Pontiff, and separate

---
[67] Merkelbach 1:955. "*Peccata contra pacem publicam.... Paci ecclesiae, schisma... Et ideo schismatici dicuntur 1) (perfecte) qui subesse renuunt summo Pontifici (cum rebellione, ita ut obedire praeceptis pertinaciter recusent), et 2) qui membris Ecclesiae ei subjectis communicare recusant (in doctrina, cultu,sacramentis); ex quo patet esse peccatum gravissimum et mortale ex toto genere.*"
[68] F. Wernz & P. Vidal, *Ius Canonicum* (Rome: Gregorian 1937) 7:398. "*Ad constituendum delictum puri schismatis requiritur: I: ut quis aut directe sive expresse aut indirecte sive factis concludentibus ab obedientia Romani Ponrificis recedat et a communione ecclesiastica ceterorum fidelium sese separet,licet separatae sectae schismaticae sese non adiungat; — II. ut recessus coniunctus sit cum pertinancia sive rebellione; — III. ut recessus fiat quoad illa, quibus unitas Ecclesiae constituitur; — IV. ut non obstante formali inobedientia et denegatione subordinationis schismaticus agnoscat illum Romanum Pontificem verum esse pastorem universalis Ecclesiae et ex doctrina fidei ipsi obedientiam esse praestandum:...*"

oneself from ecclesiastical communion with the rest of the faithful, even though one does not join a separate schismatical sect;"[69]

SSPX: Through word and action, it withdrew from any semblance of obedience to Paul VI and his successors, and it separated from communion with the diocesan bishops who represented them.

Szal: "2) one's withdrawal must be made with obstinacy and rebellion;"

SSPX: Decade after decade, it stubbornly ignored orders to cease violating ecclesiastical law, and it openly defied putative superiors, eventually characterizing them as "anti-Christs."

Szal: "3) the withdrawal must be made in relation to those things by which the unity of the Church is constituted;"

SSPX: It set up a world-wide apostolate, governed by its own superiors, laws and tribunals — an apostolate that is parallel to and independent from the hierarchy recognized by the Roman Pontiff, and that confers sacraments without reference to authorization from his duly-designated representatives.

Szal: "4) despite this formal disobedience the schismatic must recognize the Roman Pontiff as the true pastor of the Church, and he must profess as an article of faith that obedience is due the Roman Pontiff."

SSPX: At the same time, it has repeatedly claimed — indeed, *insisted* — that it recognizes Paul VI and his successors as legitimate popes and true pastors of the Church.

In 2002 Bishop Donald Sanborn concisely summed up the dilemma posed by Masses offered by SSPX and the other resistance clergy:

> "Thus the *una cum* Mass ends up as an objectively schismatic Mass no matter how you slice it:
>
> "(a) If, for the sake of argument, Benedict XVI **were the Pope**, the unauthorized [i.e., non-*Motu*, FSSP, etc.] Traditional Mass is schismatic, since it is **not said in the person of the Church.**

---

[69] Szal, 2. Only one, not both, of the two conditions mentioned — withdrawal from obedience to the pope *or* separation from communion with the rest of the faithful — is required for the delict. See Canon 1325 2: "*subesse renuit ... aut ... communicare recusat.*"

"(b) If Benedict XVI is **not the Pope**, then the *una cum* Mass is schismatic since it is **said in union with, under the auspices of, a false pope and a false church**.

"In neither case does the priest have any business saying it."[70]

The consequences for the sedevacantist who actively participates in *una cum* Masses offered by priests of the "resistance" persuasion should therefore be clear enough: he not only recognizes a false pope, but he also implicitly consents to the notion that it is permissible to refuse submission to a true pope — the essence of the sin of schism. And for these reasons, a sedevacantist should not assist at it.

IV. Objections and Responses

In the foregoing section, we have offered at least ten reasons why a sedevacantist should not participate actively in an *una cum* Mass — to wit, it constitutes a pernicious lie, profession of communion with heretics, recognition of the ecumenical church, implicit profession of a false religion, a violation of Church law, participation in a sin, offering Mass with a heretic, recognizing a usurper, the sin of scandal, and (where "resistance" clergy are involved) participation in gravely illicit Masses and the sin of schism.

Some of these arguments have already been made elsewhere and prompted several objections, which we will now answer.

A. Pope Martin V and Cardinal de Lugo

Objection: *The Constitution "Ad Evitanda" of Pope Martin V and the teaching of the theologian de Lugo permit Catholics in cases of necessity to assist at Mass with, and receive the sacraments from, undeclared heretics and schismatics when a Catholic rite is used. The priests who offer "una cum" Masses have not been declared heretics and schismatics by the Church, and they use a Catholic rite. Therefore, a sedevacantist is permitted to assist at their Masses.*

The passage in *Ad Evitanda* (1415) that is cited to support the objection reads as follows:

---

[70] "Vatican II, the Pope and SSPX: Questions and Answers," *Most Holy Trinity Seminary Newsletter* (2002), 8, www.traditionalmass.org

CHAPTER 13

"...no one henceforth shall be bound to abstain from communion with anyone in the administration or reception of the sacraments or in any other religious or non-religious acts whatsoever,... on pretext of any **ecclesiastical sentence or censure** globally promulgated, whether by the law or by an individual; unless **the sentence or censure** in question has been specifically and expressly published or proclaimed by the judge on or against a definite person, college, university, church, community or place...."[71]

But neither this passage nor de Lugo's commentary on it defeat any of the arguments against *una cum* Masses made in section III.

1. **An Irrelevant Principle.** Please note the words in the quote that we have highlighted in bold: "ecclesiastical sentence or censure..." These refer either to judgments pronounced by an ecclesiastical court or censures such as excommunication.

None of our arguments against assisting at *una cum* Masses is based on the effects of ecclesiastical sentences or censures such as excommunication. On the face of it, therefore, *Ad Evitanda*, therefore, is irrelevant to our discussion here.

This becomes even more evident from the historical context in which the document was issued.

Martin V promulgated *Ad Evitanda* at the Council of Constance (1414-1418) that ended the Great Western Schism (1378–1417), a turbulent period in Church history with multiple claimants to the papacy.

Before *Ad Evitanda*, Canon Law forbade a Catholic to communicate in any way whatsoever — either in religious or secular matters — with someone who had been excommunicated. Those who violated this prohibition incurred a censure themselves, minor excommunication, which deprived them of the sacraments. Since the various papal claimants excommunicated each other's followers, the prospect of incurring the minor excommunication caused great worry to the laity on all sides. *Ad Evitanda* removed this second censure, unless the person

---

[71] Martin V, Constitution *Ad Evitanda* (1415), *Fontes* 1:45. "...*quod nemo deinceps a communione alicuius in sacramentorum administratione, vel receptione, aut aliis quibuscumque divinis, vel extra; praetextu cuiuscumque sententiae aut censurae ecclesiasticae, a iure vel ab homine generaliter promulgatae, teneatur abstinere,... Nisi sententia vel censura huiusmodi fuerit in vel contra personam, collegium, universitatem, ecclesiam, communitatem aut locum certum, vel certa, a iudice publicata vel denunciata specialiter et expresse.*"

you communicated with had been officially declared excommunicated by an ecclesiastical judge.⁷²

As regards whether *Ad Evitanda* would still apply, the 1917 Code cites it not as a source for the prohibition against common worship with heretics and schismatics (Canon 1258), but merely as a source for the prohibition against receiving sacraments from a clergyman who has been excommunicated *vitandus*⁷³ (Canon 2261.3). It is ecclesiastical legislation on the *first* question (common worship with heretics and schismatics), not the *second* (receiving sacraments from an excommunicated cleric), that we have used as the basis for some of our arguments in section III.

2. **De Lugo's Requirements.** Be that as it may, the Jesuit theologian de Lugo (1583–1660), among others, did indeed teach that the Constitution of Martin V allowed Catholics to receive sacraments from heretics who had not been declared excommunicated.

De Lugo added two conditions, however:

1. that the rite used by the heretics must be a Catholic rite and
2. that the participation by a Catholic would not be illicit for some other reason, such as scandal or implicit denial of the faith.⁷⁴

Scandal and implicit denial of the Faith, of course, are some of the reasons explicitly adduced in section III *against* active participation in *una cum* Masses. Citing de Lugo, therefore, defeats the objection rather than supports it.

3. **Rejected by the Holy Office.** In any case, the Holy See later dismissed the liberal interpretation that de Lugo and others had given *Ad Evitanda* in the matter of common worship with non-Catholics.

---

⁷² J. Bancroft, *Communication in Religious Worship with Non-Catholics*, CUA Studies in Sacred Theology 75, (Washington: CUA 1943), 27–9.

73 *Vitandus* = "to be avoided," i.e., by fellow Catholics. This is the most severe degree of excommunication, and it is imposed on an offender only through a special decree from the Holy See.

⁷⁴ J. de Lugo, *Disputationes Scholasticae et Morales* (Paris: Vivès 1868) 2:86. "*sed quaestio est de rebus sacris nullum errorem continenti- bus… vel ipsi ritu catholico celebranti adesse,… nisi aliunde sit scandalum vel irreverentia contra fidem, aut aliquid aliud… et constat ex dicta extravaganti,… cum ergo ii haeretici non sint excommunicati denuntiati, nec notorii clerici percussores, non est cur ratione excommunicationis perhibeamur ab iis sacramenta suscipere; quamvis id aliunde possit saepe illicitum esse…*"

In a 1753 pronouncement that quoted Pope Benedict XIV, the Holy Office stated that *Ad Evitanda* permitted Catholics to communicate "in merely *civil and secular* matters" with heretics who had not been expressly declared as such by name. However:

> "Catholics should not therefore think that it is also permissible to participate together with these same heretics in acts of divine worship."

The decree went on to name several theologians who had taught the the opposite, including de Lugo, and stated finally:

> "In this matter it is **almost impossible for it to happen that Catholics who would join together in sacred worship with heretics and schismatics would be excused from sin**. For this reason, the Sacred Congregations of the Holy Office and of the Propagation of the Faith **always considered such communion illicit.**"[75]

Please note the strong language: it is "almost impossible… to be excused from *sin*," and the Holy See "always considered such communion *illicit.*"

For future appeals either to *Ad Evitanda* or to de Lugo on the question of *una cum* Masses, therefore, the 1753 decree is the final nail in the coffin.

B. No Official Declaration

Objection: *Anyone who has not been officially declared a heretic or a schismatic may still be mentioned by name in the Canon of the Mass. But Benedict XVI has not been officially declared a heretic or a schismatic. Therefore, Benedict XVI may still be mentioned by name in the Canon of the Mass. Therefore, a sedevacantist is permitted to assist at a Mass where his name is so mentioned.*

1. The hidden assumption behind the major premise is false. As we have seen above, de la Taille says:

   > "This privation of the common suffrages of the Church is by no means

---

[75] Decree *Tenos, Fontes* 4:804. "*Verum quamvis iuxta praesentem disciplinam inductam a Martino V in celebri Extravagant. Ad evitanda, de qua nonnulla inferius, liceat catholici cum haereticis, modo non sint expresse et nominatim denunciati libere conversari, et cum iisdem communicare in rebus mere profanis et civilibus; non idcirco tamen arbitrari debent catholici, fas quoque sibi esse cum iisdem haereticis consortium habere etiam in rebus sacris et divinis.… id circofere impossibile est usuvenire, ut a flagitio excusari valeant catholici sese in rebus sacris cum haereticis et schimaticis admiscentes. Quamobrem Sacrae Urbis Congregationes, Sancti Officiii videlicet et de Propaganda Fide, illicitam semper reputarunt communionem, de qua est sermo.*"

confined to the *excommunicati vitandi* alone, as may be seen from the *Code of Canon Law* (can. 2262, parag. 1)."[76]

The various Vatican pronouncements quoted above, moreover, made no distinction between "declared" and "undeclared" heretics. The 1729 decree said that Catholics who participated in rites at which heretics and schismatics were commemorated "cannot excuse themselves from the sin of evil common worship."[77] It did not then add that no sin occurred if "un-declared" heretics and schismatics were commemorated. Nor in 1756, when Pope Benedict XIV forbade commemorating schismatics and heretics in the sacred liturgy, did he limit the prohibition to "declared" heretics and schismatics.[78]

2. Nor by analogy does the major premise make any sense in light of the general rules of Canon Law and pastoral theology. These norms prohibit offering Mass publicly for a heretic or schismatic, period.[79] They do not limit the prohibition to one who has been "declared" a heretic — so you can put off planning that Requiem High Mass for your Methodist Uncle Wesley...

C. Prayed for as Material Pope Only

Objection: *According to the Thesis of Cassiciacum, Benedict XVI, because he is a heretic, is not pope "formally" (= he lacks papal authority), but is pope "materially" (= he has only the legal designation to occupy the See). One may thus understand the prayer offered for him in the Canon of an* una cum *Mass as being for Benedict XVI as material pope only. Therefore, a sedevacantist is permitted to assist at a Mass where his name is so mentioned.*

To say (as adherents of the Thesis of Cassciacum do) that Benedict XVI is "material pope only" means that he is in fact a *false* pope and *lacks papal authority* (the "form" of the papal office).

The various linguistic and theological meanings for the *una cum* in the Canon, however, can only be applied to a *true* pope who *possesses papal authority* — e.g., head of the Church, Vicar of Christ, Successor of Peter, principle of unity, visible pastor, etc.

---

[76] De la Taille 2:318.
[77] See above, III.F.
[78] See above, III.E.
[79] See N. Halligan, *The Administration of the Sacraments* (New York: Alba 1962) 134.

None of these may be attributed to someone who *lacks* this authority, as according to the Thesis, Ratzinger does. Thus, the *una cum* prayer could not be understood to refer to a material pope only.

D. Can. 2261: Sacraments from Excommunicates

Objection: *For the sake of argument, let us assume the worst about the priests who offer "una cum" Masses — that the Motu clergy are heretics, the "resistance" clergy are schismatics, and that both groups are excommunicated. But according to Canon 2261.2 the faithful may, for any just reason, ask for sacraments from an excommunicated cleric (provided he is not a "vitandus"), especially if other ministers are lacking, and the excommunicated cleric may administer the sacraments to them. Therefore, a sedevacantist is permitted to participate actively at an "una cum" Mass.*

1. The appeal to Canon 2261 (made in good faith, no doubt) is in fact an apples-and-oranges argument.

None of the arguments I have adduced against assisting at an *una cum* Mass are based on the notion that the clergy who offer it have incurred the ecclesiastical censure of excommunication.

2. Canon 2261, in any case, treats exclusively of the *reception of a sacrament*. It is indeed sometimes permissible to *receive* a sacrament (e.g., Penance) not only from a priest who is an excommunicate, but also, under certain restricted conditions, even from a heretic or a schismatic.

3. The issue of the reception of a sacrament, however, is distinct from the one I have addressed above: *active participation in common public worship*, specifically, the Mass.

In this case, as we noted in section II, the layman does not merely *receive* something (absolution, a sacramental character, etc.), but *actively participates* according to his state in offering up the Holy Sacrifice.

And therein lies the problem for a sedevacantist who would assist at an *una cum* Mass, for in so doing he participates in a pernicious lie, in communion with heretics, in the profession of a false religion, etc.

E. The Sunday Obligation

CHAPTER 13

Objection: *Catholics are bound to assist at Mass on Sundays and Holy Days, unless excused for some legitimate reason. Naming a false pope in the Canon of the Mass is not a legitimate reason. Therefore, a sedevacantist is bound to assist at Mass on a Sunday or a Holy Day, even if a false pope is named in the Canon.*

As everyone knows, Church law and moral theology admit various causes that excuse one from the Sunday Obligation.

We have already demonstrated that it is wrong to participate actively in rites at which the circumstances connote the profession of a false religion,[80] at which heretics or schismatics (whether declared or not) are proclaimed teachers of the Catholic faith,[81] or at which usurpers are recognized as possessing legitimate authority,[82] and that these conditions are present at an *una cum* Mass.

These (obviously) would fall under the heading of at least moderately serious reasons involving a "notable spiritual harm," and according to the general principles of moral theology would thus excuse one from the obligation to assist at Mass.[83]

F. Toleration of Evil for a Greater Good

Objection: *An evil may sometimes be tolerated for a greater good. Mentioning the name of Benedict XVI in the Canon is an evil, but assistance at Mass is a greater good. Therefore, one may tolerate the evil mentioning the name of Benedict XVI in order to assist at Mass.*

An evil may be tolerated only if it does not entail positing an intrinsically evil act. In this case, however, we have already demonstrated that the sedevacantist who actively participates in an *una cum* Mass engages in an action that is a pernicious lie — one that "harms God in a matter concerning religion... [a] mortal sin of its nature, due to the evil attached to it"[84] — that "signifies the profession of a false religion,"[85] that participates in a sin,[86] etc.

---

[80] See above, III.D.
[81] See above, III.F.
[82] See above, III.H.
[83] See Merkelbach 2:703. "*quaecumque causa mediocriter gravis involvens notabile incommodum aut damnum, spirituale vel corporale, proprium vel alienum.*"
[84] See above, III.A
[85] See above, III.D
[86] See above, III F.

These are intrinsically evil acts. Hence, they could not be tolerated for a perceived greater good — even that of assisting at the Holy Sacrifice of the Mass.

G. The Priest Means Well

Objection: *A validly ordained "Motu" priest, an SSPX priest or an independent who puts Benedict XVI's name in the Canon is usually acting in good conscience and means well. As regards the question of the pope, he does not know better. Therefore, a sedevacantist is permitted to assist at his Masses.*

1. The objection that the priest "means well" — Father does not advert to the objective import of what he is doing — is the argument from ignorance.

Such an argument is an implicit admission that the act the priest is performing is evil in itself: "Father [*does evil but we should excuse this evil because he*] means well…"

2. In the foregoing sections, we have demonstrated what the *una cum* phrase means and why it is wrong for a sedevacantist to participate actively at an *una cum* Mass. All this has been based on objective principles that can be found in theology books.

The mental state of the celebrant — whether he is in good conscience, means well, does not know better, etc. — is irrelevant. It does not change what *una cum* means liturgically and theologically, nor can it negate the principles that make it wrong for a sedevacantist to assist at such a Mass.

For you, a sedevacantist, the issue is not whether the *priest* knows better. Spare Father the brain scan — you know better…

H. Secret Sedevacantists in SSPX

Objection: *Some priests who offer the Traditional Mass under the auspices of SSPX are in fact secret sedevacantists and do not put the name of the false pope into the Canon. Such Masses are not "una cum" the false pope. Therefore, a sedevacantist is free to assist at such a Mass.*

Here, one thinks of the *libellatici* — the Christians during the Decian persecution (ca. 250) who did not *actually* offer the grain of incense to the gods, but who, in order to avoid persecution, gave the *impression* that they did by obtaining certificates of conformity (*libelli*).[87]

SSPX publicly recognizes Benedict XVI as a true pope and officially requires that its members pray for him as such in the Canon. SSPX chapels offer pamphlets that clearly enunciate this position, and in most cases, prominently display a photo of Benedict XVI in the vestibule.

This creates a public presumption that an SSPX priest adheres to the position of the organization to which he belongs, and accordingly, puts the name of the false pope into the Canon.

In my opinion, the only way for an SSPX priest to overcome the latter presumption is remove the photo of Ratzinger from the vestibule of his chapel, and announce at the beginning of every Mass that he is not putting Benedict XVI's name in the Canon.

(Since a sudden reassignment will undoubtedly follow, he may also want to learn how to make that announcement in, say, Burmese...)

I. Conflicting Opinions among Priests

Objection: *Some priests who are sedevacantists themselves believe it is permissible for sedevacantists to participate actively in "una cum" Masses if no other Mass is available. Since there is a disagreement even among priests over the issue, there is a "doubt," and in doubtful matters, Saint Augustine says, there is liberty. Therefore, a sedevacantist is free to assist at an "una cum" Mass.*

These priests' conclusions are only as good as their reasons. The typical arguments usually go something like: (1) the laity have nowhere else to go for Mass, (2) the priest who offers the *una cum* Mass means well, or (3) those present are not aware that the Mass is *una cum*.

My impression is that these are off-the-cuff arguments, rather than the result of any extensive research. And heaven knows, we priests all have an awful lot to do, and research consumes great quantities of time.[88]

But since the issue necessarily involves very serious questions — the identity of the Roman Pontiff, participation in evil, communion with

---

[87] See J. Bridge, "Libellatici, Libelli," in *Catholic Encyclopedia*, 9:211–2.
[88] See J. Bridge, "Libellatici, Libelli," in Catholic Encyclopedia, 9:211–2.

CHAPTER 13

heretics, and potential violation of ecclesiastical laws, to name a few — off-the-cuff arguments simply aren't enough.

If a fellow sedevacantist priest does not find the evidence and conclusions presented here to be convincing, he should research the liturgical, historical, canonical and theological issues, and then systematically present his own arguments.

J. No Place for Mass

Objection: *The number of sedevacantist priests is relatively small, compared to the large number of "una cum" Masses (Motu, SSPX and independents). Your argument is logical, but if it were strictly applied in practice, many sedevacantists could only get to Mass occasionally with great difficulty, or would have no place at all to go to Mass. They would deprive themselves and their children of the graces of the Mass, and eventually lose the Faith.*

The number of sedevacantist priests is relatively small — but it is far greater than even a decade ago and it is increasing, especially in the United States. These priests, one hopes, will be able to extend their apostolates bit by bit, just as priests ordained in my own generation did, when there was nearly *no one* — sedevacantist or otherwise — who offered the traditional Latin Mass.

As regards depriving yourself of the graces of the Mass, I will be blunt: there are none to be had for you at a Mass where you actively and knowingly participate in a sacrilegious lie.

And as regards your children, my experience tells me that one of two things will happen: either their faith will be corrupted (whether by *Motu* crypto-Modernism or by SSPX's errors on the papacy) or their respect for the Catholic priesthood will be undermined (by your attempts to correct the errors that the clergy have tried to impart to them).

I have been a priest for more than three decades, and I have seen many families that were once solidly Traditionalist surrender step by step to the new religion because of a decision to go to a "convenient" *una cum* Mass. Constant exposure to those who teach error — be it devout old Monsignor McGeezer at the *Motu* Mass, or the zealous Abbé du Fromage-Legrand at the SSPX chapel in Kalamazoo — slowly erodes your faith and all your good resolutions. It's only *one* error they teach, you figure, or it's only *one* phrase in their Mass that's bad — but this gets you ready to swallow a whole lot more.

And it is precisely for this reason that the Church— with her exquisite understanding of fallen human nature — repeatedly forbade Catholics to participate in a rite that would compromise their faith.

But even if such a danger were not present, the sedevacantist would still face the inevitable conclusion to be drawn from the weight of all the evidence presented above: active participation in an *una cum* Mass is intrinsically evil.

V. Summary and Conclusion

Th question we began with was simple: Should a sedevacantist assist actively at an una cum Mass — a traditional Latin Mass offered by a validly-ordained priest who in the first prayer of the Canon recites the phrase: *together with Thy servant Benedict, our Pope.*

Though our question was simple, we covered quite a bit of ground to answer it, so here is a summary.

I.   The Meaning of the Prayer. What, first of all, does the prayer mean?

From the perspective of linguistic meaning, putting Ratzinger's name into the *una cum* in the Canon affirms not only that he is a true pope, but also that he is a member of the true Church.

The sedevacantist firmly rejects both propositions, especially because the canonists and theologians cited to support sedevacantism state that the loss of the pontificate in a heretical pope is produced by his *loss of membership* in the Church.

The standard theological meanings attached to the *una cum* produce still more problems for the sedevacantist.

These affirm that the heretic/false pope Ratzinger is head of the Church, Vicar of Christ, Successor of Peter, the principle of unity, and our authorized intermediary with Almighty God. The mention of the heretic's name is "proof of the orthodoxy" of those who offer the Mass, and a sign they "are not separated from communion with the universal Church."

Each and every one of those propositions a sedevacantist would consider a theological horror, if not near-blasphemous.

II. **Your Participation and Consent.** A sedevacantist who assists at an *una cum* Mass cannot credibly maintain that he "withholds consent" from the odious phrase.

We enumerated at least nine ways in which a Catholic actively participates at a Traditional Mass when it is celebrated. Each of these constitutes a true form of active participation, which in turn (according to the theologians we cited) constitutes "cooperation or common action with another in the prayers and functions of worship."

Various popes and pre-Vatican II theologians, moreover, taught that the laity who assist actively at Mass, in so doing, manifest their consent and moral cooperation with the priest as he offers the sacrifice.

Finally, in this section we demonstrated that Fathers of the Church, and indeed Pope Pius XII himself in the encyclical *Mediator Dei*, teach specifically that the faithful who actively assist at Mass ratify, assent to and participate in the prayers of the Canon that the priest recites, even though they do not vocally recite these prayers themselves.

From this it is clear beyond any doubt that the sedevacantist who actively assists at an *una cum* Mass consents to and morally cooperates with the action of the priest who proclaims that he offers the sacrifice *together with Thy servant Benedict, our Pope* — the arch-heretic and false pope Ratzinger.

III. **Why You Should Not Participate.** Having established what the *una cum* means and how those present participate in its use, we then explained why a sedevacantist who actively participates at an *una cum* Mass:

1. Tells a pernicious lie.
2. Professes communion with heretics.
3. Recognizes as legitimate the Ecumenical, One- World Church
4. Implicitly professes a false religion.
5. Condones a violation of Church law.
6. Participates in a sin.
7. Offers Mass in union with the heretic/false pope Ratzinger.
8. Recognizes the usurper of an ecclesiastical office.
9. Offers an occasion for the sin of scandal.
10. In the case of Masses offered by "resistance" clergy (SSPX, its

affiliates and many independent clergy) participates in gravely illicit Masses and condones the sin of schism.

The answer to our simple question, then, is an equally simple no — a sedevacantist should *not* actively participate in an *una cum* Mass.

In light of the teachings of popes, theologians, canonists, moralists, and liturgists on the issues we have examined, the foregoing conclusion, in my opinion, is the only one possible.

The issue of how, in the absence of regular access to the Mass, sedevacantists can best maintain their faith, religious practice and spiritual lives will be the topic of another article. The task is not impossible.

Naturally, faithful Catholics dearly love the Mass and cherish it as the principal means by which God will lead them to holiness. But the Holy Sacrifice will never bear fruit for us if we purchase it at the price of truth, faith, and holiness itself — at the price of a grain of incense offered to a heretic, a false pope and his false religion. For as Father Faber warned:

> "The crowning disloyalty to God is heresy. It is the sin of sins, the very loathsomest of things which God looks down upon in this malignant world. Yet how little do we understand of its excessive hatefulness!...
>
> "We look at it, and are calm. We touch it and do not shudder. We mix with it, and have no fear. **We see it touch holy things, and we have no sense of sacrilege**...
>
> "Our charity is untruthful because it is not severe; and it is unpersuasive, because it is not truthful... **Where there is no hatred of heresy, there is no holiness.**"[89]

November 2007

BIBLIOGRAPHY

AUGUSTINE, St. *Homily de Sacramento Altaris ad Infantes* 3. PL 46:834–6.
BANCROFT, J. *Communication in Religious Worship with Non-Catholics*, CUA Studies in Sacred Theology 75. Washington: 1943.
BELLARMINE, Robert, St. *De Controversiis, Opera Omnia*. Naples: Giuliano 1836.

---

[89] F. Faber, *The Precious Blood* (Baltimore: Murphy 1868), 352–3 CUA 1943.

BENEDICT XIV, Pope. Bull *Ex Quo*. 1 March 1756. S.D.N *Benedicti Papae XIV Bullarium*. Malines: Hanicq 1827. 4:288–362.
BENEDICT XIV (P. Lambertini). *De Sacrosancto Missae Sacrificio*. Prato: Aldina 1843. 3 vols.
BESTE, U. *Introductio In Codicem*. Collegeville MN: Saint John's 1946.
BONA, G. CARD. *Le Saint Sacrifice de la Messe*. Paris: Vivès 1855.
BRIDGE, J. "Libellatici, Libelli," in *Catholic Encyclopedia*. New York: 1913. 211 2.
BRUYLANTS, P. *Les Oraisons du Missel Romain*. Louvain: CDIL 1952. 2 vols.
CAPPELLO, F. *Tractatus Canonico-Moralis de Sacramenti*s. Rome: Marietti 1951. 5 vols.
CEKADA, A. "Canon Law and Common Sense." 1992. On www.traditionalmass.org
    "Traditional Priests, Legitimate Sacraments." 2003. On www.traditionalmass.org
    Traditionalists, Infallibility and the Pope, 2nd ed. West Chester OH: Saint Gertrude the Great 2006.
Code of Canon Law. 1917.
Codicis Iuris Canoni ci Fontes. Rome: Polyglot 1923–1939. 9 vols. (*"Fontes"*)
COLLECTANEA S.C. de Propaganda Fide: 1602–1906. Rome: Polyglot 1907. 2 vols.
CROEGAERT, A. *Les Rites et les Priéres du Saint Sacrifice de la Messe*. Paris: Casterman n.d..
DE LA TAILLE, M. *The Mystery of Faith*. London: Sheed & Ward 1950. 2 vols.
DE LUGO, J. *Disputationes Scholasticae et Morales*. Paris: Vivès 1868.
DE PUNIET, J. OSB. *The Mass: Its Origin and History*. New York: Longmans 1930.
ELLEBRACHT, M. *Remarks on the Vocabulary of the Ancient Orations in the Missale Romanum*. Nijmegen: Dekker 1963.
FABER, F. *The Precious Blood*. Baltimore: Murphy 1868. FORTESCUE, A. *The Formula of Hormisdas*, CTS 102. London: Catholic Truth Society 1913.
GASSNER, T. *The Canon of the Mass: Its History, Theology, and Art*. Saint Louis: Herder 1950.
HALLIGAN, N. *The Administration of the Sacraments*. New York: Alba House 1962.
HIRPINUS. "On the Doctrine of Necessity: Does the 'State of Emergency' Really Exist?" *Remnant*. June-July 2004.
INNOCENT III, Pope. *De Sacro Altaris Mysterio*. PL 227:773–916. IRAGUI, S. *Manuale Theologiae Dogmaticae*. Madrid: Ed. Studium 1959.
JOHN CHRYSOSTOM, St. Homily *In II Cor.*, 18. PG 61:523–530.
KENRICK, F. *Theologia Moralis*. Malines: Dessain 1861. 2 vols. MAERE.

R. "Diptych," in *Catholic Encyclopedia*. New York: 1913. 5:22–4.
MARTIN V, Pope. Constitution *Ad Evitanda*. 1415. *Fontes* 1:45. MCHUGH J. and C. Callan. *Moral Theology*. New York: Wagner 1929. 2 vols.
MISSALE MIXTUM dictum Mozarabes Sec. Regulam B. Isidori. PL 85:109–1036.
MERKELBACH B. *Summa Theologiae Moralis*. 8th ed. Montreal: Desclée 1949. 3 vols.
OMLOR, PATRICK HENRY. *Sedevacantists and the "Una Cum" Problem*. Veradale WA: Catholic Research Institute 2002.
PATROLOGIA GRAECA. Migne. ("PG"). *PATROLOGIA LATINA*. Migne. ("PL"). PELAGIUS I, Pope. *Epistola* 5. PL 69:397–9.
PIUS VI, Pope. Encyclical *Charitas*. 13 April 1791. *Fontes* 2:474, PIUS XII, Pope. Encyclical *Mediator Dei*. 20 November 1947.
Acta Apostolicae Sedis 39 (1947). 521–600.
REGATILLO, E. *Institutiones Juris Canonici*. 5th ed. Santander: Sal Terrae 1956. 2 vols.
REMIGIUS OF AUXERRE. *De Celebratione Missae et Ejus Significa- tione*. PL 101:1173–1286.
SANBORN, D. "Vatican II, the Pope and SSPX: Questions and Answers," *Most Holy Trinity Seminary Newsletter* (2002). www.traditionalmass.org
────── "Una Cum," *Sacerdotium* 6 (Winter 1993). 39–75. Revised version with translation of Latin on www.traditionalmass.org
SCHUSTER, I. Card. *The Sacramentary (Liber Sacramentorum)*. London: Burns Oates 1924. 5 vols.
SC DE PROP. FIDE. Instruction *Pro Mission. Orient*. 1729. *Fontes* 7:4505.
SO (Holy Office) Instruction *Communicatio*. 22 June 1859. *Collectanea S. Cong. de Prop. Fide* 1:1176.
────── Decree *Mesopotamia*. 28 August 1669. *Fontes* 4:740.
────── Decree *Mission. Tenos In Peloponneseo*. 10 May 1753. *Fontes* 4 804.
Summa Theologica.
SZAL, I. *Communication of Catholics with Schismatics*, CUA Canon Law Studies 264. Washington: CUA 1948.
THALHOFER, V. *Handbuch der Catholischen Liturgie*. Freiburg: Herder n.d.
WERNZ, F. & P. Vidal. *Ius Canonicum*. Rome: Gregorian 1934. 8 vols.
WILSON ed., H.A. *The Gregorian Sacramentary under Charles the Great, Edited from Three Mss. of the Ninth Century*. London: 1915.

Chapter 14

The Problem of the *Una Cum* Traditional Masses

(2005)

By Most Rev. Donald J. Sanborn

A "valid" Mass does not equal a "Catholic Mass"

In my article entitled "Communion" (*Sacerdotium* V), I spoke about the problem of validly ordained priests saying Masses which were liturgically Catholic but outside the Catholic Church. This is the case of the Greek schismatics, Old Catholics (in some cases valid), even High Church Anglicans who have gotten themselves validly ordained in one way or another.

I pointed out, by citing authorities on the matter, that for *validity*, it is necessary that the minister be acting *in the person of Christ* at the altar, but for the catholicity of the Mass, he must at the same time be acting *in the person of the Church*. Saint Thomas Aquinas explains the distinction:

> And because the consecration of the Eucharist is an act which flows from the power of orders, those who are separated from the Church through heresy or schism or excommunication, can indeed consecrate the Eucharist which, when consecrated by them, contains the true body and blood of Christ: they nevertheless do not do this rightly, but rather sin when they do it. They, therefore, do not receive the fruit of the sacrifice, which is a spiritual sacrifice.

> The priest at Mass indeed speaks in the prayers in the person of the Church, in whose unity he remains; but in consecrating the sacrament he speaks as in the person of Christ, Whose place he holds by the power of orders. Consequently, if a priest who is separated from the unity of the Church celebrates Mass, not having lost the power of Order, he consecrates Christ's, true body and blood; but because he is severed from the unity of the Church, his prayers have no efficacy.[1]

Some saints and popes had some stronger words about schismatic

---

[1] IIIa q.82.a.7, corpus & ad 3um.

Masses:

> *Pope Pelagius I:* One body of Christ establishes the fact that there is one Church. An altar which is divided from the unity [of the Church] cannot gather together the true body of Christ.[2]

> *Saint Cyprian:* The schismatic dares to set up an altar and to profane the truth of the divine Victim by means of false sacrifices.[3] (He also wanted returning schismatic priests to be reduced to the lay state, referring to them as "those who against the unique and divine altar attempted to offer outside [of the Church] sacrilegious and false sacrifices.")[4]

> *Saint Augustine:* Outside of the Catholic Church, the true sacrifice cannot be found.[5]

> *Saint Leo the Great:* Elsewhere [that is, outside the Church], there is neither an approved priesthood nor true sacrifices.[6]

> *Saint Jerome:* God hates the Sacrifices of these [i.e., heretics] and pushes them away from Himself, and whenever they come together in the name of the Lord, He abhors their stench and holds His nose...[7]

Father Cappello explains this distinction clearly:

> Priests who are cut off from *the* Church, although *they* validly sacrifice in the name of Christ, nevertheless do not offer the sacrifice *as ministers of the Church nor in the person of the Church*. For the priest has the power to pray, to intercede and to offer in the name of the Church by virtue of his commission from the Church, and with regard to this, the Church can deprive the priest who is cut off from sacrificing in its name.[8]

From these texts it is clear that the validity of the Mass is not sufficient that it be a *Catholic* Mass, but rather, another very important factor is necessary: *the fact that the priest act* in the person of the Church, *that is, that he be commissioned by the Church to pray in its name.*

This factor creates a terrible problem for the *una cum* Traditional Mass.

---

[2] *Ep. ad Joan. Patr.*, P.L. 69,412.
[3] *De Unitate Ecclesiae*, c.. 17. P.L 4, 513.
[4] Ep. 72, c. 2. P.L. 3, 1048-1049.
[5] Cf. *Prosperum Aquitanum, Sent.*, sent. 15 P.L, 51,430.
[6] Ep..LXXX *Ad Anatolium*, cap.2.
[7] *Amos, V:* 22, P.L. 25, 1033-1034.
[8] Cappello, Felix M. S. I.., *Tractatus Canonico-moralis de Sacramentis*, (Turin: Marietti), 1962, I, p.462.

CHAPTER 14

If the priest is saying that Benedict XVI is the Pope, and that he is in communion with him, he is necessarily saying that the Church of which Benedict XVI is the head is the Roman Catholic Church. In order that the Mass which the priest is saying, therefore, be deemed a *Catholic* Mass, it is necessary that the priest be commissioned by Benedict XVI to say the Mass *in the person of the Church*. Without this commission, without this authorization from him who has the care of Christ's whole flock, from him who has the commission from Christ to teach, rule, and to sanctify, the Mass becomes a non-Catholic Mass. The Catholic priest must be acting as the agent of his bishop, who has the care of the diocesan flock, who, in turn, must be acting as an agent of the Pope who has care of the whole flock. The Pope, in turn, must be acting as an agent of Christ, of Whom he is the Vicar. This is the very constitution of the Catholic Church; it is this tight link of agency and authority which makes the Church Catholic. If the priest, therefore, is acting without the authorization of the diocesan bishop, he is then acting without the authorization of the Pope, and his Mass and sacraments are cut off from both Christ and His Church. His Mass is not Catholic, nor are his sacraments, for he is not acting *in the person of the Church*.

How does the Traditional priest today act *in the person of the Church*, when there is no authority to authorize him to say Mass?

He does so by carrying on the mission of the Catholic Church, which is the sanctification of souls. Thus, it is perfectly legitimate and necessary for priests to say Mass, preach, and distribute the sacraments, as they are authorized by the Church to do so through the principle of *epikeia*. This principle, however, cannot possibly be invoked if the superior is present; one cannot invoke *epikeia* against a present, acting, and ruling superior. It simply does not make sense, since *epikeia* is essentially an estimation of the mind of the lawmaker in his absence.[9]

Thus, the *una cum* Mass ends up as an objectively schismatic Mass no matter how you slice it:

a. If, for the sake of argument, Benedict XVI were the Pope, the unauthorized (i.e., non-Indult) Traditional Mass is schismatic,

---

[9] *Epikeia non potest licite adhiberi: (a) Si superior, qui dispensationem legis concedere valet, facile adiri queat."* [Translation: *Epikeia cannot be licitly used: (a) if the superior, who is able to grant the dispensation of the law, can be easily approached.*"] Prümmer, *Manuale Theologiae Moralis* I, no. 231 ff. Q.v.

since it is not said *in the person of the Church*.
b. If Benedict XVI is not the Pope, then the *una cum* Mass is schismatic since it is said in union with, under the auspices of, a false pope and a false church.

In neither case does the priest have any business saying it.

The only situation in which it would be licit to carry on an extensive, habitual, "unauthorized" apostolate is in a case similar to our own, in which there is a long-term absence of authority. The authorization for saying Mass, preaching, and administering the sacraments would then be *per modum actus*, that is, in the individual acts themselves, and would not be a habitual authority. The authorization would be from the Church itself (*Ecclesia supplet*, that is, the Church supplies jurisdiction in the absence of the competent authority).

The Society of Saint Pius X is excommunicated by the person they say is the Vicar of Christ on earth. They cannot invoke against his supposed authority the very authority of the Church (that is, they cannot invoke the principle of *Ecclesia supplet*), since he supposedly possesses the fullness of the authority of the Church. To do so is schismatic, and that is exactly what Benedict XVI considers the Society of Saint Pius X to be — schismatic.

(Internet, 2005).

Afterword

We need the sacraments for our spiritual life and growth in holiness. Through them, we receive from Christ His grace, even as we give back due honor and worship to God. The sacraments derive their significance directly from Christ, Who instituted them as means to convey grace to the members of His mystical body. Since a sacrament is a visible manifestation of an invisible divine reality, its efficacy and nature reside in Christ Himself. Each sacrament bears the imprint of Christ for its sacramental grace.

All sacraments pertain to various aspects of life. Baptism, which imparts an indelible character upon the soul, establishes the first conformity to Christ's life. The other sacraments collectively deepen and enhance this conformity. Through the sacraments, man is drawn upward to Christ, ultimately being transformed by the graces communicated, which results in the formation of Christ within him.

A sacrament is defined as *an efficacious sign instituted by Christ that bestows grace*. St. Pius X and Pope Pius XII, following the Council of Trent, affirmed that the Church has no authority to alter the substance of a sacrament, that is, those aspects that are established in Scripture and Tradition by Our Lord. While it is true that the Church does have the power to add or remove elements related to the administration of the sacraments, or make accidental changes such as the laws regulating certain liturgical movements or the material from which to make chalices, the Church has no power to change the sacraments' substance.

Without a doubt, there is a significant difference between the pre-Vatican II rites and those that followed. This book delves into the question of whether the post-Vatican II changes to the sacraments are merely accidental, or whether they constitute substantial deviations from what was instituted by Christ. Is the New Mass of Paul VI merely an accidental modification of the authentic Mass, or is it a complete invention deviating from the Sacrifice of Christ? Is the entire liturgy that emerged after Vatican II merely an alteration in aesthetics, or is it a rupture with the form of worship entrusted to the Church for its preservation and administration?

The answer was perfectly worded as early as 1969 by Cardinal Ottaviani, namely, that the changes seen in the proposed *Novus Ordo Missae* "both as a whole and in its details, [are] a striking departure from the Catholic theology of the Mass as it was formulated in Session XXII of the Council of Trent." This critique extends to the rest of the liturgical changes and the post-Vatican II sacraments. These new and invented liturgical rites transformed the fundamental concepts of the sacraments from what Christ had instituted; what remains can thus no longer be said to be from Christ.
Since Christ, as God, remains unchanged, the substance of the sacraments

cannot change from Christ's institution. To preserve the sacraments of Christ and the Church, therefore, we must reject these liturgical changes and the post-Vatican II sacraments.

Reverend Tobias Bayer
The Feast of St. Francis of Assisi MMXIV
Brooksville, Florida

www.ingramcontent.com/pod-product-compliance
Lightning Source LLC
Chambersburg PA
CBHW072233290426
44111CB00012B/2077